Nanno Marinatos is Professor of Classics at the University of Illinois, Chicago. Her publications include *Minoan Kingship and the Solar Goddess: A Near Eastern Koine*; *Minoan Religion: Ritual, Image, and Symbol*; and *The Goddess and the Warrior: The Naked Goddess and Mistress of Animals in Early Greek Religion*.

'This book enables us to see, at a level and detail of argument not reached in other works, the logic, reasonableness and force of Evans's interpretations ... Nanno Marinatos offers not simply a new but also a unique contribution.'

Peter Warren, FBA, Emeritus Professor of Ancient History and Classical Archaeology, University of Bristol

'Nanno Marinatos has pulled off a very difficult task in writing a stimulating intellectual biography of Sir Arthur Evans – excavator of the site of Knossos and creator of the Minoan civilisation – that combines a laudatory, but critical, approach with the introduction of new information about an already well-documented life. Following a broadly chronological structure – from Evans's intellectual formation in late-nineteenth-century anthropology and prehistory to his final years in the early part of World War II – this is a personal narrative in two distinct ways: first, because it links Marinatos's own quest to interpret Minoan religion to Evans's; and second, because it weaves a Greek perspective into Evans's story, drawing on personal correspondence, some never before published, of her father Spyridon Marinatos, himself famous as the excavator of the spectacularly well-preserved site of Akrotiri on Thera. Throughout, Marinatos situates her narrative effectively and readably within contemporary developments – both scholarly and historical – producing a genuinely novel picture of Evans's life, his intellectual contribution and his involvement in the world of Cretan archaeology, particularly in later life.'

John Bennet, Professor of Aegean Archaeology, University of Sheffield, author of A Short History of the Minoans *(I.B.Tauris, 2015)*

SIR ARTHUR EVANS AND MINOAN CRETE

Creating the Vision of Knossos

NANNO MARINATOS

BLOOMSBURY ACADEMIC

LONDON • NEW YORK • OXFORD • NEW DELHI • SYDNEY

BLOOMSBURY ACADEMIC
Bloomsbury Publishing Plc
50 Bedford Square, London, WC1B 3DP, UK
1385 Broadway, New York, NY 10018, USA

BLOOMSBURY, BLOOMSBURY ACADEMIC and the Diana logo
are trademarks of Bloomsbury Publishing Plc

First published in Great Britain 2015 by I.B. Tauris & Co. Ltd
Paperback edition first published 2021

A catalogue record for this book is available from the British Library.

A catalog record for this book is available from the Library of Congress.

ISBN: HB: 978-1-7807-6811 3
PB: 978-1-3501-9735-0
ePDF: 978-0-8577-2516-5
eBook: 978-0-8577-3883-7

Series: Library of Classical Studies, volume 6

Typeset in Garamond Three by OKS Prepress Services, Chennai, India

To find out more about our authors and books visit
www.bloomsbury.com and sign up for our newsletters.

This book is dedicated to the memory of those intellectuals, like Arthur Evans, Georg Karo, Erich Bessel Hagen and Thomas Mann, who were conscious of the end of civilization and who witnessed the collapse of what Thomas Mann called 'middle class humanism' ('bürgerlicher Humanismus'), *just before World War II.*

CONTENTS

LIST OF ILLUSTRATIONS

FOREWORD

Great men and women naturally attract assessments of their achievements. In the case of Sir Arthur Evans, historian by training, student of anthropology and of ancient religions, folklorist, numismatist, knowledgeable in botany, iconographer, connoisseur, as well as archaeologist, authors sometimes merely dream themselves into the trap of anachronism, passing judgements with insufficient appreciation of the time and circumstances in which their subject worked;[1] sometimes they offer psychobabble or stoop to offensive malice. In other authors' writings, while they do not hide what can be seen, with the benefit of subsequent work or discoveries, to be mistakes or misjudgements, the assessments are essentially positive, elucidating the intellectual strength of their subject and the depth and range of his humanity. One instance of the latter is Evans's continued friendship with his younger colleague and later the author of the monumental *Die Schachtgräber von Mykenai* (1930–33), Georg Karo (1872–1963), before and throughout World War I, and afterwards for the rest of his life. Among the positively appreciative assessments the late Stylianos Alexiou, after objectively reviewing Evans's Cretan work, social (active application of his Liberal principles) as well as archaeological, concluded at the November 2000 Conference in Herakleion:

> On account of all the above, let us today remember Arthur Evans with emotion, admiration and gratitude. He set the bases

of Minoan archaeology. He carried on the tradition of British
explorers and researchers in Crete, Pashley and Spratt.[2]

The present work joins the seriously appreciative and, as will be
seen, offers not simply a new but also a unique contribution. It is
therefore a pleasure to be invited to write a foreword, admittedly
somewhat personal. Nanno Marinatos, a friend and colleague for
40 years, explains that while her book is biographical it is not a linear
biography in the usual sense. Moreover it has two subjects, Evans
(born 1851), who valued above all 'the brotherhood of science', and
her father Spyridon Marinatos (born 1901), the two linked through
the relations between them revealed here.

Her approach[3] is to set out a number of major interpretations
and episodes, in approximate chronological order, central to the work
of Evans – interpretations, of course, already widely known in the
literature – and then to situate them in their contemporary and
immediately preceding intellectual contexts. Of prime importance
were the influences of the anthropologist Edward Tylor (1832–
1917), John Lubbock (1834–1913)[4] and the orientalist and biblical
scholar William Robertson Smith (1846–94). Evans was also fully
aware of but not dependent on Sir James Frazer. Evans's basic view
was that progress (a much held Victorian notion) by way of linear
evolution was not inevitable and that the causes of decline and
regression should be investigated. This book thus enables us to see, at
a level and detail of argument not reached in other works, the logic,
reasonableness and force of Evans's interpretations. It matters less
whether one accepts these interpretations (see further below) and the
validity of the wealth of comparative evidence deployed in support of
them, than that we understand (and may thus perhaps be persuaded
by) the thinking behind them. That said it is worth emphasizing that
it is Greek archaeologists – who have excavated at Knossos and in
central Crete, discovered new Bronze Age buildings and handled
thousands of their new finds – who in particular have found Evans's
interpretations convincing, building on them rather than discredit-
ing them. The present writer has enjoyed the privilege of knowing
personally each director and senior archaeologist of Herakleion

Museum after Marinatos,[5] and their views. Several of them, notably Stylianos Alexiou, Yannis Sakellarakis and Andonis Vasilakis, have also made clear their appreciations in print, while Nikolaos Platon, when introducing his own chronological system,[6] was fully respectful of Evans's overall achievement. Nanno (thus henceforward, in part to distinguish her from her father) now shows how supportive of Evans's positions Marinatos himself was too.

Within the book tree and pillar cult and the Anatolian background of Kubaba/Kybele and a young attendant leading to a Great Goddess (later Rhea) and Cretan Zeus are chosen subjects. The question of Minoan monotheism (Evans) or polytheism (Nilsson) is a closely related topic, the centrality of which in the understanding of Minoan religion justifies its separate chapter. Nanno rightly emphasizes the correctness of Evans's view, that Minoan religion should not be evaluated by any working back from later Greek religion. She has already published studies positively exploring Evans's views of baetylic cult and on links between Minoan religion and Egyptian solar religion.

The detailed stories of the find circumstances of two famous objects, the Ring of Nestor and the Ring of Minos, although told already in other publications, here make compelling reading when combined with the role or likely role of Emile Gilliéron fils, as interesting as the discussion of the iconographies themselves. For the Ring of Minos, considered modern by Marinatos and as genuinely Minoan by his young epimelete Nikolaos Platon, Nanno adduces strong arguments in support of her father's judgement.[7] Meanwhile N. Dimopoulou and G. Rethemiotakis have proposed that the iconography of the ring depicts the unity of the Minoan cosmos, of air, land and sea;[8] the Bronze Age Cretans having such a unified concept was Evans's own view, long before the ring was discovered in the late 1920s, is well demonstrated by Nanno in this book. A general point may also be made about the assessment of Minoan gold rings with engraved scenes and the genuineness or otherwise of rings not from controlled excavations. Every new discovery of an engraved ring in excavation is a wonderful surprise, since each engraved scene or depiction, although usually with observable links to others, is in itself unique. However, if the Arkhanes: Phourne ring with flying goddess and flying griffin and the original ring of the Khania Master Impression[9] and the Kato Syme ring with racing athlete[10] had come to light, not in controlled excavations but from dealers in antiquities, each would surely have aroused much suspicion.

Restorations in the Palace and other buildings are particularly well examined through their discussion as two separate episodes, those of 1901–6, contemporary with the excavation, when preservative action was absolutely necessary, and those from 1925–31, when the idea is what would today be called outreach, enabling the wider public to appreciate what a Minoan palace was like to live and move about in. The operations were throughout determined by two factors: (1) very careful and accurate assessments and measurements by the architects, Theodore Fyfe, Christian Doll and Piet de Jong, as well as by Evans and, in the early stages, Duncan Mackenzie,[11] of what actually survived: for example, the lower steps of staircases demonstrating upper floors and column bases large enough to carry columns supporting such floors; (2) the preservation of complex but collapsed structures, above all the engineering masterpiece of the Grand Staircase in the East Wing of the Palace. As Nanno also points out, Evans had the good sense to see the advantage (at the time) of ferro-concrete as against wood in exposure to the Cretan climate.

Skilfully interrelated with discussion of Evans's interpretations and his restorations at Knossos (reconstitutions was his term) is the relationship of Spyridon Marinatos not only with Evans but also with archaeologists of the British School at Athens, his close contemporaries Humphry Payne (1901–36), Edith Eccles (1910–77) and John Pendlebury (1904–41), in what is a highly interesting biography of the Greek archaeologist's years as Ephor in Crete, 1929–37, uniquely sourced by the author from personal as well as public archives. Nanno is strictly fair as she reveals the epistolary evidence and its remarkably repeated pattern. In the case of Evans, some 50 years Marinatos's senior, it began with the young ephor fully respectful but determined to take the excavator of Knossos to task over the non-notification of the excavation of two tombs. Marinatos was correct, although the unique status of Evans in relation to permits was open to more than one interpretation. However, Nanno then demonstrates how the relationship rapidly moved to one of cordiality and information freely given by Marinatos and warmly acknowledged by Evans on new discoveries, especially those of Marinatos himself at Dreros. In the case of Payne, also in 1930, Marinatos was reprimanded by his own Ministry after very sharp exchanges between the now established ephor and the British archaeologist. Nanno then shows that her father not only apologized but went on to form an excellent working relationship with his colleagues. We may add that the aptness of her linking Evans and Marinatos is confirmed by a certain parallelism in their archaeological lives. Time and chance were to deliver unimagined success for both, at Knossos and on Thera, but in the end tragedy also: for the one at the close of his life the prospect of the destruction of his achievement in the horrors of war, for the other death by accident at the height of his powers and in the midst of his success.

As she explains, Nanno Marinatos had invited our dear friend and colleague Stylianos Alexiou to write this foreword. No one could have been more appropriate. Sadly, it was not to be: Stylianos passed away on 12 November 2013, at the age of 92. Yet my standing in for him offers a degree of symmetry. Evans had written the substantial preface to Stephanos Xanthoudides's still fundamental work, *The Vaulted Tombs of Mesará* (1924). Xanthoudides died unexpectedly in 1928 and was succeeded as Ephor in 1929 by Spyridon Marinatos. The high scholarly achievements of Xanthoudides, as extensive in Cretan history, literature and philology as in archaeology, were remarkably closely mirrored in the career and range of publications of Alexiou, who as a fourteen-year-old boy had been present at and remembered the ceremony to unveil the bust of Evans in the West Court of the Palace in 1935, in the presence of the excavator. Marinatos, then 33, was of course present as Ephor. In 2004 Alexiou and I dedicated *The Early Minoan Tombs of Lebena* to the memory of Xanthoudides, which brings us full circle.

PETER WARREN

PREFACE

Although this work follows a more or less linear chronology (beginning in 1901 with Evans's 'Mycenaean Tree and Pillar Cult' and ending with his death in 1941), its aim is not to recount Evans's life, which has been successfully accomplished by other biographies. It focuses instead on his mental world and the historical and intellectual backdrop against which he conceived his boldest ideas. It is not an accident that he undertook the second phase of restorations at Knossos in the period between the two great European wars (1917–39) when many innovations were taking place in the arts, music, cinema and sciences. And yet, modernity did not influence him except in one sense: he defied its aesthetic starkness and sought to leave behind the softer beauty of another age. Consequently, the restorations at Knossos are not as much the result of his Victorian heritage as of the melancholy realization that it was nearing its end.

The ideas that Evans inherited from Charles Darwin and Edward B. Tylor have helped me greatly to construct a frame that explains the former's attitudes on time, chance and civilization. Equally, I have been much helped by letters of the interwar period derived from the archives of my father, Spyridon Marinatos (Appendices). Some of them have been donated to the Gennadius Library, Athens, others to the Archaeological Society at Athens, while some remain in my possession.

Based on these letters, the narrative presented here could have been different, however. It could have centred on the 'love and hate' relationship between the British School at Knossos, on the one hand, and the Greek Ephor of Crete on the other. Such an approach would have been in tune with the general postcolonial trend of our age but would not have done justice to the personality and ideas of a man such as Evans, who valued the brotherhood of science above all else.

The correspondence between Sir Arthur Evans and Spyridon Marinatos reveals that the former was respectful to younger scholars and not at all a nuisance to them as has been claimed in some biographies.[1] Nor does it support the theory that he was a subjective and flamboyant researcher, as one man put it (the latter statement was fortunately not made by a specialist).[2] Indeed, Evans has been subjected to extreme criticism of late – some of it based on inadequate study of his writings and notes. This negativity will no doubt eventually provoke a counter-movement.[3]

I have received generous help during my research from the Institute of Aegean Prehistory, Philadelphia. It provided a grant to organize the archives of Spyridon Marinatos (1901–74) which have formed one of the bases of the present work. Ordering and classifying the material was a task that I could not have accomplished without the assistance of Giorgos Tzorakis, Herakleion, Crete and Sebastian Anderson, Urbana, Illinois. I also thank Theodoros Eliopoulos, Athens, for providing me with evidence he had collected about British–Greek relations.

I thank the archivist of the British School at Athens, Amalia G. Kakissis, and the archivist of the American School of Classical Studies, Athens, Natalia Vogeikoff. Many thanks go also to Metaxia Tsipopoulou, ex-Director of the Archives of the Ministry of Culture, Athens. I am grateful to Nicoletta Momigliano for sharing with me documents about Sir Arthur Evans. The Ashmolean Museum, Oxford has very kindly provided me with material from Evans's notebooks. Ioannis Galanakis at the Ashmolean (now lecturer in Greek Prehistory, University of Cambridge) has helped with questions about the Ring of Minos. Diamantis Panagiotopoulos and Maria Anastasiadou, University of Heidelberg, have sent me images from the archives of *The Corpus of Minoan and Mycenaean Seals*. I thank the twenty-third Ephoreia, Herakleion for making the correspondence of the museum available to me and the Bridgeman Art Library Ltd for supplying me with an image of Elizabeth I wearing a costume that Evans would have described as Minoan-like.

Deepest gratitude for the conceptualization of this project is owed to the late Professor Stylianos Alexiou, Herakleion. He was a scholar of Cretan civilization from its Minoan beginnings to its twentieth-century development and understood all the nuances of the island's history. He personally knew many of the people who feature in this book. As I was writing the preface, news reached me from Greece that he had passed away. Just a few months back, sitting at our favourite restaurant in Herakleion, I had asked him to write the foreword to this book. Alas it was not to be! His death widens the gap between us and the age of Evans, as he was one of the last persons alive to have met him in person, in April of 1935. I doubt that I could have written the present work without the vivid impressions of Herakleion of the late 1930s that he conveyed to me during our many conversations over the years.

To Vasilios Petrakos I am indebted for advice about how to introduce the subject. Peter Warren has provided a most thorough commentary of the manuscript and has precluded errors. The University of Illinois, Chicago has provided me with funds for the copy-editing costs and for other kinds of support. I am most grateful to Sebastian Anderson for proofreading of the manuscript and encouragement throughout.

All the translations from Greek, German and French to English (and all the consequent errors) are mine.

Nanno Marinatos, Chicago, USA, 12 November 2013

INTRODUCTION

A Portrait

According to Joan Evans's biography of her brother, which must remain the most authentic one, Sir Arthur Evans was a complex man. On the one hand, he was sociable, well able to hold a salon and be an excellent host; on the other, he liked his solitude.[1] He was so private about his feelings that his sister describes his soul as a 'secret fortress'.[2] He liked music (mostly Mozart) but never went to public concerts and preferred the radio instead (I imagine that Stravinsky and Shostakovich were not to his taste).[3] As a young man he wore flamboyant, ethnic costumes to amuse himself, but as he grew older he paid little attention to his attire. His energy and physical endurance were unusual, and yet he was able to bear the waning of bodily strength with surprising courage and stoicism. He was night-blind and could not walk through a park or garden at night unaided. His ward James Candy remembers: 'Sir Arthur, all his life, had suffered from night blindness caused by his myopic sight, which was very serious, as he would blunder into the trees and bushes unless he carried a lantern or had someone to guide him'.[4] At the same time, he had great physical agility and stamina, which made a huge impression on his contemporaries. Piet de Jong, the architect of the Knossos Palace in the interwar period, describes an excursion in 1922 in which he, Mackenzie and some of the workmen took part:

On one occasion Mackenzie and I turning round as we left the table on the lookout for a suitable place for a nap saw Sir Arthur climbing up a tree. He went up with the greatest of ease and after his nap came down and presented us with three limericks which he had composed on a young lady named Tankard.[5]

Despite his slight body frame and thin voice (or because of it), Evans had a curiously powerful personality. The writer Dilys Powell, wife of the Director of the British School in Athens in the interwar period, writes that he was soft to family and friends, but that he also had a certain asperity in his character: 'Even sophisticated people were intimidated.'[6] On other occasions, though, he was delightful to be with because he had a sense of humour. Powell remembers him scratching his head and laughing heartily at his own jokes. In 1931, taking the curator's wife Hilda Pendlebury's arm, he said: 'My dear Mrs Pendlebury, don't worry, I like losing my temper!'[7] The classicist Sir Maurice Bowra described him as 'driven by a demon which made him both formidable and lovable. His remarks were infused by bursting excitement when any new problem called for solution.'[8]

Piet de Jong observed Evans astutely and described him as a very remarkable man.[9] He made a cartoon of Sir Arthur standing in front of the Blue Monkey fresco at Knossos and lecturing about apes (one imagines) with great intensity and eloquence, aided by his moving hands.[10] This cartoon is almost exactly mirrored in an actual photograph taken by Spyridon Marinatos at Knossos in 1935. There, Evans stands on the terrace of the Palace next to the governor (nomarch) of Crete and points at something in the distance (Figure 1). Is he discussing the extent of the domain of the Knossos king, or is he predicting the future? Just as we look at this picture now and wonder what his thoughts were at the moment the shot was taken, so he too wondered about the minds of the people of the past, humans who had created such brilliant art. He noticed all the small details and was able to penetrate this ancient culture of Crete because he understood its code and was aware of its uniqueness. The ability to read art went hand in hand with the ability to read people and know instinctively

Figure 1 Evans at Knossos with the nomarch, Emmanuel Lydakis, in April 1935.

when they were happy or suffering. This sentiment led him to adopt a pale boy named James Candy, a son of a neighbouring farmer, because he looked sickly. He saw to it that the boy got the best chances for a good education, so he could live a decent life. To his sister Joan he was soft, although he seemed remote at times. On one occasion, when she had lost a friend and was silently grieving, he wrote: 'I am so sorry for you'. The sympathy is expressed simply but sincerely and powerfully.[11] When the archaeologist Richard Seager died suddenly in Crete, Evans was severely affected and felt the loss deeply, people told Dilys Powell.[12] At the funeral, he got out of the carriage to walk bareheaded behind the coffin.[13]

Evans's personality had a childlike quality.[14] When Candy came to live with him at Youlbury, the boy naturally felt lonely, and Evans did not know what to do to amuse him. He therefore bought him some tame rabbits to keep him company. These were at first kept in a large cage, and then in a wire enclosure on one of the small lawns below the house. When Candy went away to school, Evans fed the rabbits himself and then sent reports about them to 'Jimmy', referring to them as Bunny 1 and Bunny 2.[15]

In other ways too, Evans was puerile. His house at Youlbury was utterly extravagant with 22 bedrooms and several fine bathrooms, one of which was a Roman bath with three steps to go down to it. On the landing outside the bathroom hung the head of a brown bear that once had attacked Evans's brother Norman in the Carpathian mountains![16]

He had outbursts of temper, but they were short-lived. Friendship was of the utmost importance to him, and this is why he kept the same friends for a very long time. It is not an accident that Sir John Myres mentions this fact as an exceptional quality in the final sentence of Evans's obituary. His 'genius for friendship and devotion to learning and truth are an ineffaceable memory.'[17]

He never forgot his wife Margaret, who died in Italy in 1893, just a few years before the excavations in Crete began. All his correspondence was written on black-trimmed stationary (see Appendix 1, Figures 45 and 46), and the letters were placed in envelopes stamped with black elephants. Elephants are said to grieve. This indirect way of expressing his sorrow and the fixation on memories was typical of Evans; he did not know any other way. As his sister Joan writes, 'he was very much alone and would not have it otherwise.'[18]

Some Personal Memories

I have my own personal impressions to add, not of Evans, of course, who passed away almost a decade before I was born, but of his visual presence in our home in Athens. As a small child in the 1950s I did not know much about the Minoans or Knossos but could not fail to notice Evans's picture on my father Spyridon Marinatos's desk. I thought he exuded calmness and the kind of contentment that sometimes accompanies deep old age. For some reason this portrait gave me peculiar comfort. As I grew older, during the time that

INTRODUCTION   5

Marinatos was excavating Akrotiri on Thera (1967–74), I remember my father mumbling to himself that Evans had been right. I had no idea what this meant, nor did I ask. Perhaps my father was thinking of the restorations and conservation problems associated with the site; for at that time Marinatos faced similar problems as Evans. How could he conserve a city so well preserved and yet so vulnerable to physical disasters and yearly rains? The excavators of Phaistos and Malia had not faced similar challenges since the latter palaces had been almost completely destroyed by subsequent habitations. But Knossos had survived almost intact, not having been subjected to the destruction caused by subsequent human habitation; it was therefore a site without precedent, and Evans had to find radical solutions to preserve it. Akrotiri was even better preserved than Knossos, but was in equal need of conservation. Marinatos did not dare utilize ferro-concrete extensively to fortify the walls of the houses since the principles of restoration had changed entirely. However, he feared – and he was right – that time would bring its revenge. This is probably the reason why he muttered that Evans was right.

In other ways too he considered Evans a remarkable personality as I remember. He described him with a special language invented to render the essence of this gifted man: 'demonic genius', 'magnificent' and '*infectious*' (emphasis mine). Evans, he wrote, was possessed by divine enthusiasm which he was able to transmit to others. John Myres writes something very similar: 'his deep enjoyment of life *infected* everyone who knew him.'[19] Since both men speak of Evans's enthusiasm as contagion, we cannot doubt the exceptional charisma that Evans must have possessed.

I have another memory, which concerns a debate. One area of disagreement between Evans and the archaeologists who worked on the mainland of Greece was the question of Knossian dominance in the Peloponnese or the opposite, the Mycenaean conquest of Knossos. Evans never believed the Helladic archaeologists Alan Wace and Carl Blegen that the Mycenaeans came to Crete, nor did they believe him that the Minoans dominated over the Peloponnese. Evans's view was labelled *Pancretism* by his scholarly opponents.

My personal memory is that unexpected support for Evans's idea of Minoan dominance in the Peloponnese surfaced during Marinatos's excavations in the Peloponnese in the early 1960s. He found a magnificent Mycenaean beehive tomb at Peristeria, Messenia and dated it to the sixteenth century BCE. It is necessary to backtrack a little and say a bit more about the dating debates that went on concerning the beehive (tholos) tombs. In the interwar period, Alan Wace had argued that sophistication of construction was a criterion for dating these buildings, and on this basis he assigned the Atreus tomb at Mycenae (the grandest and best) to the fourteenth century BCE. He also claimed that it was built at the end of the evolutionary line of development.[20] Evans had a different view. He was convinced that civilization was not the result of steady progress, and that regression in the course of time was possible. As far as the Atreus tomb was concerned, he dated it to a much earlier period than Wace, assigning it to the same time as when Knossos was at its peak, at the end of the seventeenth or early sixteenth century BCE. His main argument was the following.

A relief of bull-catching, reminiscent of the relief frescoes of the North Portico at Knossos, had been found in the vicinity of the Atreus tomb and had been transported by Lord Elgin at the British Museum. It was generally accepted by scholars that the relief had originated in the Atreus tomb. Evans argued that it was of Knossian origin and dated it to the early sixteenth century BCE, the same time as the relief frescoes of the Knossos Palace. Consequently, it testified to a strong Minoan presence and influence on the Peloponnese.[21] Wace, however, insisted that the tomb was constructed *after* the fall of Knossos and assumed that the relief was of Mycenaean manufacture. He won the debate.[22] Most scholars believed him, including Marinatos.

We return now to the excavation of the tholos tomb at Peristeria. Although it was similar in construction to the tholos of Atreus, it clearly dated to an earlier age, the sixteenth century BCE, and rendered support to Evans's theory. Marinatos also noted that the impressive ashlar façade of this tomb was ornamented with two Knossian mason's marks: a star and a double axe. He was genuinely puzzled. He was reluctant to accept Evans's conclusions that there was Minoan dominance on the Peloponnese, or that the prince buried at Peristeria was allied with the house of Knossos. Such a hypothesis would have run counter to his own reconstruction of Mycenaean history, but he had to be fair and give Evans his due and thus wrote:

> Of course the scales of the balance are tipping in favour of an Achaean invasion of Crete, but if Evans were alive now, he would have considered the Peristeria tomb as evidence that the opposite is the case.[23]

This I remember myself, although I did not have knowledge of the debate between Wace and Evans then.

In reviewing Evans's legacy, I have reflected often on how important it is to revisit some of his old theories and test them against the present evidence. Evans was never wrong, his architect at Knossos Christian Doll said once.[24] This may be an exaggeration. On the other hand, consider how the excavations at Akrotiri, Thera (in which I took part myself) have verified Evans's theory about Knossian influence in the Aegean. The architecture of Akrotiri has yielded evidence of Minoan shrines (a lustral basin or *adyton*) and of Minoan architectural vocabulary, since its larger houses are built in the technique of ashlar masonry and have pier and door partitions.[25] The script at Thera is Minoan Linear A, and its religious symbols consist of sacred horns, griffins and double axe symbols.[26] All this bespeaks of more than a superficial influence from Crete.

As for the murals that decorate almost all the houses of Akrotiri, their study is still in progress. But there is every reason to think that Evans's view about the existence of *one* major goddess, who is mother of all the young, humans as well as animals, a goddess who embodies the unity of nature, is correct.[27] I remember well when the fresco of a seated goddess was found in 1973 in a building called Xeste 3. Spyridon Marinatos instantly knew her to be the Knossian goddess whom Evans had first identified as such and noted in his daybook of 1973:

The suspicion arose in my mind that one of the seated women was a goddess. [...] The idea of the Mistress of animals emerges clearly. I gave the command at the excavation: Search everywhere in case you find pieces which look as though they belong to lions. Next day not only had animal pieces been found, but the further fact emerged that the animal was a griffin.[28]

There is another link between Knossos and Akrotiri. It is not entirely by coincidence that the project of excavating Thera was conceived by Marinatos while he was in Crete with Evans and was much inspired by him (Appendix 2). And as Evans was writing the final words of *The Palace of Minos*, intent on preserving the memory of Minoan civilization from the 'long night of man's forgetfulness', Marinatos was already planning the future excavation of Thera, which did not materialize until 1967.[29]

Truth and Happiness

All the above information helped me to construct a portrait of Evans. The picture became clearer, however, only after many years of studying his writings. I detected a certain melancholy in the work of the interwar period, a sadness that was counter-balanced by a readiness to combat opposition (political, or scientific, or aesthetic) and stand up for what he considered truth. This realization, rather than the anecdotal stories, provided me with access to his imagination, and the emotions that guided it.

One question that must be raised is why Sir John Myres singled out devotion to truth as one of his friend's most memorable qualities.[30] Was he referring to his scientific integrity, or did he imply something more than that, perhaps a moral boldness to align himself with what he felt was right? Adherence to steady principles will have checked Evans's innate tendency towards subjectivity and will have controlled his irritation against those who (unfairly as he thought) opposed him. Moreover this adherence to principle unified the various aspects of his personality and made him a steady and predictable man.

Was he egocentric? Undoubtably, he was a little. He must have noticed from a young age that he had unusual abilities of memory and perception. It sometimes happens that experience of superiority in childhood may isolate a person from his peers, and it may nurture a sense of solitude. Arthur Evans had the misfortune of losing his mother when he was a small child and this may have resulted in serious psychological trauma.[31] On the other hand, he had the very good fortune to have siblings and a very strong, intelligent and devoted father: whose integrity as a scientist and a member of society provided a good model to follow. Egocentric Arthur Evans may have been, but unfair he was not.

Was he a contented man? Probably he would have said so, despite the misfortune of losing his wife, and despite the explosions of temper which reveal inner tensions. Freud's interpretation is that events in early childhood dictate much of one's psychic state in life, and he is right. Perhaps, however, what held Evans's personality together and protected him from neurotic dysfunction — even when he was seized by anger — were his steady values and principles.[32] He recognized the symptoms of personality dysfunction in others, as he did in the case of his field director Duncan Mackenzie. The inability to harmonize behaviour with what went on in the mind was madness to him and a horrible condition.

Charles Darwin describes the relationship between scholarship and the good life so well that he is worth citing, especially since I believe that what he says applies to Evans perfectly.

My chief enjoyment and sole employment throughout life has been scientific work, and the excitement from such work makes me for the time forget, or drive quite away, my daily discomfort [. . .] I have therefore nothing to record during the rest of my life, except the publication of my several books.[33]

CHAPTER 1

TREE AND PILLAR CULT

Evans and E. B. Tylor

Before Evans excavated Knossos, the principal concern of Aegean prehistoric archaeology was the reconstruction of the proto-history of Greece, and the relationship of its mythical tradition to the story of Homer. In the eighteenth century, European travellers regarded the ruins of Greece as vestiges of this mythic-historical tradition. The French count Choiseul-Gouffier (1782), who toured the Greek islands and the Troad with a copy of Homer in his hand, constructed historical maps matching epic tradition with physical ruins, and projecting Greek history into prehistory, without second thoughts.[1] The word 'Mycenaean' did not exist yet, and scholars called the prehistoric peoples of Greece Pelasgians, a designation derived from Hecateus and Herodotus.[2] At the same time, the German scholar Karl Hoeck (1794–1877) had the clever idea to separate the cultural horizon of Crete from that of the mainland. He conceived of the people of the island as non-Greeks and therefore baptized the period of the Cretan Bronze Age 'Minoan'.[3]

Such was the state of affairs when Heinrich Schliemann made his spectacular discoveries at Troy and Mycenae in the nineteenth century, allegedly uncovering the cities of the Homeric epics. The ruins of Mycenae had been there, of course, visible through the centuries, but Schliemann's rich finds reified the myth. And when he announced his discoveries to the world, it seemed indeed to be the case that the mytho-historical method of previous scholarship had been verified.[4] The religion of the period was regarded as an early version of the Homeric belief system. When Schliemann found clay figurines in his excavations, he did not hesitate to identify them as early versions of Aphrodite and Hera, and when he found double axes, he identified them as the weapon of Zeus of Labranda (*labrys*).[5]

Evans's entry into the scene of prehistoric archaeology marks a real revolution, as he attempted to change the method of evaluating evidence almost immediately. I believe (although many would not agree with this assessment) that he liberated prehistoric Cretan archaeology from the tyranny of Greek myth.[6] However, Evans was never polemical against Schliemann or any other of his contemporaries; he steered scholarship away from Homer, gently directing it to the broader Mediterranean world.

New grounds were broken with 'Mycenaean Tree and Pillar Cult and its Mediterranean Relations,' an extensive article of approximately 100 pages published in 1901. Note that the term 'Greek' is conspicuously absent from the title, although Evans did not combat orthodoxy as represented by Schliemann and others (he actually deeply admired Schliemann). Evans always made the concession that *some* elements of Greek religion were indeed foreshadowed by the religion of Bronze Age Crete, and not uncommonly he utilized Greek myth to entice his public.[7] He knew how to write a good story and concoct clever puns: 'Amidst the labyrinth of conjecture we have here an Ariadne to supply the clue.'[8] The break with the previous tradition is nevertheless obvious.

But the innovations are remarkable. They consist first in the broadening of the horizons of Bronze Age religion by the inclusion of Egypt and the Near East. Second and more importantly, he adopts a position against the simplistic evolutionist idea that progress is steady and inevitable over time and that later cultures are *always* more advanced than earlier ones (this trend had been established in the field of Classics since the eighteenth century).[9] Contrary to the opinion of some contemporary scholars,[10] Evans had an unusual and sophisticated notion of historical progress and conceded the possibility of regression. Much of this was owed to Charles Darwin and his entourage, about which more will be said later on. Suffice it to mention here that in *Descent of Man*, Darwin argued that cultures were capable of both intellectual and moral regression and that backward steps in civilization were demonstrable in history. 'We must remember that progress is no invariable rule,' he said, because who had ever surpassed the Greeks?[11] To his friend, the geologist Charles Lyell, Darwin wrote that natural selection 'implies no *necessary* tendency to progression.'[12]

Following this line of reasoning, Evans did not find it problematic to suggest that the culture of Knossos, which was earlier by a thousand years than that of Athens, was as advanced as the latter, perhaps even more so.

To truly appreciate his originality and reaction against linear evolutionism, we must take a brief look at the work of two of his classicist colleagues at Cambridge, Gilbert Murray and Jane Harrison. Murray assigned all prehistoric religions to the 'Age of Ignorance',[13] and so did Jane Harrison. In her third edition of *Themis* (1927), she describes herself as an old evolutionist, a believer that older religions were characterized by primeval rituals and yearly demons.[14] Evans, however, found that Minoan religion did not belong to the age of ignorance, because it included anthropomorphic gods and the latter were represented in a highly sophisticated manner. These conclusions were simply ignored by the Cambridge school. A classical scholar once said, apparently in the presence of Evans, that he (i.e. the scholar) 'cared more for the products of the full maturity of the Greek spirit than for its immature struggles'. Evans reacted in anger.[15] He refused to accept that Crete had engaged in immature struggles and insisted that it had reached full maturity, if not complete perfection. Its peoples had scripts, he said, and he did not consider it unlikely that they had produced poetry and literature. He deduced this from the visual material that bespoke narratives reminiscent of the literary accomplishments of Homer. Of course, no classical scholar was willing to accept such a bold assessment, but Evans insisted to the end of his life that the Crete of that age afforded mankind a glimpse into a brilliant moment 'in the history of European civilization.'[16] He tried a different argument as well, utterly Darwinian in its tone. Greek culture did not come out of nothing, he said, but it must have had precedent in the Mediterranean, just like the organs of evolved animals had precedents in lower organisms. Thinking most likely of Darwin's revolution he wrote:

These are the days of origins and what is true of the highest forms of animal life and functional activities is equally true of the vital principles that inspired the mature civilization of Greece.[17]

As he got older, Evans became more outspoken about the superiority of Minoan religion and aggressively defended its rare brilliance.[18] But to return to 1901, his most important innovation was the introduction of a new mental toolkit for the study of Minoan religion, derived principally from the work of the anthropologist E. B. Tylor and the Darwinist group.

Arthur Evans's father, Sir John Evans, had played no small role in the formation of a social and intellectual network that concerned itself mostly with the early origins of man, and with man's mental evolution over hundreds of thousands of years. John Evans was affectionately known among his friends at the Royal and Geological Societies as 'flint-Evans' because of his important studies on stone tools in prehistoric Britain. This is how he caught the attention of Darwin, with whom he exchanged letters.[19] John Evans was also a friend of the prehistoric specialist John Lubbock, a friend of Darwin's; the group thus became further consolidated through social interactions and ideas. Another member of the Darwin entourage was E. B. Tylor, the most eminent anthropologist in Britain after the publication of his two-volume work *Primitive Culture* (1871).[20] Concerning this book, Darwin wrote to his friend Wallace: 'By the way have you read Tyler [sic] & Lecky? Both these books have interested me much.'[21] Darwin often cites Tylor in support of his own ideas about morality and religion.[22] On his side, Tylor regarded Darwin as one of the most influential figures in the development of modern thought.[23]

The ideas of Darwin and Tylor reflect similar conceptions about civilization, especially as concerned man's intellectual and moral capacities. Both stressed the unity of early mankind, and the capacity of all peoples to possess intellect, no matter how primitive. They did not doubt that the *cultivation* of intelligence and moral attitudes resulted in progress and so did not take progress for granted. The potential was there, but it did not occur automatically – it was earned by hard labour. In history, regressions did occur.

The above is what Evans inherited from his father's generation. The special influence of Tylor cannot be doubted as the latter was a personal friend of Evans the elder, often travelling with him to explore dolmens, and discover prehistoric stone tools.[24] Tylor was on his part indebted to Arthur's uncle, the anthropologist Sebastian Evans, and thus was connected by multiple ties to the Evans family. Tylor naturally became a mentor figure to young Arthur, and when the latter became famous through his excavations at Knossos, and his portrait was presented to the Chancellor of Oxford University, Tylor was among the distinguished men who attended the ceremony.[25]

What did Evans learn from Tylor and his kit of 'mental anthropology', as Tylor himself named his work?[26] One issue, perhaps the most important one, concerned the essence of civilization itself, which Tylor saw as a combination of moral and aesthetic attitudes. Was mankind from its inception capable of sympathy with other humans and even animals? The answer was affirmative. Sympathy or empathy was the ability to enter the mind of another being and share in their suffering; this constituted the basis of moral behaviour. Such a thesis had been proposed by Darwin, and there is merit to it, since it is said that criminals often lack empathy.[27]

As for religion, it exerted a benign influence on man's imagination, provided that reason was involved.[28] Tylor considered early man the mother and father of modern man, but also stressed that ethics could be improved by cultivation of customs, education, social practices, and self-discipline: this is what constituted high civilization.

Evans's view of civilization is essentially the same as Darwin's and Tylor's. It consisted in the cultivation of aesthetics on the one hand, and instinctive empathy with other live beings, even animals, on the other (this is why he considered the involvement of Minoans with nature so important). Unlike his contemporary classicists who believed that 'early' goes together with 'primitive', Evans understood the complexity of human history as a series of peaks and regressions. Minoan culture was a peak (in terms of its aesthetic and humanistic achievement), after which came a relative regression, until there was another peak with the Greeks and Romans.

He also learned from Darwin and Tylor that the study of religion is enhanced by use of comparisons and analogies across time and space, and that mankind had an essential unity. This conclusion followed from Darwin's premise that all mankind had a single origin in their remote ancestry and, as already mentioned above, that even primeval man had mental faculties similar to those of the present day.[29]

A few words must now be said about the theory of animism, which is the main theme of Tylor's work. Man was always a keen observer of nature and noted differences between live entities, such as plants and animals, and lifeless ones, such as stones. Animals and plants grew but also decayed; by contrast, matter remained static and immutable. Primitive man attributed the difference to the presence, or absence, of soul (*anima*). What was life except the insertion of soul into inanimate matter? Primitive man thus found a logical theory to explain life and Tylor called this phenomenon 'animism'. The theory had the merit of also explaining why dream-spirits entered the body of human beings at night and possessed them during sleep.[30] Even Darwin was impressed by this explanation of Tylor and adopted it to interpret phenomena of religious experience:

It is also probable, as Mr. Tylor has shewn, that dreams may have first given rise to the notion of spirits; for savages do not readily distinguish between subjective and objective impressions. When a savage dreams, the figures which appear before him are believed to have come from a distance, and to stand over him; or the soul of the dreamer goes out on its travels, and comes home with a remembrance of what it has seen. [...] Nevertheless I cannot but suspect that there is a still earlier and ruder stage, when anything which manifests power or movement is thought to be endowed with some form of life, and with mental faculties analogous to our own.[31]

Tylor explained through his theory of animism why there was tree and stone worship in antiquity. As spirits moved freely, they entered trees, stones, or pillars, and took possession of them, making them their temporary indwelling places.[32] The logic of early man was thus made accessible to the man of the nineteenth century. Apart from its value as a landmark in the history of ideas, animism is still applicable to evidence that has emerged since. We know that the ancient Hittites of Anatolia worshipped stones, the so-called *huwasi*, because they are mentioned in inventories of the Hittite king Tudhalya IV. The stones were anointed, much like cult images, and sacrifices were performed in front of them.[33] Hittite specialists have, therefore, concluded that sacred stones were indeed conceived as 'houses of god'.[34] A most surprising discovery occurred relatively recently. A stone stele from Anatolia bears an inscription which states that the soul of the deceased rests in the stele: 'to my soul which is in this stele.' The inscription provides the additional information that Katumuwa, servant of Panamuwa, was the dedicator.[35]

This mental kit was inherited by Arthur Evans from Tylor and is that which he applied to Minoan religion.

The Mental Anthropology Behind the Tree and Pillar Cult

Even before he began his excavations in Crete, Evans had looked at minute images engraved on rings and seals and realized that trees, as well as pillars, featured there prominently. After just one year of excavation at Knossos he was able to put together a synthesis of Minoan religion which he based on these images aided by the insights of Tylor. He saw representations of humans approaching a tree or a pillar. The pillars were often decorated with sacred emblems. He saw dancing figures performing in the vicinity of a tree or worshippers approaching a tree followed by huge wild animals. From the imagery he deduced: first, that tree sanctuaries existed in the Bronze Age; second, that sacred trees were depositories 'of the divine life manifested by [...] fruits and foliage'; third, that the pillar, like the tree, was a focal point of cult and that the two were interchangeable in the syntax of the visual scene. Fourth, pillars and trees were interchangeable with anthropomorphic gods. Finally, he concluded that worshippers came to the sanctuaries to bring offerings and invoke gods, and sometimes experienced their epiphany (Figures 2 and 3a–c).[36] His debt to Tylor is acknowledged:

> For the ideas underlying the widespread primitive cult I need only refer to Tylor. [...] The spirit is generally forced to enter the stone or pillar by charms and incantations, and sometimes also passes into the body of the priest or worshipper. The possession itself of the material object is only in its nature temporary. When the spirit departs the idol remains only a sacred object. When a deity is thus brought down into a tree it blends with the tree of life.[37]

Let us now see how the theory of animism helped him explain a ring from Knossos (Figure 2). A god is depicted as arriving from the sky to enter his tree-sanctuary. An obelisk is also present. The god is greeted by a female figure, possibly a worshipper. Evans considers this as an epiphany scene and notes that the female worshipper sees the god (in her imagination?). He also notes that the anthropomorphic and aniconic images of divinities exist side by side and that the two constitute alternative conceptualizations. Indeed, on the ring

Figure 2   On a ring found near Knossos, a female has a vision of a god arriving at his tree-sanctuary. Ring now in Oxford: CMS VI, 2, 281.

Figure 3a–c   Minoan and Mycenaean gems showing pillars and gods flanked by lions. Evans drew the conclusion that they are interchangeable in the imagery and arrived at his hypothesis of pillar cult. (a) CMS VI, 2, 312; (b) CMS VI, 2, 315; (c) CMS VI, 2, 384.

depicted in Figure 2 the viewer sees both the god and his obelisk-like pillar.

An equally important observation in the analysis of the visual syntax of the compositions is that gods were *interchangeable* with pillars or trees (Figure 3a–c). His final conclusion, then, was that Tylor's theory of animism was verified in Minoan art and that pillars and/or trees were worshipped because gods could enter them and make them their temporary dwelling. Also he concluded that deities were perceived as both aniconic objects and as having anthropomorphic guises: 'The idols remained aniconic, but the Gods themselves were naturally pictured to the mind of their worshippers under a more or less human aspect.'[38]

None of these conclusions would have been reached had Evans not divided cult scenes into groups and had he not classified them in an orderly and thorough fashion. In other words, the understanding of the visual syntax was a scholarly endeavour that strictly followed the rules of nineteenth-century science. Classification enabled him to establish formulas and to determine that gods and aniconic objects were visually interchangeable.[39]

Equally important were the criteria which Evans established to distinguish deities from ordinary humans, and these were size, centrality of position and attributes. To give an example: minute figures hovering in the upper field of a ring could not be humans; they had to be gods descending from the sky (Figure 2).[40]

Now we must say a bit more about how Evans was aided in the conceptualization of the cult practice of animism through analogy with other cultures. In this field, he owes a lot to the work of the scholar William Robertson Smith, whose field of study was history of Semitic religions. Due to Robertson Smith, Evans used the Hebrew Bible and sought analogies between Hebrew and Minoan cults.[41]

The Hebrews had a sacred palm tree called *Asherah*, the sacred tree of life which they used also in connection with divination. When the tree was possessed by a deity, it spoke with the voice of god, and this is the reason why the judge Deborah gave her oracular responses seated under a palm tree. Divination was attested in connection with the holy Terebinth tree near Shechem, and Robertson Smith noted that the altar stood next to the sacred tree; the entire service was carried out in the open air.[42] This is exactly what Evans saw on certain Minoan rings (see Figure 2) and he realized that in Minoan Crete the holy tree was the focal point of cult within an open-air sanctuary. When the god was invoked by a worshipper, he or she came down to enter it. The encounter occurred in front of the shrine or temple, which again matched Robertson Smith's description of Semitic sanctuaries where the divine symbols stood outside the temple.[43]

To the same scholar Evans was indebted for the understanding of the function of holy stones and pillars in Hebrew cults. The Semitic peoples poured libations on stones, anointed them, or poured blood offerings on these stones. Robertson Smith called them *masseba*,[44] but Evans renamed them *baetyls* thus introducing this term into Aegean studies. Tylor had used this term only once to designate a meteor.[45] *Baetyl* is thus an innovation by Evans. Where did he find it?

The origin of the word is Semitic, first used by Philo of Byblos and Pliny in the second century CE to designate fireballs, missiles, or meteors.[46] We may guess that Evans chose it deliberately because he wished to draw a comparison between Minoan and Hebrew religions, and thus break the monopoly of Greek terminology projected onto Bronze Age Cretan ritual. It will also be remembered that the science of religion admitted analogies as a methodological tool.[47] In any case, there is no doubt that he was inspired by a passage in Genesis concerning the establishment of the sanctuary of Bethel. Jacob arrives there and decides to spend the night. He takes one of the stones and puts it under his head as a pillow. He then dreams of a ladder reaching up to heaven on which angels of God ascend and descend. The Lord stands beside Jacob. After this stunning revelation, Jacob wakes up and names the place 'Beth-el,' which literally means House of God (Gen 28:11–13). The biblical passage matched the representation on the Knossos ring (Figure 2): here was a god descending from the heaven about to take residence in his tree or pillar. Was this not a pictorial rendition of a vision similar to Jacob's, and did it not happen next to a *baetylic* pillar?

> The obelisk here is literally, as in the case of the Beth-el set up by Jacob, God's house, and the God is seen actually in the act of being brought down by the ritual incantation of his votary to his earthly tenement of stone.[48]

Another biblical passage about King Solomon's temple shed light on the nature of sacred pillars. He (Solomon) 'set up two pillars in front of the temple, one on the right, the other to the left; the one on the right he called Jachin, and the one on the left, Boaz.'[49] The names of the pillars meant strength and stability which revealed their true significance as indwelling places of the deity Jahweh. Once again, Evans drew the analogy between biblical and Minoan pillar cults.[50]

The Pantheon on the Mycenae Ring

The analysis presented here by no means exhausts all the insights of 'Tree and Pillar Cult', but enough has been said to show Evans's remarkable originality against the background of traditional archaeology.[51] The possibilities of interpretation that he opened may be illustrated by his reading of the gold ring from the fourth Shaft Grave at Mycenae (Figure 4). Schliemann is given credit for the find although the supervising excavator was the Greek archaeologist Panagiotis Stamatakes.[52] This ring depicts a female seated under a tree whom Evans identified as a goddess since she is slightly larger than the women who bring offerings to her. Also, she is seated. He

Figure 4   Gold ring from Mycenae found in H. Schliemann's excavations. Evans identified a seated goddess receiving flowers from female worshippers. Only the goddess sees the warrior-god. CMS I, 17.

further deduced that the tree was sacred and constituted the focal point of the open-air sanctuary. Furthermore, the tree was laden with fruit. Two minute females on either side of the goddess were identified as young girls, one of them plucking the fruit of the tree, the other offering flowers to the divinity.

So far there is nothing special about this interpretation. Evans's originality consists in the realization that this scene could be read on two levels. On the one hand, it was a scene of ritual offerings such as took place in any sanctuary. On the other, it represented a vision, to which we shall return. For the moment, let us note that such a festival, involving young girls making flower offerings to a goddess, is attested on a mural from Thera; Evans was thus justified in his interpretation.

The vision encompasses all the supernatural elements: the seated goddess, the young male god covered with a shield and spear, the sun

Figure 5   Mycenae ring (abstracted). The human participants have been erased to highlight the divine and cosmic elements. Evans was able to distinguish between ritual action and mythical reality. Based on CMS I, 17.

and moon appearing simultaneously and a double axe hovering in mid-air below the astral bodies. Finally, a series of lion heads is visible on the left side (Figure 5). Evans suggested that the supernatural elements existed in the imagination of the humans who came to the tree shrine expecting to meet their gods: it was 'religious fancy' that had 'pictorially introduced the divine actors.'[53]

Having thus separated the cosmic level from the human ritual level, Evans proceeded to make a hypothesis about the pantheon. The male was a 'warrior god',[54] a possible ancestor of a Zeus-Jupiter type.[55] The female could be his wife (as we shall see, he eventually changed his mind about the relationship). As for the huge double axe hovering in mid-sky, it was a symbol rather than an implement of cult, because it held a key position in the composition exactly below the sun and the moon. The symmetrical duality of the axe reflected the astral bodies as well as the divine pair: 'The curious reduplication of the axe blades suggests indeed that it stands as an image of the conjunction of the divine pair – a solar and a lunar divinity.'[56] Later, as we shall see, he reinterpreted the same duality as referring to the dual nature of the goddess, her celestial and underworld aspects.[57]

About the six lion heads at the left edge of the field of the ring he had an interesting suggestion. Analogy from Egyptian religion suggested that lions guard the horizon and mark the space of the setting sun. This led him to propose a similar function for Minoan lions.[58] He concluded that the pantheon consisted of a divine pair whose symbol was the double axe and that this celestial pair was shown simultaneously near its tree abode on earth and within the larger cosmos.

To appreciate the novelty of the approach and the sensitivity to detail we may compare Evans's interpretation to some others. For example, when Heinrich Schliemann and his wife Sophia saw this same ring, they exclaimed that it was utterly Homeric. The seated goddess reminded them of the seated gods on the Parthenon frieze; the figure with the shield and spear reminded them of the Palladium of Athena; the lion heads they misunderstood as idols.[59]

The Greek archaeologist Christos Tsountas gave a more cautious interpretation in 1893, admitting that the meaning of religion was obscure to him:

> The nature of the subject is such that we have only the monuments as sources. Without written evidence it is almost impossible to arrive at conclusions. A special difficulty is that the monuments with religious representations are few and I personally would gladly abstain from the subject altogether.[60]

Despite his reasonable caution, Tsountas ended up projecting the Greek pantheon on the iconography, like Schliemann had done, and identified the god with the eight-shield as Zeus, the seated goddess as Dione or Demeter, or as Aphrodite in the Gardens.[61] He was at a loss to explain the row of lion heads on the margin of the scene and suggested that they were fountainheads.

Nor did the Greek archaeologist George Mylonas change this approach 65 years after 'Tree and Pillar Cult' was published. Some of the identifications he proposes for the seated goddess are Rhea, Cybele, Aphrodite, Demeter; he engages in no precise analysis of the syntax of the iconography of this most important ring.[62] The above reveals that archaeologists did not fully appreciate the novelties of approach introduced by 'Tree and Pillar Cult'. Inertia compelled scholars to fall back to the traditional prism of Greek mythology as a lens for the interpretation of Bronze Age religion.

The Artistic Side of Evans

'Tree and Pillar Cult' is an example of Evans's scientific method, since he utilizes observation, classification, and hypothesis. However, it also testifies to his unusual sensitivity to artistic detail: as though he had the ability to enter the world of pictures, and understand the meaning from the inside. This ability of imagination was manifested already during childhood and was noted by Sir John Evans, who wrote to his fiancée about his eight-year-old son:

> He is a very odd child and though I am an Evans myself to a great extent, I cannot quite understand him. Think of his burying a china doll (with its legs broken) with a butterfly and some other things in the garden, and placing this inscription over them 'KING EDWARD SIXTH and the butterfly and there cloths and things.' Whether he had some notion of resurrection or not I cannot say, but the Psyche element is very singular and the placing of the clothes in readiness for his re-existence looks like forethought.[63]

The father wondered that his eight-year-old child was able to imagine a full story with a metaphysical component, and that he enacted it with all the necessary paraphernalia. It is this quality of historical imagination that furnishes one of the keys to Evans's mind, and it was not unrelated to his abilities to observe details on objects, as well as animals and human personalities. To this effect

we have the testimony of his adopted son, James Candy, who writes
in his memoirs:

> It was Sir Arthur who introduced me to the beauty of butterflies
> and moths which were to be found in abundance among the
> flowers in the garden and on the large heath patch close to the
> old oak forest. Sir Arthur and I would sally forth each day
> armed with a butterfly net [. . .] After supper we would stop and
> listen to the night jars. If we kept quite still, we could watch
> their extraordinary flight when catching moths. Their peculiar
> way of sitting on a branch, parallel to it, I have never seen in any
> other bird, and their song was a lovely purring sound.[64]

Science and imagination complement rather than contradict each
other. Darwin was a keen observer of animals, plants, as well as
human nature (his observations on the peoples he met during the
voyage of the *Beagle* are truly remarkable) and admitted that artistic
observation does not contradict science but enhances it. 'All Science,'
Darwin wrote in his notebook, 'is reason acting on [systematizing]
principles, which even animals practically know. Art precedes
science − art is experience and observation.'[65]

CHAPTER 2

MOURNING KYBELE: ARTHUR EVANS AND JAMES FRAZER

Kybele and the Young Resurgent God

We have seen how Evans conceived of the celestial divine pair and we will now turn to more specific observations about the gods, exploring also how different his views were from Sir James Frazer's, with whom Evans is often assimilated.

First, it must be noted that the popular view of the Minoan goddess as an earth and fertility deity is not due to Evans, but to Jane Harrison and the Cambridge School of myth and ritual.[1] As to the idea that she was a mother-goddess, this fully developed in his mind only in the years between the two great European wars, and even then he hardly refers to her as an earth-goddess.[2] All this will be discussed in another chapter, but here we must concentrate on his first attempt to articulate a new mythology for the Minoan gods.

It has been noted that in 'Tree and Pillar Cult' of 1901, the goddess was not viewed as the chief deity of the pantheon, but as the consort of the sky-god; the double axe was perceived to be the common symbol of the divine pair (although later Evans explained the double axe as a reference to the duality of the goddess alone).[3] About the nature of the goddess Evans knew little at first except that she was accompanied by lions, and this led him to compare her to the

Anatolian goddess Kybele. She too was flanked by lions in artistic representations. Did this mean that the two had similar mythical personae? This is what the analogy suggested. After 'Tree and Pillar Cult' had gone to press, he found unexpected support of his Kybele paradigm during the next excavation season at Knossos. He excavated several clay impressions made by the same ring and representing a goddess atop a mountain flanked by a pair of lions (Figure 6). Facing the goddess was a male figure who saluted her respectfully. Here, then, was confirmation that Minoan mythology centred on a divine pair, thought Evans. The find was proudly announced in the annual report about Knossos in *The Times*: 'a goddess akin to the later Rhea or Cybele [who] stands on her sacred rock guarded on either side by heraldically posed lions.'[4] He compared her to other goddesses of the Ancient Mediterranean, such as Aphrodite and Rhea and, inspired by Lucian's *Dea Syria*, he conflated these deities into one single type. In some ways, he was ahead of his times because this method of translating one deity into the culture of another in the religions of the East Mediterranean is utilized by historians of religion today as a tool of modern analysis.[5]

As for the male god, Evans conceived of him as a type of early Zeus by analogy with other Mediterranean sky-gods, especially Cretan Zeus.[6] First, he observed that the Minoan deity was often depicted on rings hovering in mid-air, as though he were arriving from the sky.

Figure 6 A goddess flanked by two lions salutes a young male (ring impression, Knossos). Evans compared her with Anatolian Kybele. CMS II, 8, 256.

This showed that he was a sky-god (see Figure 2). Second, he noted that this god carried weapons, which revealed that he was a warrior and hunter.[7] Evans realized that E. B. Tylor had already collected ample evidence of male sky war-deities: Indian Indra, Zeus Kerauneios, Jupiter Capitolinus;[8] now he broadened the comparative perspective by including Near Eastern and Egyptian deities such as Horus and Syrian Reshep.[9] However, it is interesting that he also included Adonis and Attis in his conspectus despite the fact that neither of these are sky deities. The reason he chose them is because their mythical biography indicated that they were 'mortal gods', and this bore some resemblance to the story of Cretan Zeus, whose tomb was said to be in Crete. This is a very important point to stress because the analogy with Cretan Zeus led him to assume that the myth of the dying and resurgent god had roots in old Mediterranean religions and consequently also Minoan mythology.

His starting point on the aforementioned assumption was the textual evidence of the Hellenistic poet Kallimachos, who refers to a *tomb* of Zeus in Crete. Evans wondered whether some of the *baetyls* (sacred stones) which he detected in the iconography of the seals and rings did not, in fact, represent the grave markers of a Minoan god. Pillar and tombstone, he wrote, were the dwelling place of departed spirits, perhaps 'a mortal god.'[10] Kallimachos was not his only source, for he also had some archaeological data to back up the idea. A Minoan sanctuary had been excavated by the Cretan scholar Joseph Hatzidakis atop Mount Juktas, and the enclosure was said to contain the tomb of Zeus, according to old traditions.

> Dr. Joseph Hazzidakis, the President of the Cretan Syllogos at Candia, and now Ephor of Antiquities, informs me that the remains on the top of mount Juktas are still known to the country people as the *Mnema of Zia* [i.e. tomb of Zeus].[11]

Evans thus combined (a) the archaeological remains of Juktas with (b) the text of Kallimachos and (c) the monuments that he considered *baetyls* on the seals and rings. On the basis of this he proposed the hypothesis that the male warrior-god was a dying god. An ongoing

cult to Jesus Christ atop Mount Juktas fortified the impression that
there was continuity of traditions about a mortal god throughout
antiquity and that this tradition stayed alive until Christian religion
took over. The next step was to associate this mortal god with a
goddess; indeed, such associations could be found in other religions.
He writes in 'Tree and Pillar Cult':

> The survival of such sepulchral traditions in connexion with
> divinities is very widespread on Greek, Syrian and Anatolian
> ground. The tomb of Adonis was placed within the temple-court
> at Byblos. In that of Paphos the grave of Aphrodite was pointed
> out as well as her sacred cone, and with it was the burial place of
> Apollo, otherwise akin to Cilician Sandon. The omphalos of
> Apollo at Delphi became known as the tomb of Dionysos – who,
> under his earlier Thracian name was himself a Sun-God ...[12]

Evans synthesizes the evidence: there is a mortal god who is
variously named Adonis, Dionysus, or something else and is
worshipped within the shrine of a female deity, usually Aphrodite.
The mythical scheme of a divine pair where the goddess survives the
god was detected by other scholars as well in the beginning of the
twentieth century, as may be seen from the publication of a German
dissertation written on this very subject in 1903.[13] It is also worth
noting that Evans's 'Tree and Pillar Cult' was published only a year
after Frazer's three-volume edition of *The Golden Bough* (1900).[14]
Frazer had, of course, spoken about mortal gods already in his first
two volumes, but the popular reception that this volume received had
not yet taken place.[15]

The Tomb and the Rites

Where did Evans find representations of mortal and resurgent gods?
He was inspired by two gold rings from Mycenae and Vapheio
respectively (Figure 7a–b) because they represented a common theme
and had similarities in their composition. Both included the
following motifs: a sacred tree, a male worshipper grasping its branch

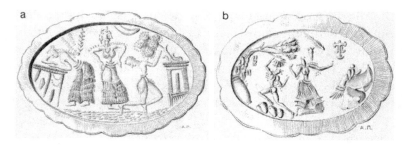

Figure 7a–b Two gold rings (a) from Mycenae and (b) from Vapheio show a dancing female in the centre. Evans believed that an ecstatic cult was represented, resulting in the epiphany of a dancing goddess. The same goddess mourns over the tomb of a departed god. These two rings were the basis for the hypothesis that the goddess had a mortal consort like Adonis. (a) CMS I, 126; (b) CMS I, 219.

and kicking up his legs, a female dervish-like figure in the centre engaged in a twirl, and a cult monument on the side. Over this monument a goddess (so the fancy took him) was steeped in sorrow and mourned: the monument could thus be identified as a tomb. It was evident on the left of the Mycenae ring whereas on the gem from Vapheio the place of the tomb was taken by a large shield at the right edge of the scene. It belonged to a departed god over whose shield a minute female figure (the same goddess) was leaning over in sorrow. In short, Evans saw allusions to the departed god and a goddess mourning for him.[16] His logic is clear but his paradigm was too wilfully imposed on scenes that may admit of other interpretations. As Evans later himself acknowledged, there was no female bending over the shield of the Vapheio ring because the motif which he mistook as a female was too small in proportion to the object. He noted 30 years later that the so-called goddess may be a sacred garment.[17] However, he retained his general thesis on ecstatic rites even in *Palace of Minos* and it may be summarized as follows.

The goddess appears to her worshipper after she has been invoked. The votary kicks up his legs and shakes the tree and becomes an ecstatic. In his ecstasy, he sees the goddess arrive and she begins to swirl. The worshipper offers her fruit and its juice. The two thus have a communion, consisting of an orgiastic dance and the common partaking of the fruit, about which more is said below.

It is hard to accept this scenario today; at the same time it must be admitted that Evans realized something very important about Minoan ritual which had no evident parallels in Greek religion. He understood that the worshipper entered a state of ecstasy when he touched the sacred tree and that he saw in his imagination a mythical version of events which the viewer of the ring was able to share. He wrote in 1901:

> The designs on both rings, which have been hitherto described as scenes of an orgiastic dance, are in fact full of meaning and depict an act of divine communion – the partaking by the Goddess of the fruit of her sacred tree.[18]

The idea that the rings showed a combination of ritual (communion, orgiastic dance) with mythic imagination (the goddess mourns the death of the god) is not modified substantially in *Palace of Minos*, although, as we have seen already, he realized that the mourning woman on the Vapheio ring represented a sacred garment. It is worth noting that by the time Evans wrote *Palace of Minos* (20 years after 'Tree and Pillar Cult'), the myth of the mortal and resurgent god had achieved great popularity due to James Frazer's *Golden Bough*; fortified by its success, Evans unhesitatingly writes:

> The mourning figure [. . .] surely indicates the death [of the god]. We are brought, in fact, into a religious domain of which Crete and Syria formed part where a mortal but resurgent God forms a principal figure.[19]

How can we judge this interpretation today when we have new gems and ring-impressions, as well as new murals? Tombs of a god have not been identified in Minoan art. Yet in other ways, Evans has been proven remarkably insightful. Take, for example, a gold ring from Sellopoulo and another from Archanes (Figures 8–9) on both of which we see men bending over *baetyls*. The figures bending over *baetyls* are most likely human visionaries and not gods.[20] Evans was

Figure 8 A gold ring from Sellopoulo, South Crete, unknown to Evans, supporting his theory of ecstatic cult. A man leans over a stone and has a vision of a bird carrying a seed. The vision takes place near the sacred tree and a *baetyl*. CMS, II, 3, 114.

Figure 9 A man leans over a *baetyl*; another man shakes a tree while a female is engaged in ecstatic dance. Both ecstatics have visions of sacred objects, huge insects as well as an eye. This ring from Archanes, excavated by J. and E. Sakellarakis, verifies Evans's hypothesis that sacred trees and *baetyls* were associated with ecstatic cults. CMS II, 3, 989.

also right that the ritual actions take place in a tree sanctuary and that
the visionaries witness an epiphany of some sort. On the Sellopoulo
ring (Figure 8),[21] the worshipper turns his head and sees a huge bird,
most probably an eagle, as well as a shooting star. Both of these signs
are manifestations of the divine. To the left of the bird on the
Sellopoulo ring we see the portal of a shrine. Thus, the cult activity
indeed takes place near a sanctuary with a holy tree, as Evans realized.
In sum, he correctly identified an iconographical formula that
represents ecstatic rituals.[22]

Communion and the Dying God: William Robertson Smith and Sir James Frazer

Evans's hypothesis entailed that ecstatic worshippers ate the fruit of the
sacred tree and that they next saw the goddess. The notion that
epiphany is a result of divine communion requires further commentary.
The fact is that nowhere on the representations of Minoan and
Mycenaean art is there evidence that fruit was eaten. Why then did he
make this assumption and how did he arrive at the idea that eating the
fruit of the sacred tree resulted in a communion between god and
worshipper? It seems that the mystery of the Christian Eucharist was in
the back of his mind, as it was also in the mind of many other scholars
at the time. The Eucharist entails communion with God because the
faithful eat a piece of bread, the flesh of God, and drink red wine, the
blood of crucified Jesus. The mysterious nature of this rite of early
Christians had puzzled Tylor, Evans's mentor, who thought that it may
have had origins in primitive cults. Tylor wrote:

> The solemn Eucharistic meal of the primitive Christians in
> time assumed the name of the sacrifice of the mass, and was
> adapted to a ceremonial in which an offering of food and drink
> is set out by the priest on an altar in a temple, and consumed by
> a priest and the worshippers.[23]

We find similar terminology in the work of William Robertson
Smith, the historian of Semitic religions whom Evans frequently cites.

Robertson Smith refers to 'sacramental communion' and 'atonement sacrifices' in connection with the rites of early Semites.[24] James Frazer also elaborated on the subject of communion. Eating the sacred fruit or the flesh of the sacred animal resulted in a bond between god and worshipper.[25] In the abridged version of *The Golden Bough*, Frazer dedicates a section to the eating of cereals and fruit.

> In all such cases, accordingly, we may not improbably describe the eating of the new fruits as a sacrament or communion with a deity, at all events with a powerful spirit.[26]

The killing of sacred animals was compared by Frazer explicitly with the Christian Crucifixion, a fact that did not escape the sharp eyes of the church, especially when Frazer published his *Attis, Adonis, Osiris* (1906).[27] These gods originated in a single vegetation deity who left the earth to enter the gloomy subterranean world and return annually.[28] The departure of the divinity symbolized the withering of plant-life, a myth echoed in ritual practice of antiquity, as when the women of Byblos wailed and wept bitterly for Adonis.[29] At Byblos, the river turned red, as if it were miraculously tinted by the slain youth's blood, so Lucian reported.[30] Frazer added that the violent reaping of the corn with a scythe re-enacted the death of the anthropomorphized god: 'the spirits of the victim die a second death at the reaping of the corn and are apt to wreak vengeance in the slayers'.[31] He compares the old fertility rites to Christian Easter ceremonies in southern Italy and describes the ritual of a waxen effigy of the dead Christ covered with fervent kisses by the mourners whilst being carried on a bier by priests. The effigy was adorned with lemon blossoms and the church bells tolled mournfully.[32]

Frazer's work abounds in bloody rituals in connection with communion and Jane Harrison follows close suit. The rites of Dionysos, the raw eater of flesh, reveal a savage god. Ecstasy, drinking wine, tearing the flesh of kid goats asunder: these rites were practised in connection with communion with this god.[33] Harrison took an interest also in the Minoan finds and specifically the sacrificed bovine depicted on the sarcophagus from Hagia Triada. Why does the bull die?

'The animal's sacrificers desired his *mana*,' Harrison answers. In other words, communion with the divine was achieved through the violent death of an animal-god.[34]

In comparison to the paradigms utilized by the Cambridge Ritualists to imagine ecstatic rites, Evans's interpretations seem very tame and utterly devoid of the violent and dramatic content that made *The Golden Bough* a bestseller in the interwar period. In Evans's reconstruction, the Minoan god is neither slain nor eaten. There are no savage rituals here, and his version of Minoan mythology is free of the anxiety that classical scholars of the interwar period associated with ancient myths.[35] He was an original mind and not a follower of trends; his vision of Minoan Crete was one of a high civilization, not of a land of savagery. However, there can be little doubt that the paradigm of the Christian Eucharist, the drinking of the blood and the eating of the flesh of Christ, was an inspiration for both Evans and Frazer.

The Oriental Goddess

A major difference between Frazer and Evans is their respective conceptualization of the goddess Kybele, to whom Evans assimilates the Minoan goddess. Was Evans influenced by Frazer, as has been often claimed?[36] Not much, it seems, although it is certain that he read *The Golden Bough* before he wrote 'Tree and Pillar Cult' since in one place he writes, 'nor with Dr. Frazer's *Golden Bough* before us need we linger in the Arician Grove'. The difference between the two is that whereas Frazer adumbrates a violent goddess, Evans's Minoan Kybele is neither violent, nor sexually wanton. The only two common points the Minoan deity has with Phrygian Kybele are the ecstatic worshippers associated with the tree cult and the lion attendants.[37]

Frazer's Kybele is accompanied by a young lover or devotee, variously named Adonis, Attis or Kumbabos. The lover is killed, or maimed, or suffers some other kind of violence, even castration by the goddess. Sometimes he castrates himself. The early religions of mankind, as Frazer imagined them, were obsessed with fertility and renewal of life and this had to occur at any cost. Kybele's eagerness to mate and the eventual destruction of all her lovers was nothing but a realistic reference to the relentless cycles of nature.[38]

Since none of the above describes Minoan mythology as reconstructed by Evans, *The Golden Bough* is not a particularly helpful guide to Evans's thought.

Consider also the following. During the interwar period, Frazer was honoured with a series of lectures and Evans was asked to give one of them at Oxford (1930).[39] He spoke on the 'Earlier Religion of Greece in the Light of Cretan Discoveries' and presented a new and more reflective synthesis than previously, thus honouring his esteemed colleague. The odd thing is that there is no single reference to *The Golden Bough* in this lecture.[40] Why? The omission is certainly not a sign of disrespect to his colleague (whose book he had elsewhere characterized as a 'masterly monograph').[41] Rather, it reveals Evans's view that primitive cults were irrelevant to the comprehension of Minoan religion. Frazer had been in search of savagery in *The Golden Bough*, but Evans had discovered instead a high civilization in Crete:

> Broadly comparing it [the Minoan religion] with the religion of the Ancient Greeks it must be said that it had a more spiritual essence. From another aspect it had a more personal bearing [. . .] Here indeed, we see a religious symbolism such as was never carried further in Christian times.[42]

Tree Cult and a Wounded Goddess from Thera?

In conclusion to this chapter, we shall look at Evans's theory of the mourning goddess in relation to the highly enriched (through excavations in Crete and Akrotiri, Thera) iconographical repertoire of Minoan culture. It has already been mentioned that the theory of the mortal god has not stood the test of time. On the other hand, the idea that the goddess experiences pain and sorrow has found unexpected support.

The evidence is a fresco found in 1973 by Spyridon Marinatos on the island of Thera. It depicts a seated female figure with a wounded foot from which blood is dripping (Figure 10). The excavator described the scene thus shortly after the discovery of the mural:

> This figure is perhaps the most surprising of all. [. . .] This young girl has met with an accident. Sitting on a rock, she holds with her right hand her bare foot. A few drops of blood are visible on the ground. The left hand is brought, palm open, to the forehead in a characteristic gesture denoting pain and especially distress – a gesture observed in our days amongst Southern peoples. Did the girl stumble on a stone? Was she hurt by a thorn? Or was she bitten by a snake, actually a venomous one, and her gesture suggests the fearful consequences of that bite?[43]

It is clear that Marinatos was seeking a mythical narrative behind the image, and perhaps he was right. Now that we know much more about the architectural context of this fresco, we can ascertain with some confidence that the wounded female is situated in such a way as to be the focus of the visitor who descended into the *adyton* shrine (Figure 11). To the left and right of the wounded figure are two

Figure 10   Wounded goddess from Xeste 3, room 3, ground floor at Akrotiri, Thera.

Figure 11   Reconstruction of the *adyton* or Lustral Basin, a type of Minoan sacred space, from Xeste 3, Akrotiri, Thera. The murals depict a seated goddess with a bleeding foot, two worshippers and her shrine on the east wall. After N. Marinatos 1993, Fig. 214.

women. The left one carries a necklace (which may be an offering). The last woman to the right looks behind her at the east wall and sees something that startles her: a sanctuary with a large gate topped by the so-called sacred horns. Behind its walls is an olive tree with foliage so luxurious that its branches spill out (Figure 12).

The mural fully confirms Evans's understanding of tree sanctuaries as enclosed by solid walls and as having impressive portals, but this one from Xeste 3, Akrotiri, supplies new information. First, it is decorated with red lilies and spirals, certainly alluding to the symbols of its divine dweller. Second, it has the startling feature that the sanctuary is bleeding: red streaks of blood trickle down from the horns to the façade and stain the door. It is as though (so the fancy takes one) the horns bleed in sympathy with the wounded seated figure of the adjacent north wall; in other words, the bleeding shrine echoes the blood of the wounded female. This is what the young girl engaged in the twirl sees and understands. The vision shocks her (Figure 11).

This set of murals is a glimpse into mythology and ritual simultaneously and once more shows how correct Evans was to

Figure 12   Sanctuary façade on mural of the east wall of *adyton*, Xeste 3, Thera. The shrine has a large gate topped with horns; behind its walls a sacred tree is visible. The tree is bleeding in sympathy with the wounded goddess of Figure 10.

connect ecstatic rites with tree cultism. He inferred a blend of mythical imagination and ritual action for the Mycenae and Vapheio rings (Figure 7a–b). And this idea (the blending of ritual reality and mythical imagination) raises the question of how to identify the wounded figure seated on a rock of the north wall. Is she a mortal, or is she a suffering goddess who has hurt her foot? In my previous work, having noticed the visual echoes of blood between the north and east walls, I suggested that she is a mortal maiden undergoing a trial of initiation into womanhood.[44] I now believe I was in error. Those days many of us were under the influence of initiation theories, first introduced before World War I by Arnold van Gennep's *Rites of Passage*[45] and then by Jane Harrison's *Themis*.[46] These theories were revived and revised in the 1980s and 1990s under the impact of the Paris school of structuralism headed by Jean-Pierre Vernant.[47] Many scholars then turned to puberty rites as a frame of explanation for rituals depicted in Minoan art, but perhaps many of us overstated the case.

It is thus worth considering another scenario, that will bring us closer to Evans's views. Suppose the wounded female is not a mortal maiden but a goddess; suppose that the painting is a reference not to a rite but a myth now lost. We are at a loss to interpret it, of course, but that ought not to discourage us, since a viewer of that age would be fully able to understand it.[48] In any case, there are four reasons for adopting the interpretation that the figure is a divinity. First, she is seated, which is rare for humans in Minoan art. Second, and most importantly, she has a central position in the wall and this position *exactly corresponds* to the seated goddess painted on the wall of the second floor, directly above her. Third, she is painted on a larger scale than the other two females. Fourth, the narrative context suggests that she is invisible to the two females who accompany her: indeed, they seem entirely unaware of her presence. I found this lack of interaction between the three women to be a problem with my previous initiation scenario and had wondered why the two girls do not rush to help their wounded mate. For all these reasons, the scene makes best sense if the two girls are mortals who are not aware of the wounded figure simply because she is a goddess situated in a different sphere and because she exists *only in the imagination of the worshipper* during the ritual.

However, do gods suffer? A sceptic may legitimately ask this question. The issue can be addressed only briefly in this context but suffice it to state that parallels are not lacking. Did not Egyptian Isis suffer for the loss of her husband Osiris and the mutilation of her son by Seth? Was the latter not killed and torn to pieces by his rival?[49]

Thus, the seated figure with the bleeding foot from Akrotiri, Thera may well be a goddess and the protagonist of a hitherto unknown myth. And if so, Evans's ideas about the mourning goddess may have some substance (compare Figure 7a). Let us be clear: the Theran fresco does not verify Evans's theory of a mortal god and his mourning mother, but it does suggest that he intuited something important about Minoan mythology. Old ideas may be useful when modified in the light of new evidence.

CHAPTER 3

THE WHIRLIGIG OF TIME: THE NARRATIVE OF THE PALACE OF MINOS

> The whirligig of time brings in his revenges
> Shakespeare, *Twelfth Night* (Act 5, scene 1,
> 372–8)

A Single Story

Evans says that he conceived of *The Palace of Minos* as 'a single story' and, indeed, it deals with the birth, childhood, adulthood, and old age of this culture.[1] The narrative is structured according to the social-biological model of growth-maturity-decline which was utilized by many archaeologists and historians of the nineteenth century.[2] Yet there is greater complexity in Evans's narrative, partly because of its reflective tone (that owes much to Edward Gibbon's *Decline and Fall of the Roman Empire*) and partly because of its unusual angle regarding the causes that lead to the decline of civilization. The historical circumstances under which *The Palace of Minos* was written surely influenced its author. Evans was no longer a young man when he began writing the first volume, but a man close to 70 who had recently experienced the devastating effects of

World War I. He had also witnessed great changes in Europe's politics, morals and aesthetic attitudes. By the time he wrote his last volume, he had reached his mid-eighties. His greatest achievements lay behind and the foreshortened perspective of age, as well as the criticism which some of his views had received in certain quarters, had given him cause for pessimism. *The Palace of Minos* is about an age coming to its end, just as the European intellectual world-order as Evans knew it in his youth was nearing its own end. The sadness is sensed by the reader when the author speaks of 'a deepening twilight' and the very real possibility of 'universal darkness'.[3]

Let us backtrack and trace the development of his thoughts. He began as a scientist who examines the layers of his excavation: 'an entirely new perspective on antiquity has here opened, and the superimposition of the successive strata is as clear as in any geological section'.[4] At that time his primary aim was the clear assessment of the stratigraphy of the site and the comparison to geology supplied him with a clear model. In parenthesis, we note that the end of the nineteenth century saw much interest in the history of the Earth's strata. He baptized the culture 'Minoan', adopting a name given to the island culture by the German scholar Karl Hoeck but using it primarily because he wanted to honour Cretan patriotism (many Cretans named their sons Minos).[5] Later he divided the history into three phases, Early, Middle, and Late, a division of which he was very proud since it was based on full mastery of archaeological stratigraphy correlated with pottery styles. This is Evans's undisputed scientific achievement.

Next, Evans engages in history. The threefold division into Early, Middle, and Late, appears (on the surface) to follow traditional evolutionist models of growth, progress, and decline. But a closer analysis reveals that this division is an attempt at making history. The author is less interested in the process of growth and decline of civilization[6] and more in the synchronicity of Crete with other cultures, especially that of Egypt. Anchoring Minoan culture to Egyptian history made the civilization more real, and this is the reason why he is keen to mention names of Egyptian pharaohs in association with Minoan strata when the evidence warrants it. One example is the association of the Second Intermediate

Period/Hyksos/fifteenth-Dynasty pharaoh Khyan with the corresponding Middle Minoan period.[7]

Thus, at the beginning of the excavations at Knossos Evans was a scientist classifying and ordering his data, but in *The Palace of Minos* he is very much a historian. Here is one example which shows his heightened sense of imagination on what had happened in Crete.

After he experienced an earthquake in Crete in 1926, Evans realized that natural catastrophes could change the course of Minoan history. He noted that every major change detectable in the archaeological record at Knossos coincided with a major earthquake.

In June 1926 [...] I shared the dramatic and awe-inspiring experience of a fairly severe earthquake shock — overdue according to the local reckoning — in the head-quarters house on the actual site of Knossos, and the vivid experiences there gained have greatly assisted my own realization of the tremendous destructive force that has been operative on the site at perpetually recurring intervals.[8]

There are some important thoughts contained in this paragraph. One is the observation that earthquakes occur during set intervals because they are the result of the relentless law of nature. The geological perspective owes much to the scientists of Charles Darwin's entourage, which included the geologist Charles Lyell.[9] Darwin was himself interested in earthquakes and wrote that 'all-powerful time can grind down mountains [...] into gravel and mud.'[10] Another observation is that natural catastrophes are not always a bad thing. Sometimes they give unexpected opportunities to society to renovate and improve its institutions. Catastrophes give a chance for new technologies to develop, whereas art may be re-conceptualized under the challenge of reconstruction. Such a positive change occurred in Knossos after the grand earthquake of Middle Minoan III A.[11] On the other hand, earthquakes may deliver a fatal blow to already weakened systems: the earthquake of Late Minoan II (*c.*1400 BCE) at Knossos signalled the final decline of the Palace.

However, let us start from the beginning, the first volume of *The Palace of Minos*. Evans began with the Neolithic era, a cultural period that he considered unified in its material culture and religion. The unity was inferred from the similarity between all Neolithic cultures of Anatolia and Europe – due perhaps to the great length of this period. At Knossos some of the peoples lived in caves, others in houses; traces of habitation bespoke a rudimentary settlement-life.[12] Next came the Early Minoan period, in which a distinctly Minoan cultural idiom is recognizable. Evans not only describes it, but he asks the question of why it was created at that time and not another. He arrives at the conclusion that new stimuli from Anatolia caused the change, and that immigrants from the north coast of Africa, Egypt, and Libya also arrived on the island.[13] What a contrast to those scholars who advocated theories of purity of race! Evans speaks of an 'Early Nilotic impulse' and tracks down all the common elements between Nilotic and Early Minoan cultures: artefacts, tombs, weapons, and religious elements. He points to the portraits of 'negroized Libyans' found in the Messara and envisages multicultural and multi-ethnic groups in the fertile valleys and coast of southern Crete.[14]

The stimuli from abroad were not the only nor a sufficient explanation for the formation of a distinct Minoan idiom, however. It was the openness of Crete to the outside world that made the island so special. To illustrate this phenomenon of openness, he contrasts Cretan settlements to the small Neolithic town of Dimini in Thessaly, which remained static because of its geographic seclusion which in the end caused it to become inward-looking.[15] Crete, by contrast, acquired a navy, and this made it reach out to other worlds, civilizations that broadened its intellectual and aesthetic horizons. At first, the contacts were mainly made with the Cycladic islands, but soon the navy sailed outside the familiar Aegean seas to explore Egypt and beyond.[16] The encounter with superior and literate civilizations of the East gradually transformed the old insular society to a cosmopolitan centre. Importation of artefacts, evident since the Early Minoan period, became more conspicuous when the palaces were founded.

The foundation of the Old Palaces in the beginning of the Middle Minoan period marked a new era of cosmopolitanism; even a king from Babylon sends a seal, perhaps as a gift.[17] Foreign ideas (as opposed to motifs) became assimilated to local idiom, and Evans found evidence of ideograms which were not only appropriated by the Minoans but were reinterpreted by them. The double axe was brought from Anatolia, the tree of life (palm) from Syria and Mesopotamia, and the waz papyrus from Egypt.[18] As the new Cretan elites became international, they learned how better to organize themselves and how to make consumption more conspicuous. In sum, the growth of the Minoan palaces was due to an organic development from the inside, whereas the *stimuli* and *models* came from abroad, acting as decisive catalysts for change.[19] Evans puts it thus: 'The establishment of a direct contact with the East about the close of the Early Minoan Age may be said to usher the Age of the Palaces in the Island of Crete.'[20]

The First Palatial era met all the standards of what Evans considered a civilized society. It had two hieroglyphic scripts, possibly of Egyptian inspiration, high aesthetics as evidenced by the decoration of its pottery, high technology, well-planned towns and harbours.[21] This period came to an end when an earthquake struck Knossos in the seventeenth century BCE (Middle Minoan III A). However, the catastrophe did not cause a huge rupture in the continuity of Minoan culture but, on the contrary, stimulated further growth and resulted in higher levels of aesthetic achievement. The Palace was rebuilt on a more splendid scale than before. Early in the sixteenth century BCE (Middle Minoan III B), the new Palace was refurbished and Evans could hardly conceal his bewilderment at the high standards of the civilization that he had unearthed: this was the golden age of Minoan culture. He spoke of 'brilliant friezes', 'elegant vases' and 'remarkable house-planning'.[22] The central Palace gave evidence of impeccable organization, and yet it did not give signs of strict military autocracy: 'at that time, at any rate, the Priest King seems to have exercised a beneficent dominion'.[23] Art displayed an unusual freedom of spirit, especially when compared to the more rigid art of previous ages, or to that of Egypt and the Near East. Yes, Knossos was a centralized power, but it did not stifle all other administrative units since smaller palaces existed in various parts of this large island. Along with the mansions or villas, they functioned as mini-centres of administration and economic activity to which Knossos must have delegated its power for the distribution of goods. In terms of religion, the Palace promoted a unitary type of cult. Because its religion was benign, it had a motherly appeal and took an emotional hold on its adherents, Evans claimed.[24] The high standard of material living was demonstrable by finds in the houses of Knossos. Large bronze hoards, for example, were found in several houses.[25] The House of Frescoes covered an area of $c.120\,m^2$ in its ground floor alone, a large house even by modern standards. Its owner was literate, as shown by an inscribed ladle found there. Evans surmised that he was not only a wealthy man but that he had 'cultivated taste' because the murals in his house were, 'unrivalled [...] for picturesque setting and [...] many coloured effect'.[26] As for the town itself, it was an *immense* settlement even by modern standards:

> The size and disposition of the houses of the inner town have themselves been so far sampled that I have ventured – with a proportionate estimate for the poorer outer quarters – to come to some conclusions as to the actual population of 'broad Knossos' in its great Minoan days, which if we add the Harbour Town, can hardly be safely reckoned as having included less than 100,000 inhabitants.[27]

He observed and admired details of town planning. Despite its large size, Knossos had been skilfully divided into three zones of habitation with alleys that allowed air and light between the houses; this showed that its rulers adhered to rules of urban planning. Was this not a mark of a civilized society?[28] Provisions for water were made through a complex drainage system, carefully designed to avoid contamination. Was this not evidence of communal discipline and mutual respect of one burgher to his neighbour? Finally, Evans noted no great discrepancy between social classes, and he inferred this by the sumptuousness of the architectural remains found everywhere in the countryside and the integration of the richer mansions within the towns.[29]

This age of unprecedented prosperity and well-being was designated as *Pax Minoica*. I note here that the kings, whom Evans called 'priest-kings', were conceived as being very different from the 'priest-kings' of James Frazer's *Golden Bough*. The Minoan monarch, far from being a savage and cruel magician, was a civilized ruler restrained by the ordinance and rules of divine justice. He was additionally an organizer of processions and ceremonies, similar to the Egyptian pharaoh. In short, divine kingship was a civilized institution and civilizing to others.[30] Finally, it is reasonable to assume that Evans thought of the king as the supreme leader of the fleet, although he does not say much about this.

The meaning of *Pax Minoica* has been misunderstood in some of the literature about Evans. It is assumed that he envisaged a peaceful, non-warrior culture, but quite the opposite is the case.[31] Evans did not imply that the Minoans did not practise war: had he not found plenty of evidence in the warrior graves of Knossos? (By the way, he did not consider the graves Mycenaean.) *Pax Minoica* referred to peace made possible because of the strong naval power of Knossos. Only a powerful fleet would have been able to eliminate the constant threat of piracy. This theory explained why Crete did not need major fortifications.

Although Knossos was strong, it seemed to Evans that it opted to exercise a minimum of violence or at least not to display it in the form of visual intimidation-propaganda, in contrast to the pharaohs of Egypt. In this respect, he likened the Minoans to the Romans, who also built an extensive network of communication within the Mediterranean and homogenized the cultures they encountered:

> Everywhere at this epoch we meet with signs of intensive intercourse and conformity of cultural forms that finds its explanation in the methodical extension of the Minoan system of built ways to the remotest districts.[32]

By 'methodical extension' Evans must have meant conquest or the gradual establishment of a commercial empire. It is not out of the question that he remembered the words of Pericles in Thucydides's

Funeral Oration where Pericles says that, 'all sea and land has been forced to be accessible through our daring' (Thuc. 2.41.4) It is more likely, though, that he remembers Gibbon's historical judgement that when law is exercised by benign emperors, it improves the general condition of mankind: 'the general principle of government was wise, simple and beneficent'.[33]

The civilizing force of Knossos also reached Mycenae: 'a great and civilized city was only just in the making at the hands of Minoan conquerors and colonists'.[34] All this shows that Evans envisioned the Aegean as a network of Minoan highways traversed by the royal fleet of Knossos, enhancing trade and facilitating communication between the islands and distant lands. The fleet eliminated pirates and ensured safe passage. *Pax Minoica* thus refers to a way of life, a peace made possible by the rule of order and law, all essential for prosperity. That Evans was inspired by Gibbon's notion of *Pax Romana* may not be doubted since Evans draws this analogy himself.

> Never again till the Roman Governors put a final stop to the internecine feuds of the Greek cities did Crete enjoy throughout its length and breadth such uniform prosperity. There is much in all this that recalls to mind the general well-being fostered by the *Pax Romana* in the best days of the Empire.[35]

There is a passage in *Palace of Minos III* which throws much light on how Evans viewed the *Pax Minoica* and concerns his interpretation of a scene embossed on a silver vessel found in one of the Shaft Graves at Mycenae (he considered it an import from Crete). The representation shows a fortified town with Minoan architectural features under siege (Figure 13). Some of its people stand in front of the gate, defending the city, whereas others are standing on top of the walls watching the spectacle in despair – one woman wears a distinctly Minoan dress. The peoples are ethnically mixed; Evans deduces this from the bristling hairstyles and the nudity of natives.[36] A force of archers aids the besieged town. At the lower part of the largest extant fragment, a ship arrives to aid the town, its commander wearing a Minoan helmet. Evans concluded that the ships were

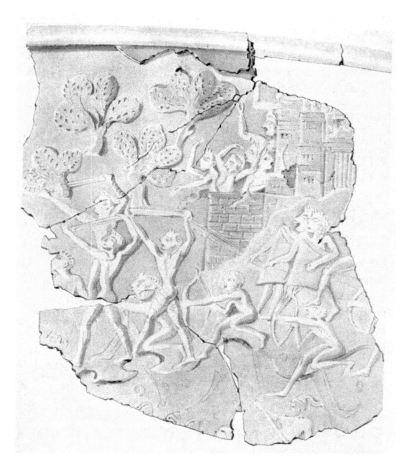

Figure 13 Town under siege engraved on a silver vessel from Mycenae and named 'Silver Siege Rhyton'. Evans detected a multi-ethnic population in the town including a woman in Minoan dress. At the bottom right of the scene a ship with a Minoan warrior arrives to aid the besieged town. The interpretation of Evans has been strengthened after its remarkable parallel on the ship fresco, West House, north wall of room 5. After Evans, PM III, 93, Fig. 52.

Minoan and that the Knossian force arrived to protect its own colony from some barbarian invaders.[37]

> The subject of the whole design is thus the relief and delivery of some Minoan outpost outside Crete, hard pressed by a barbarian onslaught from the land side [. . .] It is a real record, and whether we place the moving scenes [. . .] on the European or Anatolian side, [it] brings into strong relief the superiority of Minoan civilization.[38]

The clash is conceived as a conflict between civilization and barbarism which recalls Gibbon's narrative of the fall of the Roman Empire when it was invaded by barbarians. One is also reminded of Darwin's description of 'naked savages' in *The Voyage of the Beagle*: nudity and hairstyle constituted criteria by which scholars of the eighteenth and nineteenth century determined ethnicity.[39] On the other hand, the attempt of Evans to detect ethnic categories is not entirely off the mark, and his notion that the East Mediterranean population was multi-ethnic deserves further investigation. We must be careful not to dismiss his interpretations as anachronistic or Victorian, because he was careful to show that analogous depictions of historical events are attested in Egypt and other civilizations of the Near East. Since Early Dynastic times, Egyptian reliefs showed the enemies of the Egyptians as less 'civilized' than themselves: Bedouins, Asiatics, Sea-Peoples, etc. All had inferior armament, peculiar dress and hairstyle.[40]

Was Evans influenced by his own culture? Did he have in mind the naval supremacy of the British Empire in his construction of the paradigm of *Pax Minoica*?[41] To be sure, Evans was the product of his generation, and the same may be said of Gibbon, Darwin and Tylor. Recent biographers of Evans think that projection invalidates the hypothesis regardless of observation.[42] Yet, we (including the critics in question) are also products of our own age and the same criticism may apply to us. The validity of a hypothesis may only be tested by data, and the data support the idea that Crete held an extraordinary role within the East Mediterranean. It seems to me that the evidence produced by the excavations at Akrotiri, Thera is particularly valuable in this respect. This harbour-town was thoroughly Minoanized in its architecture and iconography. Moreover, one of its houses (West House) yielded a ship-fresco with a narrative similar to the Silver Siege Rhyton. All this has lent great support to Evans's theory of the *Pax Minoica*.

Peter Warren has admitted of Evans:

> His vision of a Minoan empire must have reflected, consciously or unconsciously, the British imperial age in which he lived. But, and this is the main point, he possessed an extraordinary ability, based on a remarkably wide and deep range of interests, to see the larger picture, including its myriad details, of the Minoan world, a picture formed not from preconceived theory but inductively or empirically from highly perceptive evaluation of what he found.

'Many have felt', Warren further states, 'that his picture or vision of the Minoans stands close to reality, as hundreds of subsequent discoveries testify'.[43]

The End of Knossos

The important question of why and how the *Pax Minoica* came to an end was answered at the end of *The Palace of Minos*. The answer was not confined to one single cause but was attributed to a combination of natural disasters and social upheaval.

Evans identified an earthquake in Late Minoan I (*c*.1500) and realized that it caused major damage to the Palace and its surroundings and that 'far-flung blocks' testified to the magnitude of the disaster. Still, only the Domestic Quarters were affected severely whereas the rest of the Palace was spared severe damages.[44] More serious was the destruction inflicted on the Royal Temple Tomb, which partly collapsed, trapping within its ruins several human victims.[45] However, he did not associate this earthquake of Late Minoan I A with the volcanic eruption of Thera and the tsunami, and it is not known if he knew of the theory of Spyridon Marinatos, formulated at the same time. Marinatos made a case that this eruption resulted in the abandonment of all the lesser palaces that were dependent on Knossos (see Appendix 2).[46]

Evans, however, thought of the decline of Knossos in political terms. It seemed to him that the institution of kingship was weakened after the natural disaster of Late Minoan I and that this caused the multi-palatial society to collapse and give way to a more authoritarian regime centred on Knossos. He thought that it was symptomatic of a changing age that the smaller palaces were never rebuilt whereas Knossos was redecorated in a splendid fashion with military emblems such as large shields, and that its corridors were adorned with grand formal processions reminiscent of Egyptian theocratic schemes. The graves of this period were full of panoplies and long swords. All this betokened a new 'aggressive spirit'.[47]

He also noticed that the archives of the Palace were written in a new script, Linear B, derived from Linear A. He did not recognize it as Greek, but it did not escape his attention that the tablets recorded inventories of weapons, chariots, and swords and that they revealed a general concern with arms and armour.[48] Evans would never agree with his German friend Georg Karo that the new dynasty was Mycenaean.[49] He saw complete continuity of religious symbols and iconography with the previous age: no, the last phase of the Palace gave ample proof of its purely Minoan character, but it was an authoritarian Minoan government.

Thus, during the last era of its life (which Evans designated as Late Minoan II) Knossos flourished but became autocratic. It cultivated intense contacts with Amenhotep III of the Eighteenth Dynasty of Egypt, and the Knossian king (so it seemed to Evans) copied the methods of his Egyptian counterpart.[50]

Evidently the priest kings of Knossos in some sort regarded themselves as Pharaohs overseas. Is it too much to say that they may even have cherished pretensions to a lineage reaching back to kings before Mena?[51]

While this militaristic and authoritarian dynasty was on the throne, another major earthquake struck the city, and this one fatally destroyed the Palace — for it was never rebuilt. It was followed, as earthquakes often are, by a widespread conflagration, traces of which were still visible in Evans's time on the orthostats of the western façade. This was the end of the all-powerful Knossian rule, although Minoan culture was not yet at its end.

> But the immediate importance of this huge disaster as regards the general course of Minoan culture must not be exaggerated [. . .] By no means did it portend the final ruin of all that the Great Palace had stood for. Old Civilizations die hard. A falling off compared with the golden age [. . .] there certainly was already, but a disaster now suffered was far from heralding the Reign of Chaos.[52]

It has been mentioned already above that Evans denied vigorously that Knossos was invaded by Mycenaeans. 'We have *not* here the indications of a violent intrusion at the hands of some foreign power,' he said,[53] and, as an afterthought, he added that the residence of the priest-kings was transferred to a mainland site, quite probably to Mycenae.[54] This view has not found general acceptance. We have already noted that he was called a 'pancretist' and that he saw Minoan influence everywhere. Moreover, it was said that he was prepared to go to extremes to defend the military superiority of the Minoan civilization over the mainlanders, and that he fought scholars who thought otherwise.[55] Consider, however, what evidence he had at his disposal. The strongly Knossian artistic spirit of the palaces on the mainland was hard to explain if Knossos had been conquered. Why imitate a conquered people? Consider also that Linear B is derived from Linear A and that the earliest specimens of this script so far have been found at Knossos and not on the mainland.[56]

The most interesting aspect of Evans's theory, however, is not about who exerted influence on whom abroad, but how the autocracy of the last dynasty undermined Minoan social balance. He argued that the authoritarianism of the last regime was the deeper and truest cause of the downfall of Knossos. The earthquake was nothing but a mere catalyst that prompted an insurrection against an unpopular tyrant. Such a view is historically more nuanced than the alternative theory that Knossos was invaded by Mycenaeans.[57]

His historical reconstruction of absolutist monarchy at Knossos involved analogies with more recent history. After the earthquake of 1926, he decided to research documents from the Venetian occupation of Crete in the fourteenth to sixteenth centuries CE. He realized that the unpopular Venetian governors had to flee Crete after major earthquakes because they could not assuage the populace and feared attacks by the mob.

> Nor can the possibility be ignored that these great natural convulsions had political consequences, and that they may have been productive of the uprising of depressed elements in the population, or of a change of dynasty. An actual example, indeed, of such a result is supplied by the records of a great earthquake that took place in 1304, in the early days of Venetian dominion, the violence of which was such that it destroyed a great part of the city walls. It was followed by an insurrectionary movement among the subject Greek population of the island which was checked, however, by the prudent council of Alexios Calergos.[58]

In another place he writes:

> Experiences such as those of the Venetian Duke of Candia on the occasion of the earthquake of 1508 may well have been shared three thousand years earlier by a Minoan Priest King, escaping in the same way from his crumbling palace.[59]

Darwin too had noticed that 'earthquakes are sufficient to destroy the prosperity of any country'.[60] Historical events of our days lead to similar thoughts. The Prime Minister of Japan Naoto Kan resigned after the tsunami that afflicted the country in March 2011.

Leaving earthquakes aside, Evans's involvement with the political scene of Europe sparked another thought about the end of Knossos. The generation of Darwin and Tylor had a deep faith in the superiority of European civilization and the benign rule of Britain. Darwin felt blessed to have been born an Englishman.[61] Evans was more critical towards the politics of his country and noticed that British policy did not always support the weak. He always fought for the rights of ethnic minorities in Albania, Bosnia, Ragusa and Kosovo.[62] He defended the rights of Greeks and Cretans under the Ottoman Empire; he protested the barbarities committed by the neo-Turks against Greek minority populations in Asia Minor, and he supported the liberal politician Eleutherios Venizelos against the absolutism of King Constantine.[63] He disapproved of the selfish and aged king of Montenegro, who had looked after only his own dynasty and neglected his people. When this king was finally deposed, Evans felt sorry for him on the one hand; on the other he passed a hard judgement on his character. He wrote to *The Times*:

Sir, The sympathy of all men – even, we may believe, of his enemies – will follow the aged king of Montenegro in his tragic fall. *Sunt lacrimae rerum*! But in recent years the constant preoccupation has been less the realization of national aims than the preservation of the Petrovich dynasty.[64]

A deep melancholy permeates the last chapters of *The Palace of Minos* and stems from the author's conviction that *all* civilizations are doomed to extinction, and that their contribution to history is rendered trivial by the vast perspective of time. Disaster will come at the end either in the form of a natural catastrophe or a social disturbance. This was the legacy of the generation of Darwin and Tylor who had a vast perspective on the effects of time on human culture. And the same realization led James Frazer to say that 'we must adjust our little life to the awful mysteries of the universe'.[65]

Evans used instead the phrase the 'whirligig of time' to express similar thoughts.[66] The civilization of Crete, miraculous as it was, was an accident of cultural evolution rather than a step in the ladder of progress. And this was actually a Darwinian idea, since the evolution of species had an element of randomness when viewed from the perspective of a huge time-scope of over a million years. Human civilization was especially fragile because it was a product of the artifice of culture, exercised by man and owing to his ability to empathize with others. Civilization led man to act for the general benefit of his community. However, since man was led also by primeval and selfish instincts that prompted him to struggle for his existence and to dominate others, he destroyed his own achievement.[67] Although Darwin made a case for the advantages of civilized over barbarous communities, he was also conscious of the tendency of humanity towards regression. Indeed, in some ways decline was easier to explain than the attainment of high civilization because it came automatically every time the delicate balance between authority and freedom was upset.

Evans's metaphor of the whirligig, a spinning machine, is derived from Shakespeare and symbolizes the ever-changing circumstances of the human condition.[68] Events succeed one another rapidly, as if they were scenes viewed from the perspective of a person seated in the machine. In this constantly changing world, all civilizations, even the most brilliant ones, had to come to an end.

In the whirligig of time [...] it was ordained that this resting place of the old priest-kings should not thus be re-occupied by the newcomers.[69]

CHAPTER 4

MONOTHEISM

God is day [and] night
Heraclitus[1]

The Goddess [is] Queen of the Underworld and of
the starry vault of Night.

Arthur J. Evans[2]

Revision of the Paradigm

Evans's original idea that the Minoan Goddess was similar to Anatolian Kybele did not entirely satisfy him, and he revised his paradigm substantially after World War I. This shift has been rightfully noted but it is assumed, wrongly in my opinion, that the change occurred under the impact of Sir James Frazer's work *The Golden Bough*.[3] It has been shown here that Frazer and Evans followed quite distinct interpretative paths and that whereas the former was interested in the savagery of the past – the early stages of human thought and ritual – the latter was interested in its most brilliant achievements.

If not to Frazer, to what cause may we attribute the revised view of the goddess? As we shall see, it was the evidence itself that led him to reconsider his earlier template, but let us for the moment simply note the four changes that were made in the original paradigm. First, the goddess was given the primary role in the pantheon. Second, she was named the mother of all living things, including the young god, whereas in 'Tree and Pillar Cult' of 1901 the goddess was a consort of the god.[4] Third, she embodied all aspects of the cosmos: sky, earth, sea, underworld, day and night. The polarity between antithetical concepts, such as up and down, day and night, sun and moon, explained the perfect dual symmetry of the divine symbols: the double axe, the sacred horns, the split rosette, the incurved altar and the eight-shaped shield.

The Unity of the Minoan Cosmos

Evans called his new version of Minoan religion monotheism. It is a term that needs explanation because, as we shall see below, it was influenced by contemporary studies in Egyptology. Another term he might have chosen was *henotheism* (the predominance of one god over others during worship) or *monism* (unity of all gods in one).

For Evans monotheism meant basically this: there was one principal goddess who had many manifestations. He arrived at this conclusion through sheer observation and not a preconceived paradigm, because he noted that images of female deities in Minoan art were not diversified enough to warrant distinctions based on their respective attributes or costumes. The same iconographical formula kept recurring, its singular elements being derived from a steady pool of signs and motifs. The goddess was often enthroned. If she was standing, she was worshipped by a human or was flanked by animals. She was associated with sacred plants: lily, papyrus, crocus, palm, fig tree and olive tree. Her cult symbols were the double axe, ankh sign, split or whole rosette, pillar, incurved altar, sacred garment, or knot. She shared the sign of the eight-shaped shield with the male god. Sometimes she was associated with stellar bodies: the sun, moon and stars.[5]

The visual motifs merged into one another and hybridized: for example, the double axe merged with the sacred garment on the Vapheio ring (Figure 7b), constituting an Egyptian ankh symbol. The lily merged with the double axe.[6] Thus, symbols were combined and recombined, revealing that the Minoans made highly sophisticated abstractions to express their beliefs. The symbols alluded to the entire cosmos: the earth and its plants and animals; the sea with fish; sky with its birds and stars. In short, when Evans called the religion monotheistic he did not deny multiple gods but argued instead that the unity of its cosmos was embodied in one principle female deity with many manifestations.[7]

A different question was how historically to explain the predominance of this one goddess. Evans imagined two possibilities. The first was that the unity was due to a relic of a primitive deity of Neolithic times, when one single matriarchal goddess prevailed. But such a relic did not fully explain her complex character as mistress of heaven and the underworld, and this made Evans lean towards a second possibility, that Crete developed theological monotheism under the impact of Egypt. He put his thesis thus:

> Clearly the Goddess was supreme, whether we are to regard her as substantially one being of varied aspects, celestial, terrestrial, or infernal, or partly differentiated divine entities. As a working hypothesis the former view has been here preferred.[8]

The Unity of the Goddess

The insight that the goddess united celestial and infernal aspects was gained after Evans realized that she was queen of the underworld. This was based on the finds of the Tomb of the Double Axes, which he excavated in 1912, before the outbreak of World War I. The tomb was part of a cemetery in the vicinity of the Palace and had an unusual plan encompassing both a grave and a shrine. Its antechamber was fitted with benches on which stood ritual vessels and cult implements, and it also contained a central pillar. The cultic function of the room was additionally testified by two sizeable double axes and an ox-head rhyton.[9] In other words, the tomb gave the impression of a sacred pillar crypt-chamber, such as those found in the Palace and surrounding mansions.[10] But its most curious aspect was the burial pit that was formed like a double axe, as though the shape of the latter guaranteed eternity for the interred body. Surprised at this fact, Evans drew the conclusion that the double axe was a chthonic symbol and that the goddess reigned in the underworld, as well as on earth and sky. He writes:

> On the intimate connexion of the Great Minoan Goddess with the cult of the dead, much light was shed by the discovery of the 'Tomb of the Double Axes' near Knossos.[11]

A few years later, he began writing *The Palace of Minos* and matched up this evidence with certain other finds he had made earlier in the century in the West Wing of the Palace within the cists that he named 'Temple Repositories'. He had found there an assemblage of faience statuettes of deities or their votaries, pottery, burned matter, and other objects, all of which constituted relics of cultic material. One of the faience statuettes represented the divinity with snakes entwined around arms and body. At first he did not realize the full significance of the serpents for the comprehension of the nature of the goddess, and in a public lecture delivered to the Society of Antiquaries in London (1903) he does not mention anything about the underworld. He notes, however, that some of the associated material depicted suckling animals.

> It was a surprise to come upon faience figures of women in strange costume beautifully embroidered. Votive rites with snakes were figured in this faience, which showed the extraordinary perfection of the art of the middle period [...]
> There was also a very remarkable faience relief of a wild goat and kids.[12]

Twenty years later, as he reviews the same evidence, he understands that the faience statuettes of the goddess refer to her chthonic side. He also understands why the divinity is associated with reliefs of a wild goat and a cow, both suckling their young: the goddess is a mother but at the same time she is a protectress of the

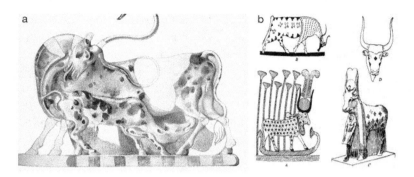

Figure 14a–b Comparison between Minoan and Egyptian cows made by Evans. (a) Evans PM I, 511, Fig. 367. (b) Evans PM I, 513, Fig. 370.

dead. He realizes that he must construct a new model for the Minoan deity and that the best parallel is Egyptian Hathor or Isis, both of whom have the form of a cow in Egyptian art (Figure 14a–b). Additionally, he notes that Hathor was a goddess of the necropolis at Thebes and a protectress of the dead.[13] Evans wonders in the first volume of *Palace of Minos* 'how much of the spiritual being of the Egyptian Mother Goddess may not have been absorbed by her Minoan sister?'[14]

The Cow of Heaven

Hathor was the divine cow who nurtured Horus and his earthly counterpart, the king. Assimilated with Nut as the Cow of Heaven, she bore the solar god in her belly, giving birth to him in the morning.[15] Evans put it thus:

> The group of the Cow and Calf of the Egyptian Mother Goddess, enlisted here in the cult of the analogous Cretan divinity, leads to another interesting comparison of a symbolic character. The Egyptian Goddess as lady of Heaven appears as a cow of the underworld, the body of which, in place of natural spots, shows asterisk marks or simple crosses, symbolizing the starry firmament of Night.[16]

What if the Minoan goddess was a queen of heaven while simultaneously she was a queen of the underworld? Already in 1901 Evans had observed the curious co-existence of sun and moon, day and night, together with the double axe on the gold ring from Schliemann's excavations at Mycenae (see Figures 4 and 5). In 1921, in the first volume of *The Palace of Minos* he interpreted the images further: the goddess, whose emblem was the double axe, had a dual nature. She was simultaneously 'queen of the underworld' and the 'starry vault of night'.[17]

Another symbol pointed to the unitary nature of the goddess: a large marble cross that was found in the Temple Repositories. Evans interpreted it as a stylized solar disc with symmetrical rays identical to the sign of the sun-god Shamash in the art of the Near East.[18] The discovery of the cross caused a great sensation among the workmen at Knossos, and Evans remembered the local priest of Knossos saying that it was a true miracle.

> No Minoan votary would have regarded it with greater veneration than did the orthodox Greek pope whose parish included the remains of the Palace-sanctuary, and it did much to confirm the views of his flock that the fresco figures found were icons of Saints of old.[19]

The cross sign featured also in Linear A as an ideograph of the solar/heavenly aspect of the goddess, so Evans thought.

A cultic assemblage from the smaller 'Shrine of Double Axes', stemming from the latest phase of reoccupation at Knossos, reinforced his conclusion that the entire cosmos was unified in the persona of the goddess. The shrine contained a raised bench on which stood several statuettes *in situ*. The largest was naturally the goddess, and her celestial aspect was indicated by a bird perched on her headdress. Yet there was also a double axe, lying close by on the same bench. Evans surmised that the double axe unified the chthonic and heavenly realms:[20]

> the Snake Goddess herself represents only another aspect of the Minoan Lady of the Dove, while the Double Axe

itself was connected with both [i.e. the underworld and heavenly sides].[21]

A shrine at Gournia, excavated by his American colleague Harriet Boyd Hawes, also yielded a group of goddesses and snakes. Evans connected these relics with small clay figures of doves and with a relief from the shrine showing the double axe; thus, here too the two diverse spheres of the cosmos were joined.[22] By the early 1930s, Evans was certain that he was on the right path and could pronounce himself with clarity in his lecture in honour of Sir James Frazer about Minoan religion: 'It seems to me that we are in the presence of a largely Monotheistic cult, in which the female form of divinity held a supreme place.'[23] In summary, Evans meant by monotheism first that the goddess was supreme in the pantheon and second that she embodied the unity of the entire cosmos.

The Mother of the Young God

Another idea was that the benign side of the Minoan Goddess was expressed primarily through her aspect of motherhood. This led Evans to think over an image on an electrum ring from Mycenae that represented a seated female together with a young standing male, and when he looked at it again, he revised his previous views (Figure 15). The seated deity had broad hips and heavy breasts and was substantially larger than her partner. The two seemed engaged in agitated interaction, pointing their fingers at each other. In 'Tree and Pillar Cult', Evans had identified the pair as a conjugal couple making gestures of 'plighted troth.'[24] But in *Palace of Minos* he reinterpreted the scene as one of filial interaction, the whole impression of the design indicating 'rather the relationship of a son to a mother than of a husband to a wife or mistress.'[25] He states this even more clearly in his Frazer lecture:

The youthful male personage who is coupled with the Minoan goddess stood to her, according to the persistent

Figure 15   Seated goddess faces young male whom Evans identified as her son. Electrum ring from Mycenae. CMS I, 101.

tradition of Rhea and the Cretan Zeus, in filial relation and none other.[26]

Only if the goddess was a mother would the ample body proportions and prominent breasts be explicable, and this provided one more link to the two Egyptian cow-goddesses, Isis and Hathor. As for the seated posture of the deity, it signalled her status as an enthroned queen and the supreme goddess in the pantheon. Despite her high position she was foremost a mother:

> No Astarte, no Paphian Aphrodite, no 'Syrian Goddess', stands here in the background. Rather, the image speaks clearly of the simple and natural relationship of the divine Child to his Mother.[27]

He concluded that the religion of the Minoans had a motherly appeal and that it produced 'an emotional hold on its adherents, anticipating a good deal of the Christian Church at the present day.'[29] The Minoan mother evoked the image of the Christian Madonna, Evans added, because she was a mother, a nurturer, and a protectress of the dead all at once.[30]

In short, his views on monotheism were reached on the basis of observations on the imagery, the analysis of archaeological contexts and analogies with Egyptian religion. They were arrived at over a long period of time and not because of personal feelings (a syndrome of mother-deprivation);[31] nor were they due to the influence of Frazer, whose mother deities were conceived quite differently, as we have seen; nor is it correct to say that his mother-goddess reflects modernist female archetypes.[32] It must also be noted that the theory of monotheism developed *before* the rings of the Thisbe treasure, and the so-called Nestor and Minos Rings appeared in the market. The various ivory statuettes had not circulated yet, and this means that his views were *not* shaped by possible forgeries. But when he saw all the above-mentioned objects, he derived great satisfaction because he thought that they confirmed his theories.[33]

The Debate over Monotheism and Polytheism

In the background of Evans's hypothesis of monotheism lurks a historical debate concerning the nature of early religions and the association of monotheism with a high ethical and civilized standard. Monotheism is *not an ancient* term. It was invented in the seventeenth century to describe spiritual and civilized religions (Judaism, Christianity, and Islam) as opposed to pagan idolatrous cults that were considered savage.[34] When Evans compared the religion of Minoan Crete to the Christian religion, he found them almost equal.[35] He must have annoyed some Christians and certainly classical scholars who thought that nobody could have been more advanced than the Greeks. Evans, however, bravely maintained his position and became combative:

> We see here an abode of light rather than darkness. We have not here the Hades of primitive Greek tradition – the gloomy Under-World of pale shadows and gibbering ghosts. This is the true Elysion, un-Hellenic in its conception.[36]

E. B. Tylor had also devoted a few pages to monotheism and had granted that certain old religions were civilized. Egyptian Ra/Re, Greek Zeus and the Persian Ahura Mazda were dominant gods in their respective religions, and the latter tended to monotheism.[37] Still, they differed from Judaism, Islam, and Christianity in that they lacked *consistent ethical systems*, whereas advanced monotheism entailed divine sanction of ethical laws, theological enforcement of morality, moral government of the universe, and providence for the doctrine of a future life.[38] These were the criteria that Tylor utilized in order to explain true monotheism, and Evans had to answer them.

And he did! Minoan religion passed the ethics test. Did not the Tomb of the Double Axes prove that the Minoan deity cared for the dead? Were not the Minoan larnakes (clay coffins) painted with symbols of the goddess? Therefore the deity was a mother to the dead as well as the living.

At about the same time as Evans was developing his paradigm about monotheism, the American scholar James H. Breasted (with whom Evans was in regular correspondence) was engaged in defending the moral aspect of monotheism in Egyptian religion. In *Development of Religion and Thought in Ancient Egypt* (1912), he devoted an entire chapter to the ethical nature of Egyptian gods.[39] He emphasized the importance of the solar deity of the Amarna age, the Aten, because it united the entire inhabited world as well as the cosmos in one entity and had the remarkable epithet, 'a mother, profitable to gods and men': this was solicitude for mankind.[40]

Breasted's conception of Aten is quite similar to that of Evans's Great Goddess. As mentioned above, the two scholars were in touch and each obviously read the other's works. Breasted writes in 1927 that Evans recognized the fact that 'Ancient Egypt itself can no longer be regarded as something apart from general human history'.[41] Evidently this meant that Evans regarded Egyptian civilization as a landmark in the entire history of mankind, and by adopting some of the insights of the Egyptologists of his day he could apply the same principles to Minoan religion.

The Challenge of Nilsson

However, in 1927, Evans was challenged by the Swedish historian of Greek religion, Martin Persson Nilsson, in his book called *The Minoan-Mycenaean Religion and its Survival in Greek Religion*, a major accomplishment even by today's standards. Nilsson discredited the fundamental assumptions of the English scholar, although it is certain that he intended no disrespect for his older and much revered peer. First, argued Nilsson, there was no solid evidence for a mother-goddess in Minoan religion: 'whether the name "Mother" is permissible needs proving'.[42] Second, he denied that the chief deity represented a fusion of all others on the grounds that it was an unparalleled phenomenon (he discarded Egyptian analogies).[43] Third, although he admitted that Egypt and Crete had contacts, he denied that Egypt supplied vital clues for the understanding of Minoan religion.[44] Fourth, Nilsson regarded Minoan religion as primitive and argued that it had its basis on vegetation cults and cycles of nature; thus, he denied the moral content that Evans ascribed to it. Finally, he claimed that his own method was sounder because it was based on purely archaeological facts rather than 'indulgence in hypotheses'.[45]

On the surface, Nilsson's work appeared more systematic than Evans's. It consisted of a thorough – albeit dry – collection of all the known data about Minoan and Mycenaean cults and was accompanied by pictures and a thorough commentary. Yet, the method is deficient without proper classification of the images, and this is where Nilsson is at his weakest. His assignation to categories is based on premises that are neither argued, nor demonstrated. One example is his chapter on the 'Epiphanies of Gods in Human Shape'. How does he define epiphany and what distinguishes epiphany scenes with humans witnessing them from divine representations in general? This question is not answered. Moreover, the chapter includes so many categories (anthropomorphic gods, animal demons, women carrying animals) that a definition of the phenomenon in Minoan-Mycenaean terms eludes the reader.[46] By contrast, Evans attempted to present epiphany as a phenomenon of ecstasy and divine communion taking place at a specific location next to a sacred tree or a *baetyl*. This has been now fully verified by a fresco from Thera (for a sacred tree in a sanctuary see Figure 12).

In other ways too Nilsson's work is deficient. He curiously strips the most conspicuous religious emblem of the Minoans, the double axe, of its symbolism and interprets it as a mere instrument for the sacrifice of the bull. But no image exists to date that shows a bull being killed by a double axe.[47]

The truth is that Nilsson had an agenda: he was trying to prove that Minoan and Mycenaean religion was the primitive stage of Greek religion. This is revealed in the subtitle of his book 'Survival in Greek religion.' Being a classical scholar, it was natural that he would be mostly interested in the Greeks and that he would utilize the mythological prism of the Classical Age to interpret Bronze Age Cretan material. He admits this much in his preface when he states that the book was the result of somewhat prolonged studies that originated in the Olaus Petri lectures on the History of Greek Religion (1921). In the following years, he enriched his knowledge of Cretan artefacts with a visit to Crete and gave a series of lectures at the University of Wales, Aberystwyth (1923) on the topic of origins. Finally, all this material turned into a book on Minoan and Mycenaean Religion. The collection was thorough, but the prism of interpretation was a reversal to the pre-Evans era when Greek myth was projected onto the past, an assumption that was not argued.

Evans did not let Nilsson's assertions go unchallenged, although the two men maintained excellent relations throughout their life. Evans rebutted: 'Any criticism which excludes the probable reaction of Egyptian elements on the early Cretan religion stands today self-condemned.'[48] And:

> it is dangerously misleading to regard the Minoan Goddess from the standpoint of Greek and Roman religion. [...] This criticism applies in part to the attitude adopted by Prof. Nilsson in his valuable work.[49]

Despite this, Nilsson's impact was major. Already upon the publication of the monograph in 1927, the Harvard professor Arthur Darby Nock wrote a glowing review, praising the Swede's method without being in the least bothered by his Hellenocentric lens. He found Nilsson's chapter against Evans's theory of monotheism very welcome.[50]

Evans still had some followers, however. D. G. Hogarth accepted his basic premise but modified it a little, speaking of the 'dual monotheism' of goddess and god.[51] Spyridon Marinatos found Evans's perspective very valid since it explained many of his own finds but admitted that the notion of monotheism had been 'repeatedly subjected to criticism'.[52] The Greek archaeologist Nikolaos Platon followed the idea of the one goddess,[53] whereas Stylianos Alexiou undertook a systematic reinvestigation of the question exactly 23 years after the publication of the last volume of *The Palace of Minos*. Alexiou noted the contradictions in Nilsson's model and those of others who followed him. With great clarity he saw how Evans's theory was supported by a goddess statue found at a mansion at Gortyn in southern Crete: she had a bird perched on her cheeks and snakes entwined around her arms (Figure 16). Could there be doubt that she embodied two diverse spheres of the universe, the sky and underworld?[54] Alexiou concludes that the best hypothesis is that of one goddess with many manifestations:

> There has been an effort to demonstrate distinct areas of worship as evidenced by statuettes and Minoan sanctuaries and to argue that they support a distinction between cycles of worship. Thus, Banti notes that snakes and birds are never found in the same sanctuary. This view has been proven wrong by the sanctuary of Gortyn in which a statuette bears both snakes and a bird.[55]

However, the tide was against Evans after the end of World War II. The monograph of the Swedish scholar Axel W. Persson, *The Religion of Greece in Prehistoric Times*, marked a clear return to the notion that Minoan religion was primitive, characterized by fertility vegetation

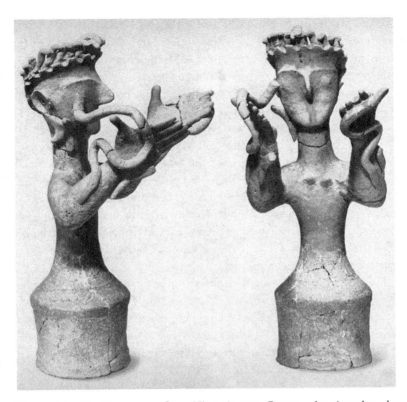

Figure 16 Goddess statue from Khannia near Gortyn, showing that the goddess embodied both underworld and heavenly symbols as Evans suggested. After Marinatos and Hirmer 1976, pl. 133.

cycles.[56] Many people did not even realize that this notion was *not* due to Evans but to the Cambridge Ritualists and especially Harrison and Frazer. Persson accepted Evans's theory of the mourning goddess but situated it in a primitive setting dominated by magic and nature-allegory, while he attuned it with the theories of Frazer and Nilsson. At this stage in the history of scholarship a major transformation occurred. The benign goddess of the high civilization, as Evans had conceived her, became a primitive earth mother, a relic of matriarchy. She was impersonal, prolific and savage.[57] She had a son who was also her consort. Sexual union between goddess and young consort were reflected in primitive rituals termed *hieros gamos*, a rite with connotations of unspeakable sexual unions and savagery. As Frazer put it in *The Golden Bough*, 'the civilized Babylonians, Egyptians and Greeks inherited it from their barbarous or savage forefathers'.[58]

The model of the earth-fertility-vegetation goddess found expression in the French-speaking world through Charles Picard's *Les Religions Préhelléniques*, written after the end of World War II (1948). Like Nilsson and Persson, Picard regarded the Minoan pantheon as the embryonic stage of Greek religion and spoke of deities as forces of nature. He envisaged fertility rites, matriarchal institutions and sacred marriage rites.[59] He found Evans's ideas about the purity and spiritual side of Minoan religion unconvincing: 'he could not supply decisive proof.'[60] W. K. C. Guthrie's general book *The Greeks and their Gods* (1950) also ascribes sacred marriage and fertility rites to Minoan religion.[61]

In the 1980s, scholars thought they found evidence of human sacrifice.[62] The theories were cautiously formulated by the excavators, but the media, seeing a chance to cause sensation, amplified the cases.[63]

Minoan religion mutated further under the impact of feminism. It was a refreshing change when Colin Renfrew attempted to systematize the study of cult by setting solid criteria of what is image, what is ritual, what is a communal ceremony.[64] However, even such clear-headed criteria seemed out of place when the fashion was determined by anthropological theories. The verdict of the 1980s may be summed up in a paragraph written by an eminent authority on prehistoric archaeology who states that 'the model of Minoan religion developed by Evans, centring upon a universally recognized great goddess and her consort [...] runs counter to a lot of evidence.'[65] As for the verdict of the twenty-first century, it has been even more severe as it denies the possibility of attempting any reconstruction of religious beliefs.[66]

Three main conclusions emerge from this discussion. First, Evans had a particular definition of monotheism in mind. Second, his theory was based on hard-core evidence. Third, his original views were distorted by the subsequent works of Nilsson and Persson, both of whom combined Frazer's approach with the traditional pre-Evans notion that Minoan religion was the primitive stage of Greek religion. Finally, it is evident that the above scholarly trends coloured the perception of Evans's actual writings with the result that little of the original thought has remained. Add to this another fact: postcolonial narratives do not particularly appreciate the praise of civilization.

CHAPTER 5

THE RING OF NESTOR

A Clever Forger?

The publication of the first volume of *The Palace of Minos* in 1921 (which included Evans's theory of monotheism) had the unexpected consequence that shortly after its appearance Minoan forgeries flooded the market. They consisted mostly of ivory statuettes, gold rings and seals. As these objects are of varying quality, it has not proved easy to dismiss all of them as forgeries, and this issue will not be the primary concern here. Suffice it to note that all the above-mentioned objects had an undocumented provenance. Here we shall examine only the so-called Ring of Nestor because it ended up in Evans's hands and became one of his favourite pieces. He parted with it only in his deep old age at which time he donated it to the Ashmolean Museum. He named it Ring of Nestor because of its alleged provenance from a large beehive (tholos) tomb in the southern Peloponnese.

The reason he favoured the Nestor ring above all others is that he was drawn to the mental universe of the picture. He saw in the engraving a complete narrative of the belief system of his beloved culture with all its benevolent demons and the Great Goddess. He therefore published it many times, first in a preliminary article, then in the third volume of *The Palace of Minos*, and finally in the lecture he gave in honour of Sir James Frazer. He also exhibited the ring in London as a testimony to the sophistication of Minoan religion.

It must be admitted that nobody since Evans has interpreted this ring as eloquently as he did; all the subsequent discussions have focussed either on the style of the engraving or on the parallels for each single motif without the consideration of its complex visual syntax and overall interpretation.[1] For this reason, Evans's explanation remains the *only* solid and comprehensive one. If the ring is genuine, as many scholars think, it proves once again that Evans's intuition was astoundingly sharp. If it is a forgery, his interpretation is still of great interest for the biography of Evans because it sheds light on his inner world and shows the manner of his thinking. It must also be said that the style of the engraving is convincingly Minoan so that, even if it proves to be a forgery, this fact will not discredit Evans's sharp eye. Rather, it will highlight the extraordinary skill of another man, one of Evans's own collaborators, who managed to deceive him. And this relationship is very interesting for the assessment of his character. Evans, it must be noted, was not lacking in shrewdness about human nature but was too honest to conceive of the possibility that one of his most competent artists was working in conjunction with forgers.

The present discussion of the gold Ring of Nestor will now introduce Evans's restorer Emile Gilliéron fils and it will be hinted at that he was a dealer of antiquities and possibly also the designer of the Nestor ring. He was the son of a famous father by the same name whom Evans had employed at Knossos since the beginning of the excavations and whom he appreciated deeply, not just on account of his technical skill but also because of the successful way that he rendered Minoan art.[2] Gilliéron père was not a stranger to profitable business. He established a workshop on Skoufa Street 44, Athens, where he and his son together produced copies of Minoan and Mycenaean art pieces and sold them abroad for private profit. When the father died, the son took over the family business. Evans employed the son as he had the father and was very happy with the results.[3] There is nothing to suggest that they were emotionally close because their correspondence is cool and restricted to formalities. However, we do know that Evans held him in as high esteem as he had held his father.

A second person who will be involved here is the German archaeologist Georg Karo (Figure 17a), a scholar about 21 years

Figure 17a–b   (a) Georg Karo, German archaeologist, University of Halle *c.*1928. (b) Spyridon Marinatos *c.*1928 (at that time Karo's student in Halle).

Evans's junior but one who felt close to him. Karo was born in Venice in 1872 and died in Germany in 1963. A Jew by origin, he was baptized Evangelical and made his career in Germany, becoming more German than the Germans. Before World War I, having earned a solid reputation as an archaeologist, he was chosen to be Assistant Director of the German Archaeological Institute in Athens. This is when he met Evans and became a regular visitor at Knossos, the observer of his excavations and the first phase of his restorations. Subsequently, he was made Director of the German Archaeological Institute and held this position twice, between 1910 and 1919 and between 1930 and 1936. In the end, he was ousted by the Nazi regime because of his Jewish origins. He managed to immigrate to America where his life was not happy and returned to Germany after the war.

During his long stay in Athens in the interwar period, Karo became well acquainted with the same people as Evans and acquired suspicions about the Gilliérons, father and son, after they worked with him in preparing the drawings for the publication of the Shaft

Graves of Mycenae. Between 1920 and 1930 Karo returned to Germany and held the professorship at the University of Halle, Germany. One of his graduate students then was the young Greek archaeologist Spyridon Marinatos (Figure 17b), whom he singled out as one of his best. The relationship lasted for a lifetime; surely they discussed their common acquaintances and the increasing power that Gilliéron fils accrued in his hands. Marinatos met the latter in Herakleion in 1926 and had polite but cool relations with him. In 1928, he wrote to his boss Xanthoudides that this man was self-serving and made profit by copying Greek antiquities, selling them to foreign museums.[4]

The Find Circumstances of the Ring of Nestor

We shall see next how Gilliéron was involved in the story of the Nestor ring, which came into Evans's hands in the following way. The ring was first brought to the National Museum in Athens around 1924 by an unknown man. Karo was asked to be a member of the evaluation committee that examined the ring (the other members were Greeks). Karo was instantly convinced that it was a forgery and that it should be returned to the man who brought it.[5] A few years later, Karo discussed this incident with Marinatos at the University of Halle. The occasion was Martin P. Nilsson's publication of *Minoan-Mycenaean Religion* (1927), which included the Nestor ring as evidence regarding religion.[6] Karo apparently told Marinatos what had happened three years before in the National Museum and expressed his disappointment that Evans did not heed his advice. Marinatos reports this fact to his boss in Crete, Stephanos Xanthoudides, and stresses that Evans was criticized because he was prone to accept forgeries as genuine and thus misled other scholars: 'the whole thing [about forgeries] has become too much and everybody has a duty to tell the facts for the sake of science, since even a scholar such as Nilsson has been deceived'.[7]

The letter shows that some German scholars were critical of Evans's gullibility. This is confirmed by what the German Hittite specialist, Helmut Th. Bossert, writes in the preface of his book on Minoan and Mycenaean art a few years later:

> Only a few experts who live permanently in Greece and who observed the processes [of production of antiquities] are in the position to decide about forgeries. They came to understand how to identify the forgers in the course of time and to distinguish their style and technique. In this respect I relied on the observations of Prof. Dr. Karo in Athens and the advice of the Director of the Herakleion Museum Dr. Marinatos.[8]

How did Evans get hold of the ring that was rejected as a forgery by the Greek authorities? In 1925, someone whom he calls a friend tipped him off that the gem had been viewed in the Peloponnese.[9] Evans went there, presumably accompanied by the same 'friend', and upon seeing it was thrilled. Here was an object rich in iconographical motifs and furnishing new clues about the Minoan afterlife in a style that seemed genuine even to his expert eyes. His first impressions are evident from the sketch and notes he made in his original notebook, now in Oxford (Figure 18).[10] He evidently saw a map of the other world because he refers to the sea, a river of paradise, fishes, a boat (the latter he later re-identified as a dragon whereas the river became a tree; see Figure 20). In the same notebook, he notes a dancing goddess but does not mention that she is almost exactly copied from the ring from Vapheio (Figure 21). He notes a griffin on a throne and observes that this monster is adored by griffin-women; he observes that this is paralleled by bird-women on sealings that had been found by David G. Hogarth at Zakros. Note that the latter were published in 1902 and republished by Evans himself in the first volume of *The Palace of Minos*; therefore the forger could potentially have known them.[11] For Evans, though, this parallelism constituted proof of authenticity. He was very impressed by the group of humans and griffin-women: they furnished a clue that the topography represented the netherworld. He started interpreting the scene but the crossing out of some of the sentences in the notebook shows a certain hesitation and a struggle to find coherence.

Figure 18 Ring of Nestor. Evans's drawing from his Knossos notebook, Ashmolean Museum, Oxford, 42, pp. 82–3 (Box 10).

Figure 19   Ring of Nestor. CMS VI, 277.

This is what he wrote:

Dance. Girls put hand on wrists of two youths. But one holds
the waist of the other. The other lays (?) hand on girl's shoulder
[crossed out]. Woman griffin seems to peep at dancers.
Enchanted bower of sacred lion or griffin [crossed out] . . .

Figure 20   Ring of Nestor. Watercolour painting made by E. Gilliéron
fils. Evans, PM III, pl. XX A.

Figure 21   Comparison of the dancing goddesses on Vapheio and Nestor rings. If the latter is a forgery, the comparison reveals the designer's prototype.

In the end he concluded that this was a Minoan paradise and writes to his cousin that it depicts 'a map of the Elysian fields of my old people' (his old people are the Minoans).[12]

And yet he had been warned by Karo that the Nestor ring was a forgery and Karo probably hinted that Evans ought to be cautious about a man in his own entourage who knew his ideas. Evans argued back that the iconography was too unique to be the creation of any forger. Within a few months he had published the ring in the *Journal of Hellenic Studies* and writes: 'We have [. . .] the first glimpse into the Elysian fields of Minoan and Mycenaean religion; it throws a singular light on the eschatology of the pre-classical age in Greece'.[13]

It is obvious why the content of the scene excited him, since it furnished prospects of great mental discovery. Besides, he was told a convincing story about its find context. It had supposedly been found 20 years before by a peasant who obtained it from a beehive tomb in the excavations of the German archaeologist Wilhelm Dörpfeld. Upon the death of the finder, the ring was passed on to other persons and Evans reproduces the story as follows in his publication:

On the death of the peasant who had the good luck to find it,
the ring passed into the possession of the son, who in course of
time ceded it to the owner of a neighbouring vineyard.[14]

What is curious about this story is the extraordinary chain of
transmission of ownership that has the advantage of bridging the gap
between 1907, the time when Dörpfeld excavated the tomb, and
1924 or 1925, when the ring came to Evans's possession. Also note
the involvement of several persons, which means that serious
investigation of the original find circumstances was impossible. The
discoverer was dead and his son had passed the ring on to a third
party, a 'neighbour'. There was no way to test the veracity of the story.
Evans forgot the complexity himself and simplified it in *Palace of
Minos III* (1930) five years later.

[The ring was found] in a large beehive tomb at Nestor's Pylos
by a peasant in quest of building material, somewhat previous
to its investigation of its remains there by the German explorers
in 1907. The discovery, however, was kept dark, and on the
death of the original finder the ring passed into the possession
of the owner of a neighbouring vineyard.[15]

In this last account, the son of the peasant has been omitted, and
the narrative has become simplified. The question *we* must ask is who
the intermediary was. Who convinced Evans to go to the Peloponnese to
interview the dealer and to acquaint him with its owner?

In his first account of 1925, Evans names this man as 'a *trustworthy
source*'[16] but in the second, in 1930, he speaks more specifically about
a friend who lived in Athens: 'Thanks to the kindness of a friend, I
saw an imperfect impression of the signet ring at Athens'.[17] And this
friend must have been a very competent man since he had the presence
of mind to have malleable material in his pocket to make an imprint.
When and how did 'the friend' see the ring? The possibilities are not
many; it is almost certain that the friend cannot be anyone except Emile
Gilliéron fils who was at the time Artistic Director of the Athens

National Museum and who could have made an imprint in order to show it to Evans. Note that he did not want his name to be revealed.

We may criticize Evans about the following. When he produced his report in 1925, he described the tomb excavated by Dörpfeld in such detail that it is easy for the reader to forget that the origin of the ring is not certain. However, as far as the engraving went, it was indeed excellent in quality. We must now look at the narrative of the scene through Evans's eyes, better to appreciate his enthusiastic endorsement. And it must be noted that if the ring is forged, it was crafted by someone who knew what he was doing and understood very well Evans's interpretation of Minoan religion and its affinities with Egypt.

Evans's Interpretation: An Egyptian Prototype for the Ring?

In the centre of the composition is a sinuous design which, as we have already seen, Evans identified at first as the river of paradise viewed from above (Gen. 2:10; see Figures 19–20).[18] It has also been mentioned that females with eagle heads and an enthroned griffin constitute elements of the unusual iconography of the gem. Also strange is the huge lion lying on a podium and receiving worship from two minute females. However, Evans had an explanation for all of the above. The lion was a guardian of the underworld, according to Egyptian parallels which he had published in 'Tree and Pillar Cult'.[19] Actually, all the motifs of the representation cohered if one were to use the template of Egyptian afterlife-beliefs: in Egyptian funerary art it is often the case that the deceased couple arrives at the court of the seated judge-god Osiris and his wife Isis (Figure 22).[20]

And this matches exactly the syntax of the Nestor ring. A young couple meet again in the underworld after having previously been parted by death. The couple is shown twice. First, they appear on the upper left panel where they meet each other in the presence of the goddess and her handmaiden. Above them is pair of butterflies that Evans interpreted as souls. The man and woman are represented a second time in the lower half of the scene and a female griffin-demon leads them to the 'court of judgement'. Evans considers the griffin a

Figure 22   Arrival at the court of judgement. Comparison of the Egyptian Papyrus of Ani and the Nestor Ring. The forger must have used the Egyptian papyrus as his prototype.

'gentle judge' because he allows the couple to move on to the presence of a dancing goddess. It has been noted above that this dancing figure is almost an exact replica of the supposed goddess on the Vapheio ring (Figure 21). This is a suspicious parallel: why would the goddess (assuming she is one) be engaged in an ecstatic dance in the netherworld? Evans saw this as logical because she takes the place of Osiris in the equivalent scenes of the Egyptian funerary papyri.

No doubt he was aware that the visual syntax (note that I am speaking of syntax and not style) was highly reminiscent of Egyptian funerary scenes as represented on the papyrus of Ani, where the subject usually was the journey of a deceased couple to the court of Osiris (Figure 22).[21]

What about the two butterflies? There is no compelling evidence that they ever represent souls in Minoan and Mycenaean art, as was indeed pointed out by Karo in his publication of the Shaft Graves from Mycenae. He writes there that such a designation is an unproven assumption although it was proposed by Schliemann himself. It rested on the fact that in the Greek language *psyche* means both soul and butterfly, a pun which may not have held true for the Minoan language.[22]

Evans had his own reasons for following Schliemann. He had been concerned at that time with a butterfly depicted on the priest-king relief fresco from Knossos and this happened before he saw the Nestor ring, namely around 1924. At that time, he got the idea that the Minoan priest-king was situated within an Elysian landscape of huge lilies and butterflies. When he saw the Nestor ring, it provided him with the unexpected verification that the Minoan Elysium included butterflies.[23]

This leads us back to our suspected forger. Prior to the ring's appearance, Gilliéron fils had been working on the restoration of this very fresco of the priest-king and must have had discussions with Evans about the role of the butterfly in the composition. This coincidence makes it more than likely that the Nestor ring was fabricated especially to suit Evans's taste and to confirm his hypotheses about butterflies and souls in Elysium.

There is another curious fact. The ring surfaced shortly after Howard Carter opened the sealed doorway of the tomb of Tutankhamun in Egypt, on 23 February 1923. Evans had been disappointed that he had found nothing similar at Knossos, but he was thrilled that so much evidence about the beyond was being discovered in Egypt. On 11 December 1923, while the tomb was being excavated, he presented a lecture at the Egypt Exploration Society stressing the close connections between Crete and Egypt.[24] What a happy coincidence that a ring of Minoan manufacture should present a funerary scene that looked so Egyptian! Or is it not a coincidence that shortly afterwards the Nestor Ring appeared, the concoction of a clever forger?

The Tree of Life and the Golden Bough

So far we have seen that Evans's interpretation of the Nestor Ring was entirely coherent because he intuitively comprehended the Egyptian paradigm behind its design and therefore he could read the visual syntax like no other. There is little doubt that the scene also struck an emotional chord in him because he expected Minoan religion to have been gentle and to have included humane afterlife beliefs. Yet, even *he* did not understand all the motifs of the iconography and had to correct himself on certain points as time went by. The first mistake was this: the design in the centre of the ring did not represent the four rivers of paradise, as he thought at first.[25] At some point he gave up the idea and realized that the features of the object are those of an old oak tree, gnarled and barren, and that the latter is guarded by a dog or monster or some other such dragon (Figure 20). He corrects himself:

> The convex formation of the upright dividing object in the middle of the field has no resemblance to water, but its rough and sinewy surface shows the unmistakable features of the trunk of an old tree.[26]

Who suggested this alternative explanation to him? Gilliéron fils was preparing the definitive design of the gem at the time as well as a watercolour version (Figure 20). Was he the one who intimated the correct interpretation about the tree? In any case, Evans admitted that the size and shape of the tree was un-Minoan and that parallels for it came from 'a very distant quarter', by which he meant Nordic myths.[27] He missed another detail which may prove crucial for the evaluation of the ring's authenticity. Although the tree was barren, it had a single *leafy branch* growing from the upper right corner of its trunk. The regenerative power of the single branch would make a lot of sense to viewers who understood the fashionable themes of the time, primitive tree cults and cycles of life. However, Evans had thought of trees not merely as regenerative sources but as abodes of the deity; in their vicinity humans had communion with the divinity and experienced epiphanies. And given his frame of interpretation, he missed the significance of the single leafy bough. He was right to have missed it because no such a bough has ever appeared to date in Minoan art and therefore most likely expresses the forger's understanding of what the Tree of Life was.

It seems, however, that by 1930 Evans was told by someone that the bough on the tree was significant; perhaps it was even suggested to him that it was the golden bough. So Evans revises his thoughts and writes, 'The religious character of the scene is further enhanced by the bough'. He adds references to Frazer's work.[28] Was this idea casually mentioned to him by our suspect? In any case, he expresses his gratitude to Gilliéron for his insights in the same volume: 'I had at hand not only a competent artist but one whose admirable studies in Minoan art had thoroughly imbued him with its spirit'.[29]

One has to wonder if it is an accident that the abridged version of James Frazer's *Golden Bough* appeared just a few years before the discovery of the Nestor ring. In this elegant volume, the educated non-specialist would have become familiar with the theory that nature dies but regenerates anew in the spring.[30] Frazer discusses there the worship of the oak, a tree that, although barren in the winter, stays green because of the parasitic mistletoe intertwined in its branches.[31] Frazer's ideas caught the popular imagination, as may be shown by an article in *The Times*, December 1920.[32] On 21 November 1921, Frazer was awarded an honorary doctorate from the Sorbonne together with Rudyard Kipling. The same year he was knighted at the age of 71.

It is difficult to avoid the suspicion that the Nestor ring was fabricated to suit tastes current in the 1920s and that *The Golden Bough* was the inspiration for the single fresh branch attached to the barren tree trunk in the centre of the scene. The forger used Frazer as an inspiration but basically relied on an Egyptian iconographical funerary formula for meaning. The only man who could have had the knowledge and artistic skill to design such a ring (if it is indeed a forgery) is Emile Gilliéron fils. By creating this masterpiece of art and universal themes, he crafted 'a key to all mythologies'.[33]

Contemporary scholars who are now convinced of the ring's authenticity will argue that the technique could not have been known in the 1920s. Not so. Here is the testimony of Edith Eccles, a British archaeologist who worked at Knossos in the early 1930s and who assisted Evans (see Appendix 2). In a letter addressed to Sir Arthur in November 1935 she included photographs of highly magnified gems and wrote that:

they might teach us a good deal about the technical methods used by the Minoan gem cutter and possibly help us occasionally to detect a forgery by showing up cuts and grooves made by instruments which we could prove were unknown to the Minoan gem cutter.

Upon reflection, however, Eccles realized that this method was not sufficient since a good forger would have avoided this very trap: 'I think now that this test is a pious hope. I think the modern forger is astute enough to confine himself to the few tools and emery in use in ancient times'.[34]

It is impossible to tell if she had concrete suspicions about Gilliéron fils. Still, it is clear from letters addressed to Spyridon Marinatos that she had no great regard for him (see Appendix 2, letters 3 and 8).

It remains to examine Gilliéron fils's motives, if he is indeed the designer. He perhaps collaborated with goldsmiths in Herakleion, about whom more will be said in the next chapter. Father and son had many contacts in Greece and abroad, and as noted above they made copies of rings and other artefacts in their workshop on Skoufa Street, Athens.[35] These copies gave them the chance to study the technique of ancient objects carefully, and for this reason some scholars have suspected them for forgeries of rings before.

[The forgers] must have been close to Athens dealers and have had a substantial workshop there and an outlet to collectors in Europe, perhaps through Switzerland. That they were artists of calibre familiar with engraving techniques and metal working is obvious, and it should not be too difficult on the basis of this evidence to guess who they were, but, as the evidence is so far circumstantial, the guess should perhaps not be set down in print here.[36]

The motive is more difficult to determine since it is not at all clear whether Gilliéron fils made money from the transaction. His motive may have been mere ambition to create something so perfect that it could be mistaken as genuine by all experts, even by Evans.[37] Did he have a sense of stifled creativity? Was he convinced that he understood Minoan art and technique better than anyone else and that he could prove it? These are possibilities but cannot be verified. All we can say is that if the Nestor ring is a forgery, it symbolizes the conflict of two great minds, that of Evans and that of his restorer.

The last word will be given to Georg Karo, who hinted even in public that the Nestor ring was a forgery but never said so explicitly so as not to offend Evans while the latter was alive.[38] However, in his memoirs (published in 1959) he writes that he warned Evans and adds with a tone of regret, 'Despite all this, Evans bought the ring shortly afterwards and published it'.[39]

CHAPTER 6

THE RING OF MINOS

Malice was to a person of Evans's character truly
incomprehensible.

Georg Karo[1]

The Discovery of the Minos Ring

A few years after Evans bought the Ring of Nestor, another one of
similar make made its appearance in Herakleion and was eventually
baptized the Ring of Minos. Evans knew instantly that the two were
twin products of the same workshop, but the possibility that the
workshop was modern did not cross his mind.[2]

The ring was brought to the Herakleion Museum in 1930, but
before we turn to the specifics of its discovery some other
information will hopefully throw light on the case. We go back to
1928, when Spyridon Marinatos was in Germany studying with
Georg Karo at the University of Halle. Each week he sent a report
of his activities to the Director of the Herakleion Museum,
Stephanos Xanthoudides, and his letters which have survived
reveal that the two men had information about the existence of a
forger's workshop at Herakleion. Marinatos writes to Xanthoudides in 1928:

I am so glad that the matter of the forgeries is beginning to be resolved. I am often put in a most difficult position about the matter and I had to refuse reviewing Nilsson's book because I would have been compelled to touch upon the matter of forgeries and I would have made Evans my mortal enemy — imagine how he could harm us.[3]

In another letter he writes:

Concerning the forgeries now: I urge you fervently to tell Evans everything, or if it is too late, tell Mackenzie to write him. [...] Karo is forced to tell him something. I myself have been compelled to take a stand [on this matter] and write a very long footnote about the forgeries in an article [...] I mention there explicitly that all my colleagues in Crete have been suspicious of many objects for a long time, and that they have unambiguous evidence about the fabrication of several pieces but said nothing so as not to displease Evans. But now the whole thing has become too much and everybody has a duty to tell the facts for the sake of science, since even a scholar of the status of Nilsson has been deceived.[4] I wrote nothing definitive about the Boston goddess, since you asked me not to do so.[5]

From this letter we surmise that Xanthoudides had serious reservations about the authenticity of the 'Boston goddess', a gold and ivory statuette launched in the market after World War I. Xanthoudides also knew that there was a forger's workshop in Herakleion.[6] Also worth noting is the fact that another gold ring from Archanes (illegally obtained by a local) had been brought to Evans around 1924. Marinatos writes about this to Xanthoudides from Germany:

The Archanes ring had been brought to the museum long before Evans bought it and [...] it had been justly rejected by us as a forgery. As an afterthought I omitted the name of the man who had brought it, Kefalogiannis, in case you would be displeased [. . .] there is no reason why Evans should get angry since he is getting reprimands from everyone and from all directions.[7]

Apart from the fact that Marinatos considers Evans gullible in this letter, we also get the information that Evans had bought the ring *after* it had been rejected as a fake by the Greek authorities. This detail ought to be noted because it establishes a pattern: Evans bought antiquities *after* they had been inspected by the Greek authorities.

From the letter we also learn that a man named Kefalogiannis, a well-known goldsmith in Herakleion, had brought the Archanes ring to Evans.[8] This man was not just a goldsmith but also a dealer. Despite his suspicions, Xanthoudides unfortunately never got the chance to tell Evans his true opinion about the rings; because by the time the aforementioned letters by Marinatos were received, Evans had already returned to Britain whereas later that year, Xanthoudides suddenly suffered a heart attack. This was a great tragedy for Cretan archaeology as he had been a learned and moderate man and a friend to Evans. It was quickly decided by the Archaeological Council in Athens to recall Marinatos back from Germany in 1929 and offer him the post. And this is how he entered the scene as director of the museum and began dealing with forgeries.

It was under those circumstances that the Ring of Minos was brought to him a year later, on 19 May 1930, by the parish priest of the Knossos district, a man by the name of Nikolaos Pollakes. He was not only a priest but had additional offices doubling as a teacher and supervisor of archaeological activities in his district.[9] Apparently his supervising was not always blameless (see Appendix 5).

We now return to the first appearance of the Minos ring at the Herakleion Museum. Upon seeing it, Marinatos instantly suspected it to be a forgery, recalling what Karo had told him. However, his assistant Nikolaos Platon, who later became a famous archaeologist, had a different opinion. Platon had actually seen it before in Pollakes's hands, had been convinced of its authenticity and had persuaded Pollakes – not without considerable effort – to bring it to the authorities.[10] Now Platon felt a sense of embarrassment that

Marinatos considered it a forgery. Yet when the archaeologists asked the priest where the ring had been found, the informants were vague. Platon was told that a boy had found it in a vineyard many years earlier. Since this information was hearsay, involving a chain of informants, Marinatos remained unconvinced.

Another question must be answered now. Who tipped Evans off about the ring's existence and when did he actually see it? The standard view (still current in the Cretan press) is that Evans was the first to see it and that he sought to buy it; that he refused to buy it in the end because of the high price requested by the priest.[11] This scenario is in need of revision as far as the proper sequence of events goes because, as Gibbon said once, there is no history without proper chronology.

Three points must be considered. First, it is not at all likely that Evans would buy a ring illegally without informing the Greek authorities. Such an act would cast the English archaeologists in a very bad light. In the previous year, Evans had clashed with Marinatos on another matter, about which more will be said in the next chapter; it is thus very unlikely that he would risk another confrontation with the young director of the museum. Second, it was a matter of principle for Evans not to support thieves of Cretan antiquities (if an object had been discarded as a forgery, of course, he considered himself released from any obligation). It will be remembered that he bought the Archanes and Nestor rings only *after* they had been rejected by the Greek authorities as forgeries. Third, and most important, there is solid evidence that Evans saw the ring for the first time the same year it was brought to the Herakleion Museum. This is indicated by the date of his entry in the Knossos notebook of 1930 (Figures 23–4). The entry consists of two pages of notes and one full page of a drawing.[12]

'Ring of Minos'. Found on E. slope of Gypsades? below Hogarth's House (Small chamber tomb then much plundered.) Spanos owner sold to Papa Ni-kola for DR 25,000 = £68. Weight 29.5 grammes (R. of Nestor 31.5) Interior size Gilliéron. 16.5 cm × 14. R. of N. p. 47. 17 cm × 12

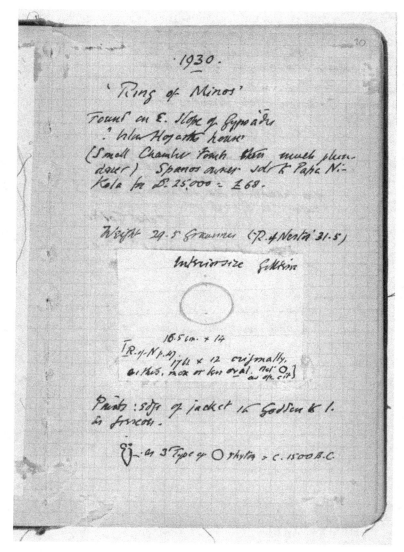

Figure 23   Evans's notes about Ring of Minos, 1930. Knossos notebook 41, p. 10a, Ashmolean Museum, Oxford.

Figure 24 Sketch of Ring of Minos by Evans. Knossos notebook 41, p.9a, Ashmolean Museum, Oxford.

originally, this more or less oval not O as op. cit. Prints: edge of jacket of Goddess [? writing illegible] frescoes.

At the bottom of the page Evans sketched an oval rhyton with the note 'type of O rhyton c. 1500 B.C.'

It is evident from the above that Evans was excited about the iconography and this is why he made a detailed drawing. Note that the latter is based on an impression rather than the ring. This was normal practice but, in this case, I have some reasons to believe that he had not seen the actual object at the time he made the entry. First, it is strange that there is no information at all about the surface of the gem, the condition of its preservation, or the quality of the engraving whereas the notes include information about the interior dimensions and the weight of the ring. Second, next to the entry we note the name 'Gilliéron'. Does this not suggest that Gilliéron fils was the man who brought Evans the imprint as well as information about its exact dimensions and weight? This must have happened while the original was in the Museum of Herakleion.

Emile Gilliéron as the Mediator: Conflicting Stories about the Origins of the Ring

In the spring and summer of 1930, Gilliéron was working at the Herakleion Museum in the double capacity of artistic director of all Greek museums and Evans's restorer for the murals of Knossos; he would have been present at the museum when the gem was presented to Marinatos by the priest Pollakes. Thus, it is most likely − if not outright certain − that he made a plaster imprint and showed it to Evans. The pattern of events recalls exactly the case of the Nestor ring since in both cases Gilliéron fils makes imprints and brings them to Evans.

Another fact is interesting. Evans was told different stories about the find circumstances of the ring at different times. In his first entry, he writes that a man named Spanos had sold it to the priest Pollakes. Later, however, he adds a second entry, at the end of the same notebook: '8-years son of Emm. Papadakis 3 years ago. Ring found below Kouskouras steep slope in vineyard N. of Π (south of the Palace). Kouskourades name of spot "Paris" hamlet'.[13]

This entry agrees with what Platon remembered years later. He was told that the ring had been found by a boy next to, or hanging from, a vineyard. Platon, however, recalled the name of the boy as Stratakes in one account, and Apostolos Diakakis in another.[14] He was evidently served different stories by different people, and he was trying to combine them in his memory 50 years later when he wrote his account of the Ring of Minos.[15] When Peter Warren made his own inquiries in the 1990s, he was told by a reliable source that the boy was Michalis Papadakis, the son of Emmanuel Papadakis.[16] This agrees with the entry made by Evans and represents the story as it crystallized; but is it a true story? In any case, it does not accord with Evans's first entry. Conclusion: there was no agreed upon version in 1930, when the ring was found.

Another fact is interesting. Evans notes that the boy was eight years of age. Does this refer to the boy's present age or the time when he made the discovery of the ring? It is not clear; in any case, a small boy is not a reliable witness and cross-examination is difficult. All this reminds of the case of the Nestor ring, the finder of which could not be cross-examined because he was dead by the time Evans came to the Peloponnese. In short, there is a definite pattern here concocted by men of no mean intelligence.

Marinatos became suspicious of the authenticity of the Minos ring for this and other reasons and the idea occurred to him that it was produced in a workshop in Herakleion.[17] Still, he felt that it was his duty to invite Evans to examine it in the museum in the spring/early summer of 1930, because Evans did see the original and writes so in *Palace of Minos IV*.[18] Marinatos witnessed his enthusiasm and decided to send the ring to Athens to have it examined by the National Archaeological Council. Gilliéron fils carried it there in his capacity as the artistic director of all the museums of the Greek nation. He signed a receipt (which has survived in the Ephoreia archives), and we thus know the exact date of its conveyance to Athens: 26 June 1930.[19] After the object was examined, it was rejected unanimously by the council as a forgery.[20] Marinatos requested from the ministry that the ring be returned to the priest, as this was the fair thing to do. And so the priest received the ring back in Herakleion and signed a receipt dated to 21 December 1930.[21] After this Pollakes took it and hid it away.

We now turn to Evans's own account of these events in *Palace of Minos IV*, and we shall see that it is in full accordance with the story as reconstructed here. He writes:

> The ring was purchased from the finder's father by a local priest, unfortunately of unbalanced mind, and no exact account of its whereabouts is at present obtainable. His favourite answer to inquirers was that he had given it to his wife, who had buried it and forgotten where! In any case it was worth 'twenty million drachmas'.[22]

When did Evans have a chance to negotiate with the priest? By December, when the ring was returned to Pollakes, Evans was back in England. This means that he must have communicated with him through a mediator, which is clear from the wording, 'his [the priest's] favourite answer to inquirers.' Who are the inquirers if not Gilliéron fils? The latter emerges once again as the possible mediator, as though he wanted to see the Minos ring published by Evans.

There is one more curious fact. Since the ring was too expensive to buy, Evans asked Gilliéron to make a copy based on the impression (see Figure 25a). However, now two copies exist in the Ashmolean Museum, and they are not completely identical. The difference is that the shrine in the centre of the ring is rendered differently in each: in one version there is a guilloche pattern in the building, on the other there is none. The copy that eventually resurfaced (and which is considered the authentic one) has the guilloche pattern and so does the sketch drawn by Evans (Figure 24); the other version exists in the Ashmolean. Note, however, that the drawing executed by Gilliéron fils (Figure 25a) does not show the shrine with a guilloche pattern whereas Evans's sketch shows it. Note additionally that a sketch found in Marinatos's archives, made on the basis of what was brought to the museum in 1930, does not include the guilloche pattern of the shrine (Figure 25b).

As mentioned already, the copy of the Minos ring with the guilloche pattern and bearing a distinct cut-mark eventually

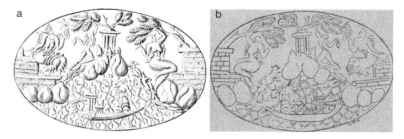

Figure 25a–b   Ring of Minos. (a) Drawing by E. Gilliéron fils, based on imprint. After PM IV, p. 950, Fig. 917. (b) By unknown, found in Sp. Marinatos's archives. Based on the original.

resurfaced. It was discovered by a descendant of the priest inside a jar and was brought to the Greek authorities. Subsequently, it was examined by a committee of Greek and international scholars and was pronounced genuine, reversing the judgement of the scholars in 1930. The ring is now on permanent exhibit at the Herakleion Museum.[23] The puzzle of why two different versions were circulating in 1930 has not yet been solved.

Perhaps some facts will reveal its true origin in the future. For the moment another detail must be added to its history. In 1931, Marinatos prosecuted the priest Pollakes for engaging in illegal activities concerning antiquities. The priest knew he had gone too far and wrote a letter pleading with Marinatos:

> Stop the inimical actions against me; directly withdraw your accusation against me; do not take me to court, a place to which I have never been before [. . .] stop this unholy war and rest assured that I shall always be your most ardent mediator [*euxetes*] towards God. (See Appendix 5.)

In the end, Marinatos won the case, and Pollakes was removed from his parish in the Knossos district. That Pollakes was engaged in illegal antiquities trade does not prove either that the ring was genuine or the opposite. However, it does show that there was a network of illegal dealers and possibly forgers in Herakleion.

Evans's Interpretation of the Minos Ring

Why did Evans regard the Minos ring as genuine? He was convinced by its exquisite style no doubt, but at the same time understood the visual syntax of the motifs in a way which matched his ideas, indeed confirmed them. According to Evans, the narrative centred on a series of episodes revolving around tree cult and divine epiphany, a combination that he had ascertained since the publication of 'Tree and Pillar Cult' in 1901. On the Minos ring, he saw the goddess navigating in a boat and eventually arriving at her shrine. She and one of her devotees shook a tree and partook in a ritual of communion. Finally, the goddess took her seat on her shrine and saw an epiphany of herself.

To the eyes of some, including the present author, the motifs seem too loosely connected to be products of a Minoan religious narrative. Evans, however, solved the problem by postulating a story about the advent of the goddess from across the sea to partake in ecstasy rites with her worshippers. This is unparalleled but not utterly impossible; still, a problem remains. The epiphany of the goddess to herself which Evans calls reinforcement is difficult to comprehend: 'Simultaneously with this sacramental act the divinity of the seated personage is reinforced, as it were, by a small descending figure of the same sex'.[24]

How can a goddess have an epiphany of herself? Evans linked the image to his theory of communion assuming that the juice of the fruit of the sacred tree would be consumed: 'a small male attendant [...] pulls down a branch of another sacred tree and tenders a flask containing its juice'.[25]

Be that as it may, there is a serious mistake in the syntax, which, oddly enough, Evans did not catch. The dragon-shaped boat in which the goddess navigates has the dragon head at its wrong end. The mistake is this: Minoan dragon boats travel in the direction of the tail, not the head, as shown by depictions of Minoan boats on other examples. The paddlers or rowers face the tail. In other words, the head of the animal is in the stern not the prow. Consider the ring from Mochlos as well as a ring-impression from Hagia Triada (Figures 26–7).[26] In both these cases we see that the direction of travel is determined by the tail, not the head of the monster and that the rower faces the former. However, the maker did the opposite and engraved the goddess as facing the head of the dragon boat.

The model of the maker is thus probably the Ring of Mochlos (Figure 27), which the Gilliérons knew well because they made copies of it and sold it in their workshop, on Skoufa Street. If Gilliéron fils was the designer of the Minos ring, then he knew Evans's ideas exactly because in the second volume of *Palace of Minos* (1928) Evans had discussed the marine aspects of the goddess.[27]

Figure 26   A figure with a tall hat (a god?) rows a dragon boat facing the tail of the animal. Ring imprint from Hagia Triada. CMS II, 6, 20.

The Minos ring verified many of Evans's theories about Minoan religion: tree cult, epiphany, the role of the goddess as a protector of ships and mariners. Only Georg Karo understood how much of the design was inspired by Evans's ideas and writes:

> With great skill the forgers brought their products in the market, golden engraved rings and seals with deeply engraved images mostly of mythical and religious content (they were allegedly chance finds made on the mainland). [...] The objects always confirmed Evans's own ideas about Minoan religion. And he never doubted their authenticity, because – as he wrote me once – nobody knew about these ideas since they were as yet unpublished.

Figure 27   The ring from Mochlos (now lost). The goddess faces the tail of the dragon; the forger used this ring as his model but misunderstood this detail. CMS II, 3, 252.

Karo explains:

> That men to whom [Evans] must have intimated something
> [about his ideas] and who received benefits from him for many
> years should repay him with such malice was to a person of his
> [Evans's] character truly incomprehensible. And the successful
> efforts of Spyridon Marinatos, Ephor of Crete, to expose the
> petty goldsmiths who worked on commission, did not affect
> these high-standing men.

Their greatest achievement, Karo continues, 'was an enormous gold
ring, which Evans studied and photographed but could not acquire:
the ring of Minos'.[28]

This was Karo's judgement on the matter, and it carries some weight
since he knew all the people involved. It remains to clarify one
important detail. Karo mentions above that Marinatos made a huge
effort to dismantle the mafia of Herakleion but that he did not
succeed in catching the high-standing men. Did he mean by high-
standing men the Gilliérons, père and fils? Almost certainly this is
what he implies.

Marinatos, however, exposed another man, Kefalogiannis, the
goldsmith who brought the Archanes ring to Evans in 1924. The
story will be presented below; for the moment let us note that the
arrest of this man and his accomplices signified the abrupt end of
gold-ring trade in Crete.

Theft at the Herakleion Museum

To discuss the arrest of this man, Kefalogiannis, we must move eight
years ahead to 1938, a year before World War II erupted in Europe.
By that time Nikolaos Platon had become the Director of the
Herakleion Museum whereas Marinatos had moved to Athens to
assume the post of General Director of Antiquities of Greece.

One day, Platon noticed that a piece of gold jewellery, a small deer,
was missing from one of the display cases of his museum, and much
as he looked around, he was unable to find it. A suspicion began to

arise in his mind that it was stolen, and he began a meticulous search of all the cases, checking each for their contents. To his horror, he realized that several dozen hard-stone gems, some of the very best seals in the museum, were also missing. He sent a telegram followed by a letter to Marinatos in Athens: 'As you will have gathered from my telegram, the situation here has developed into a real tragedy. The pain that I and [the assistant] Petrou feel is beyond description'.[29]

Platon immediately informed the police. He surmised that the theft had taken place during the night and that seals had been removed from the cases slowly and methodically whereas the remaining ones had been rearranged so as to leave no detectable gaps. There was a rumour circulating in Herakleion that some of the pieces had been substituted by forged ones. Platon discovered in addition that certain gold rings, which had been judged to be forgeries and were kept in the safe of the Museum, had been stolen as well. He suspected the two guards of the Museum and wrote to Marinatos: 'It would be impossible to conduct all these manoeuvres during working hours of the museum. My suspicions are centred now on the chief guard M. Pantouvakis'.[30]

When the police searched the houses of both guards, however, they found nothing. It seemed that a third person was involved, and it occurred to the police that he was the one who had hidden the treasures away. This proved to be true and, as we shall see, the man in question was the aforementioned Kefalogiannis. He was probably the same man whom Evans had met at Archanes.

A few days later, Marinatos received a letter from the assistant of Platon in the Herakleion Museum, a younger archaeologist by the name of Christos Petrou.

From the letters of Mr Platon [...] you must have been informed of our great misfortune, the theft at our museum. What has happened here is unprecedented. The methodical organization, the boldness of the execution and the measures of precaution taken by the thieves surpass every other case. It is not only the disappearance of the small golden deer that disturbs us (it has now found its explanation), but the malice of the affair which has poisoned our soul. Anxiety made us lose our mind when we discovered that the best seals of the museum had been taken. Despite our agony, we did not omit to take every action that could possibly lead to the unmasking of the perpetrators. [. . .] What is certain is that we are dealing with a most audacious and mysterious theft executed on the bases of a well thought-out and ingenious plan; it would take many pages for me to explain it. Our conclusions are that the theft was carried out by people who were in the service of the museum and over a long period of time. And that the perpetrators are the two guards: Spanoudakis, and his superior, Pantouvakis.

Petrou adds with anxiety:

I fear greatly that we ourselves will be blamed and sent to court and be pronounced guilty. I don't know what will become of us. I am going crazy with fear and I curse the hour which made me decide to leave my ex-profession as a teacher in order to become an archaeologist with the bitter result that I taste the poverty which accompanies this miserable profession of ours.[31]

Whilst the operators and thieves were plotting in Crete, Marinatos was weaving his own counter-plot in Athens. He and Nikolaos Platon realized that the two guards would never confess to whom they sold the antiquities as long as they had the backing of their local communities. They thus suggested to the police that the two suspects be brought to Athens for interrogation with the hope that they would reveal everything. And so indeed they did. On 10 February 1939, the Athenian newspaper *Athinaika Nea* reported that one of the guards, M. Spanoudakis, had confessed instantly to everything and had named the man to whom he had sold all the stolen goods: it was the goldsmith Kefalogiannis.[32] He was consequently arrested and not only confessed to his crime but returned most of the stolen seals and more besides (evidently he had obtained them from elsewhere).

And this is the climax of the story because it ties the beginning with the end. This man, Kefalogiannis, must be the same goldsmith who brought the Archanes ring to Xanthoudides first and then to Evans in 1924. Possibly, the two gold rings of Nestor and Minos were handled by the same mafia that controlled a workshop in Herakleion. Still, Marinatos felt that he had not exposed the most high-standing man behind the gang and wrote to Platon after the case was resolved, in February 1939:

> The report of the police insists on the fact that a man of great power hides behind Pantouvakis and this is why the gold deer has not reappeared; this is why money for his bail has been found. Obviously he blackmails that he will 'reveal all.' The entire affair is dirty but we should not let it rest. I thought for a moment that we would get rid of this patron but he escaped this time also.[33]

Who was the man of great power? Was it the same man whom Karo named? Unfortunately we shall never know for sure.

Evans and Forgeries

Whether they are forgeries or not, the Nestor and Minos rings supplemented Evans's ideas about Minoan religion; this is very evident from the prominent place they both hold in the last two volumes of *The Palace of Minos*. His renewed enthusiasm about the subject is reflected in a letter to Marinatos dated 3 April 1930 where he clearly refers to the two rings: 'I am going to lecture at Athens on some new evidence on Minoan Religion'.[34]

Unfortunately the inclusion of so many objects of doubtful provenance in the last volumes has had a negative impact on Evans's scientific reputation and has laid him open to the accusation that he was gullible and subjective, a charge which his recent biographers have utilized to maximum effect. But this subject ought not to receive undue emphasis since even the ivory statuettes appeared *after* Evans had already developed his principal theories on monotheism. Hopefully the arrangement of events and ideas in their proper chronological sequence that has been attempted here will lead to a better understanding of his work and scientific method. It has also been stressed that the rings are of such exquisite craftsmanship and technique, that the final judgement about their authenticity is very difficult.

CHAPTER 7

THE FINAL YEARS: EVANS'S RESTORATIONS AND HIS VISION OF KNOSSOS

The Vision of the Palace and its Reception

We shall now look at the final years of Evans at Knossos. The principal argument will be that he was determined to conserve the ruins because he felt the need to preserve the Minoan aesthetic vision which he considered truly unique in the entire history of mankind; moreover he was motivated to do so because of the onslaught of modernism to which he could not entirely relate. He sensed that his own civilization (the nineteenth century) was giving way to another era. The pessimism which he felt in his older age about the future of Europe is a backdrop that we must keep in mind.

Given the above, it is an irony of fate that many people among the intellectual and artistic elite of Europe got exactly the opposite idea of what he intended to convey; rather than admiring Minoan civilization for its high standards and uniqueness they considered the restored Palace as exotic, ugly or decadent. Some did not realize the basis for the reconstructed features and considered them scientific fantasy. At the same time, modernism questioned the aesthetic principles of the restorations (which by the way are *not* modernistic).

Let us begin with the 1920s when a German architectural historian by the name of Fritz Krischen visited Knossos. Impressed by the ruins, he decided to design works of art representing the people in the Palace.[1] One of his lithographs was inspired by a Minoan vessel from the mansion of Hagia Triada, the so-called Chieftain's Cup (Figure 28).[2] Krischen depicts the two men of the ancient work as exotic officers standing in front of the Palace. Their muscular half-naked bodies and heavy facial features give them a foreign look and they remind of paintings about the tropics, such as, for example, Gauguin's Polynesian scenes. Evans, however, imagined the same men very differently; in his mind they were members of a sophisticated European court, as may be inferred from what he writes about the original scene on the Minoan cup.

Figure 28   Chieftain's cup, sketch made by the German artist F. Krischen in *Ein Festtag am Hofe de Minos* (1921).

The young Minoan Prince is shown outside the gate of his residence here indicated by the pillar of rectangular blocks behind him, giving orders to an officer of his guard. Though in this case there seems to have been nothing more on his head than a band or a simple diadem, the superior rank of a youthful chieftain is shown not only by his greater stature but by the decoration that he wears around his neck and arms. In addition to the double ring or torque around his neck that he shares with his subordinate, there hangs from his shoulders across his chest a jewelled collar which, like the broad armlets and bracelets, have the appearance of having been set with medallions.[3]

The meticulous description of the jewellery is not just a sample of Evans's ability to detect artistic detail; it additionally reveals his belief that the figures are members of a highly civilized and hierarchical court society where each piece of jewellery is a carefully crafted *insignium dignitatis*.

The same discrepancy between Evans and Krischen applies to females. The German artist's women are exotic as we may infer from an etching of Minoan ladies bathing in the queen's quarters of the Palace (Figure 29a). They are plump and naked, with pretty pouting faces. They mutually anoint each other, an act which suggests sensuality. Evans would not have liked these images had he seen them; for, as he often remarked, nude figures were systematically avoided in Minoan art, and its people were more restrained in matters of sexual sensuality than their Near Eastern neighbours. A rendition such as Krischen's was out of tune with the true spirit of Minoan society. His own version, executed by Gilliéron fils for the frontispiece of *Palace of Minos III*, is entirely different (Figure 29b). The two ladies there are fully clothed and their elegant dresses, despite deep décolletages, discreetly cover the breasts with a diaphanous gauze, a practice that is paralleled in Elizabethan costume. Indeed, a portrait of Elizabeth I shows her with exposed breasts (Figure 29c).[4] Note also that the ladies in the painting by Gilliéron wear gloves: again we note a similarity between

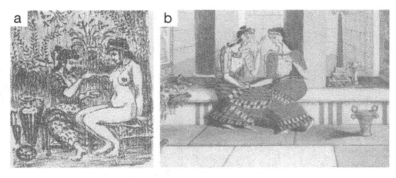

Figure 29a–c Contrasting visions of Minoan civilization: (a) Krischen's sensual view of Minoan women. F. Krischen, *Ein Festtag am Hofe de Minos* (1921). (b) Evans's version of Minoan women as civilized court-ladies in the Queen's Hall. Evans PM III, frontispiece. (c) Rainbow Portrait of Elizabeth I, Hatfield House.

Minoan and European female dress. Evans had consulted the art historian of the Ashmolean Museum and concluded that Minoan ladies wore close-fitting bodices that were sometimes covered by light linen cloth. The full flounces of the skirt were ornamented by diverse pieces of fabric, and the whole costume was enhanced by ribbons, garlands and beads.[5] Again, the comparisons were closest to the dress of European court:

> The sleeves are puffed and the constricted girdles and flounced skirts equally recall quite modern fashions. A narrow band appears above the chest, which suggests a diaphanous chemise, but the nipples of the breasts indicated beneath these [...] give a décolleté effect. A curiously artificial atmosphere of social life pervades these highly polite groups of Court ladies.[6]

In short, the aforementioned German artist of the interwar period, as well as other artists inspired by Minoan art, imagined the Cretans inhabiting an exotic and sensual world, whereas Evans had them dwell in a sophisticated (he called it artificial) court society. In the gestures of the ladies on the paintings he detected pointed and lively gestures, but never violent, never over-passing the limits of 'what is permissible in good society'.[7]

Consider how he discusses a mural found just north of the central court, the so-called Grand Stand Fresco. The women in this painting either stand or are seated among the Palace pillars. Evans senses what kinds of conversation those ladies had and brings the scene to life:

> the latter [lady] points her statement by thrusting forward her right arm so as almost to lay her palm on the other's lap, while her confidante raises hers in amazement. 'You don't say so!' – the sense of the words can be supplied, though we may never decipher the language.[8]

Such a society, spontaneous and artificial, sophisticated and yet close to nature, was hard to parallel.[9] And this combination is what made it unique in Evans's eyes and is why he attempted to capture it with his architectural restorations. The Palace is a building open to sunlight, nature and colour. It incorporates gardens and vivacious paintings, and yet it is also solemn and imposing. It is conspicuous in the landscape and yet it blends within it. This vision of Minoan aesthetics could not have been made concrete except by a man who had thought deeply about it. And yet, it must be stressed again and again that almost every detail was based on evidence.

We know that his efforts were not always appreciated. When the English writer Evelyn Waugh visited Knossos in 1931, he felt aversion rather than awe, especially when he entered the room of the throne, which he describes as a place of oppressive wickedness.

> This squat little throne, set on a landing where the paths of the palace intersect; it is not the seat of a law-giver nor a divan for the recreation of a soldier; here an ageing despot might crouch and have borne to him, along the walls of a whispering gallery, barely audible intimations of his own murder.[10]

This example (and one could find many more) is enough to illustrate the gap that separated Evans from the artistic public he tried to reach. Perhaps this is an inevitable consequence of the popularization of ideas.

The First Phase of Restorations

Turning now to the question of whether the restorations have a scientific basis, we must distinguish between two phases. The first took place before World War I, between 1901 and 1906, and was driven by the concern to conserve what was found *intact*.[11] We have Evans's own testimony to explain what motivated him to restore the Palace. It had been his extremely good fortune, he wrote, to have come across such a curious and unexampled phenomenon: the upper levels of the Palace had been found completely preserved because they had not been destroyed by any physical disaster, nor had they been carried away by floods. It was simply the case that the wooden beams that once supported the upper floors had eventually rotted away, and the floors had collapsed as a result. It was as if the levels of a doll's house had been compressed into one compact mass. In the East Wing at least, the picture was complete. A dilemma presented itself then: should he allow rain and wind to erode the remains? Should he leave the ruins to time and chance? Should he remove the floors, layer by layer, and thus destroy them? Or should he rebury the site? He decided that the only way to preserve the remains of the upper floors was to re-erect the rotten columns and the beams of the roof and replace them with wood and to preserve the entire complex. Thanks to his excellent architects, Theodore Fyfe and Christian Doll, who meticulously studied the architecture and proposed solutions, he was able to accomplish the task. Doll first experimented with wood (since the latter was the original material), but when he realized that it did not stand up to Cretan weather, he experimented with iron. Yet that too was incompatible with the Cretan climate since it disintegrated through corrosion after the first few seasons.[12] It was only after World War I that Evans saw the advantage of ferro-concrete buildings and decided that this material was the most enduring.

The Restorations of the Interwar Period

In the interwar period, between 1925 and 1931, Evans tried to do more than just conserve, since greater possibilities were furnished by ferro-concrete. The architect during this phase was the Briton of Dutch origin Piet de Jong.

The restorations of this period are bolder. They include paintings and are geared towards creating an overall impression of Minoan life, which is not to say that they are not scientifically based. For example, it is seldom admitted that cement was used mainly for the horizontal elements of the roofs and not for the erection of vertical walls, which were built by stone according to the original conception of Minoan architecture.[13] The result was a palace that was accessible to the public and which made Minoan civilization comprehensible even to the uninitiated. Another aim was to highlight the beauty of Minoan art. The contrast between the rejection of nature in modernist visual arts and its exuberance in

Knossian murals must have struck Evans. Hilda Pendlebury, the wife of John Pendlebury, the curator of Knossos, wrote to her father-in-law in the spring of 1929:

> Sir Arthur took us over to the site which has altered enormously since last year as more excavations have been done in some places and reconstructions in others. It is really becoming a habitable place and I think it is a good thing that the reconstructions should be done on the site so as to give people a clear idea of what a Minoan palace was.
> I do think Sir Arthur ought to live there in the end.[14]

We have another eyewitness of the restoration works of 1929. As a recently appointed Ephor of Antiquities of Crete, Spyridon Marinatos supervised the restorations as a representative of the Greek authorities and wrote reports about them to the Ministry of Education and Culture in Athens. He lists all the works: the roofing over of the west magazines, the northern Lustral Basin, the erection of the walls of the South Propylon, the building of a storehouse near the House of Chancel Screen, the roofing over of the Middle Minoan magazines near the 'School Room' and the Room of the Throne. He reports that Emile Gilliéron had been painting fresco replicas in the Queen's Megaron and Grand Staircase (Figure 30).[15] At that time the young Marinatos was not entirely convinced that all these restorations were absolutely necessary and writes a private report to his ministry in Athens:

> As regards my personal opinion, I have difficulties expressing it responsibly without deeper knowledge which at present I do not possess. Nor do I have the time at present to engage in deeper study of the matter. But I can state that I am absolutely in favour of the building restorations which have the advantage of securing the antiquities lying underneath. On the other hand, it is unfortunately not to be doubted that, on many points, Mr Evans takes liberties beyond what is desirable. And it must be admitted that the painted decorations are motivated more by a desire for show than by scientific necessity. In both his

Figure 30   Spyridon Marinatos, 1932, in front of the freshly painted shields of the East Hall. In the beginning he was sceptical of the restorations but then converted to Evans's views.

restorations and his writings, Evans takes into account the general public rather than the researcher. Thus, there is no scientific criterion for the restorations of doors and window openings and placement of certain murals.[16] All this creates a fanciful impression of the ruins but certainly misleads the researcher.[17]

In a separate letter he requests that the Director of the Archaeological Service, Professor Konstantine Kourouniotis, visit the site himself because he (Marinatos) could not take the entire responsibility on his own shoulders.[18]

Thus, the opinion that Evans over-restored was shared by experts and non-experts alike and is certainly the view that has prevailed in our days as the *communis opinio*. And yet, Evans had also his defenders.

Marinatos himself turned fully around when he became more familiar with the Palace and when he had a chance more fully to study the bases of the restorations. For when he wrote the report cited above, the Greek ephor was unaware of Evans's full arguments, which were published only later in the third volume of *The Palace of Minos* (1930). Once the detailed plans of the Queen's Quarters were made available, Marinatos understood the scientific bases for the restorations. He realized why the doors and windows were placed exactly where they had been; only careful study enabled the young archaeologist to appreciate Evans's brilliance and de Jong's accuracy.

Leaving the divided opinions aside for the moment, we return to the question posed at the beginning, namely why Evans felt the need to initiate the second phase of restorations and reify his vision of the high civilization he had unearthed. In 1925 Evans was 74 years of age; by 1931 he was 80. On the aesthetic level, modernism signalled a new age. On the political level, European instability could hardly go unnoticed. Did Evans attempt to rescue Knossos from the incertitude of time and chance? This, in any case, is what he wrote in the last volume of *The Palace of Minos*.

> It seemed a duty of the excavator to preserve, wherever possible, the history of the building by replacing *in situ* – even when it entailed some reconstitution of the walls – replicas of the fresco designs as completed from the existing fragments.[19]

That World War I affected his perception of history and opened his eyes to the fragility of civilizations may be inferred indirectly from the references he makes to the end of the golden age in the last volume of *Palace of Minos*; I suspect he meant also his own.[20] We also know that when his field director, Duncan Mackenzie, visited the site after the end of the war, he found it in very bad shape: weeds covered many of the ruins while the place had turned into a sanctuary for goats to graze freely.[21] What Evans could not have foreseen is that a series of natural disasters was about to occur during the interwar period and that his restoration plan saved the ruins from destruction.

Two Earthquakes (1926 and 1930)

In the summer of 1926, Evans experienced the first major earthquake at Knossos, which shook the entire Mediterranean, reaching as far as India. Evans described the drama of the incident as follows.

> On June 26 of that year, at 9.45 in the evening of a calm, warm day the shocks began. They caught me reading in a basement room of the head-quarter house – the Villa Ariadne – and, trusting to the exceptional strength of the fabric, I decided to see the earthquake through from within. Perhaps I had hardly realized the full awesomeness of the experience, though my confidence in the strength of the building material proved justified, since it did not suffer more than slight cracks.
>
> But it creaked and groaned, heaved and rocked from side to side, as if the whole might collapse. A dull sound rose from the ground like the muffled roar of an angry bull: our single bell rang, while, through the open window, came the more distant jangling of the chimes of the Candia Cathedral, the belfries as well as the dome and cupolas of which were badly damaged. As the quickly repeated shocks produced their cumulative effects, the crashing of the roofs of the two small houses outside the garden gate made itself audible, mingled with women's shrieks and the cries of some small children, who however were happily rescued.[22]

Eyewitnesses reported that once the earth stopped trembling, Evans emerged calm from the Villa Ariadne surrounded by a cloud of dust.[23] He was greatly relieved to see that the Palace had suffered no damages and considered it a miraculous coincidence that he had finished the works just in time; he determined to do more. In a paper given at the Society of Antiquaries a few months after the event, he explained to the audience the advantages of ferro-concrete as earthquake-proof material and one that endured even physical catastrophes of great magnitude.[24]

On 14 February 1930, the second major earthquake took place causing further damage to the town as well as to the archaeological museum at Herakleion. We have the testimonies of Marinatos on the severity of the situation. The museum had been already weakened during the first quake of 1926, and now the new tremor destabilized it further, turning it into a veritable death-trap for visitors and antiquities alike. The Greek ephor realized at that moment that Evans's mission had been the preservation of this ancient civilization for posterity and decided to join him with all his forces. The imminent collapse of the museum alerted him to the possibility that the treasures of Minoan civilization were about to perish and his fears increased when more tremors occurred during the next two months. He wrote to the ministry in Athens on March 8, 1930:

I have the honour to report that the day before yesterday, Thursday, another strong earthquake occurred, around 11:30AM, which resulted in the destruction of two more vases. The museum was full of visitors then and the ensuing panic among the guards and the public almost resulted in damages even more severe than what has hitherto been suffered. Luckily I happened to be on the entrance stairway and from the position where I stood I tried to calm the crowds down by shouting and forbidding the guards to come down the stairs and flee the building. Once the danger was over, I closed the museum for the day. [. . .] In general, I must report the sad fact that this museum is a complete wreck and we hardly have time to repair one damage before the next one occurs.[25]

Evans was in England at the time but was informed directly by Marinatos about the state of affairs. Something had to be done also about the Throne Room at Knossos because it had been damaged and a more solid and permanent roof was necessary. All Marinatos could do at the time was to shelter it provisionally and wait for Evans to come personally and propose a better solution. Evans writes back to Marinatos on 3 April 1930:

I was glad to hear that you have not suffered more from the Earthquake, also that you are taking steps to secure an Earthquake-proof wing. That was promised by the Government after the 1926 earthquake but never executed. Now I have got through my proofs of Vol. III I hope to hasten to Crete so I shall have an opportunity of talking over these things with you personally. I want to have the Room of the Throne at Knossos better roofed over − together with Antechamber, the Gypsum slabs of which are suffering greatly from exposure to dampness. M. de Jong has gone ahead to prepare this.[26]

The letter shows that Evans's intention at the time he wrote the letter was simply to cover the Throne Room better. However, when he came to Crete and reflected upon the situation, he decided that a solitary room with a ferro-concrete roof would look aesthetically out of place.[27] He consulted with de Jong about the possibility of constructing an upper storey and they decided to do so. Their reasons were four. First, a second storey offered permanent protection to the Room of the Throne. Second, it enhanced the aesthetic impression of the West Wing, integrating it with the rest of the Palace. Third, the upper storey gave the possibility to the visitor to enjoy vistas of the environs of the Palace. Fourth, it enabled Evans to install a gallery and exhibit there the best of Minoan fresco replicas.

All this must be viewed in connection with the imminent danger of earthquakes that was hanging over the archaeologists' heads in 1930−1. If the precious murals (which were stored in the crumbling Herakleion Museum) were to be damaged in the event of another earthquake (which in fact happened), the gallery would have preserved at least the replicas of brilliant Minoan paintings.

There have been objections to the procedures, and some of them are no doubt well stated.[28] And yet it must be noted that the upper floor was not entirely conjectural. Its presence was justified by the existence of the service staircase next to the Room of the Throne, as well as by objects fallen into the Lustral Basin.[29] The positions of the pier-and-door constructions of the upper storey were not arbitrarily decided but concluded on the basis of the weight-bearing pillars or the solid walls of the ground floor. In other words, a student of Minoan architecture realizes that Evans's scheme entails predictable plans and that the latter follow consistent rules and templates.[30]

The Responses of Georg Karo and Spyridon Marinatos

When the restoration of the Throne Room was complete, murals of griffins against a landscape of reeds were placed on the walls executed by Gilliéron fils. It has already been mentioned above that visitors kept flocking in to look at the miraculous Palace and the throne of its king and that their reactions were mixed. Once more Evans found himself to be an object of controversy rather than admiration. Unfortunately, most of the travellers arrived during a cruise and spent just an hour or two in the Palace.

In 1933, the Greek poet Kostas Ouranis arrived in Crete on a cruise ship and visited Knossos. The Palace was a priority, but Ouranis was so disappointed with what he saw that he published a negative piece about his impressions in an Athenian newspaper. How exaggerated the importance of Knossos and its ruins had been, he wrote, and how little the Palace had lived up to his expectations! When his ship docked in the harbour of Herakleion he and his fellow French tourists were most eager to see that great marvel of Minoan civilization and therefore skipped all other sites of historical importance, heading directly to Knossos. However, disappointment began right away: the road was dusty, the landscape barren and uninviting, the day dark and cloudy. When the party arrived, Ouranis realized to his horror that not a single room was 'genuine' and that everything seemed to be the product of the unbridled fantasy of the archaeologists. The stone throne of Minos was a crude and narrow seat which a French lady, his fellow traveller, named unworthy of her entrance parlour! The bathtub of the Queen was nothing but a small stone trough! 'With or without Evans's restorations, the Palace of Knossos does not speak to the soul of the visitor'.[31]

When Marinatos read this piece, he was moved to anger and wrote a response in another Athenian newspaper defending Evans's restorations, his scientific method and his vision of a truly brilliant civilization.[32] Marinatos did not question the subjective judgement of the poet (everybody was entitled to their own opinion), but he was upset that the latter expressed his uninformed views with such confidence. A poet was not trained to be an archaeologist and did not understand on what bases the restorations had been made. Perhaps, wrote Marinatos, Mr Ouranis was moody that day, bothered by the wet and dark weather; perhaps he found no pleasure in the visit – this was his right and privilege. However, pronouncing a scientific judgement on the work of a man who had spent his entire life thinking about details and calling Evans's work unbridled fantasy was irresponsible. Had he studied the architectural evidence? On what kind of expert knowledge did he base this verdict? Worst of all: why had he not sought the guidance of an archaeologist as he was visiting the site? Marinatos was equally bothered by Ouranis's doubts about the quality of Minoan civilization. Did he not observe its complex drainage system unsurpassed in antiquity until Roman times? Was not exceptional cleanliness evident from the presence of water-troughs, bathtubs and hydraulic installations throughout the Palace and the town? Was not the Palace built by architects who had adjusted their design to the physical beauty of the Cretan landscape? The Throne Room had appeared humble and dark to him because he had looked at it through his own moody dark goggles. Beauty had to be felt inside the heart before the mind.[33]

In another newspaper article, Marinatos further defended Evans's restorations when he had the occasion to compare them with the minimalistic restorations of the Italian archaeologists at the Palace of Phaistos. He found the latter adequate, but in some respects inferior to those of Knossos. It is true, he wrote, that at Knossos sometimes the restorations went beyond what was necessary. Yet, nothing at Knossos was done without some reason. There was no ideal solution anyway. In the case of Phaistos, problems arose due to the minimalist intervention of the architects. For example, they left the exquisite floors and the magazines in the West Wing unprotected from the weather. One could have sheltered them with a simple roof, of course, but then the aesthetic impression would be distorted.[34]

It is not known how much Evans was aware of these debates, but we may suspect that he knew of them because his sister mentions that around this time he was conscious of a sense of failure.

Georg Karo, however, was and remained one of his most ardent defenders, and this is how he explained Evans's decision to restore. Evans had realized already in 1901 that some of the materials of the Palace, especially gypsum and alabaster, were particularly vulnerable to the Cretan climate and needed immediate conservation; indeed, conservation was the key behind his entire project. Only a few people knew as well as I, Karo writes, that each phase of the excavation brought a new headache and that Evans had constantly to devise ingenious solutions, always relying on the most expert and reliable collaborators. It was a lucky coincidence that the site had fallen into the hands of a man of such scientific expertise and unbounded personal generosity, a man who was able to dedicate both his life and fortune to Knossos. Karo believed that Evans had not only the necessary scholarly insight but also the boldness to execute the plan. Additionally, he had the necessary stability of character to maintain the same collaborators for decades and thus keep the project consistent.[35]

Given the above, one understands why Knossos is considered so controversial today but one also may wonder if people today realize how much thought and study was put into the project. Such knowledge may easily get lost, and for this reason the testimony of people who witnessed the process is important.

The Third Earthquake (1935) and the Fate of the Herakleion Museum

A postscript must be added about the fate of the Herakleion Museum.[36] Its situation was made worse when a third earthquake struck Crete in 1935. It was most severe, and because it occurred during the early hours of the day, it resulted in several human victims. The first report published in *The Times* gave the human casualties as three, but later the numbers rose to six dead and 60 injured. More than 200 houses collapsed, and some 500 were at the point of so doing.

Tents were sent from Athens to shelter people exposed to the heavy rain that followed the earthquake.[37] The museum was now at the point of collapse, and Evans heard the bad news from his curator at Knossos, R. W. Hutchinson. He immediately sent a note to *The Times*, and the newspaper reported to its public:

> Sir Arthur Evans informs us that the curator of the museum at Knossos has advised him that the Minoan Palace and the British headquarters house, the Villa Ariadne, and the hostel are safe. The curator makes no mention of the museum, in which, according to a message from Athens, some damage had been done by a fall of plaster due to the earthquake.[38]

Marinatos's assessment of the situation was more pessimistic, as may be seen from a letter he writes to his Dutch friend, Mme Suzanne Goekoop.

> We have suffered very much from the earthquake. I am now fully occupied with reparations which will last a long time still. The antiquities have suffered enough, although not as much as it appeared at first. In any case we have much to reconstitute and re-assemble.[39]

Evans too became anxious that the museum would collapse but trusted that 'the energetic ephor of Crete', Marinatos, would do his best.[40] The latter informed him that the old building would be soon demolished but that his efforts to build a new museum had met with the stubborn resistance of local people. He was losing patience, he confided to Evans, and was almost ready to resign from his post. One of the leaders in the resistance was the old pottery-restorer of the Herakleion Museum, Manolis Salustros, a man whom Evans knew personally because he had worked at Knossos in earlier years. It is not clear why Salustros resisted the demolition of the old building with such vigour; apparently he had some issues with Marinatos which the latter discloses to Evans:

The new Museum has not yet found its beginning, as Mr. Salustros, who is now not more [sic] in the service, has caused in the newspapers and in the coffee-houses a terrible reaction. He is pretending that the old Museum must not be demolished. As it is impossible to found [sic] another place, he tells to built [sic] the new Museum out of town. He has excited much people [sic] but I have too, my partisans and a mortal duel is being [fought] now in the Ministry. I have mentioned that I shall go out of Crete, better, than to undertake the danger of the transport of the museum far away from its actual place. I think that this week we shall begin to put down the great flight of the old building, that is already free from cases. It has not been possible to go to Kephallonia excavation this year. The new museum absorbs all my time and I have put aside every other work.[41]

Marinatos struggles with his English in this letter but manages to convey the intensity of his emotions and his frustration. He expresses the same view of despair in a local Cretan newspaper where he attempts to rally the emotional support of the local public for the erection of the new building. The state of affairs is indeed lamentable, he says in an interview. Everything conspires against the materialization of the new museum and every time an agreement on a particular plan is reached, something or someone stops it: e.g. financial crises, civil unrest, changes of government, etc. The work is postponed for the indefinite future while irresponsible people propose solutions concocted in five minutes in the coffeehouses. The most urgent matter was this: the inestimably precious treasures of European civilization were stored in a deadly trap and they had to be rescued immediately.[42]

Evans, now at the age of 85, felt he was running out of time and that something needed to be done, but he was unable to interfere. On 12 December 1935, however, he received the good news from Marinatos that the battle had been won and that the question of the new museum had happily ended. Half of the old building had already been demolished, and Marinatos hoped that by April a new flight of stairs would be in place. He adds with sadness in his letter to Evans:

But the unexampled demagoguery of Mister Salustros and his similars has caused to me much trouble. I have been called a not indigenous (*anemozoxaris* in their own dialect) and I have been invited by a newspaper to go away from Crete. I am sorry that I am obliged to abuse still of their hospitality![43]

Evans had himself experienced local rivalries in the past when he had a conflict with the rich Herakleiote merchant Minos Kalokairinos; he was the first man to have dug the Palace and resented Evans's intrusion into local affairs.[44] Now Evans calmed Marinatos down and wrote back: 'I am sorry to hear that you have had this trouble with Salustros but I hope that by now you have really been able to set to work'.[45]

In the end, everything went well. The necessary money for the new museum was supplemented by private donors, two bankers from the island of Kephallonia named Spyridon and Dionysios Loverdos. The architect was the prize-winner Patroklos Karantinos, who also came from the island of Kephallonia.[46] The new building was modernist and lacked all the embellishments and grandeur of the old one, but it was practical and functional. Karantinos also made provisions for underground casements designed for the protection of antiquities from earthquakes. As it turned out, these casements saved the antiquities during the war.

The museum opened officially on 16 February 1939, exactly four years after the earthquake of 1935 and just before the outbreak of World War II.[47] The efforts of Evans and Marinatos to preserve Minoan civilization must be regarded as parallel since they both believed that this culture was one of the most precious ever to have been produced in human history. Nowhere does Evans state this more clearly than in the preface he wrote for John Pendlebury's guide on the Palace in 1933:

It may be confidently said indeed, that no equal plot of Earth's surface has been productive in such various directions of so many unique records bearing on our own culture. Not only have we here the first evidences of an advanced linear script, but architecture is already fully developed on novel lines, and with a no less original form in fresco decoration carried to great perfection, while masterpieces of sculpture and moulding have come to light [. . .] which for instantaneous spirit and truth to natural forms have in their own line never been surpassed.[48]

As has been mentioned before, Evans's goal was to make known the beauty and sophistication of the ancient culture of Crete to the general public. His decision must be viewed against the backdrop of the anxiety, financial poverty and aesthetic innovation of the interwar years as the nineteenth century was giving way to a new order: revolutionary aesthetics and uncertain values. This anxiety was communicated by expressionist artists as well as by the bolder cubist painters, such as Pablo Picasso. It was also represented in Weimar cinema, in the films of Georg Pabst and Fritz Lang, notably in *Metropolis, The Testament of Dr. Mabuse* and *M.*

Evans undoubtedly sensed the insecurity and anxiety of the interwar years and found great solace in another age and another type of beauty. His restorations will ever be contested, and whatever position one takes, a counter-argument will easily be produced. And yet time has shown that he was both insightful and wise. Not only did the Palace survive three major earthquakes, but thanks to its solid walls it endured World War II without major damages. As for the museum, it was hit three times by the explosives dropped by the planes of the German forces in 1941. However, the ancient objects of Minoan civilization were hidden in the casements of its solid basement and were therefore saved.[49] It was not time and chance that preserved these antiquities but the foresight of men who understood the fragility of civilization and took measures to prevent its decay.

CHAPTER 8

SIR ARTHUR EVANS AND SPYRIDON MARINATOS

A Quarrel and an Apology

The relationship between Evans and Marinatos had not always been cordial. It will be remembered that in 1928–9, when Marinatos was barely 30 years of age, he had expressed scepticism regarding the Knossos restorations and that he had been critical of Evans's attitude on forgeries. In a 1928 letter to his boss, Stephanos Xanthoudides, he had mentioned that Evans was doing harm to scholarship by publishing forgeries, and that it was the duty of the Greek archaeologists to say 'all they knew' about the forgery workshops in Herakleion. In the same letter one senses that he was afraid of Evans: 'I would have made Evans my mortal enemy and he could harm us in many ways.'[1] Given this background, it is not utterly surprising that when Marinatos assumed the directorship of the Herakleion Museum after the death of Xanthoudides, he did not accommodate all of Evans's wishes.

In the spring of 1929, the Director of the British School at Athens, Humfry Payne, conducted at the behest of Evans a small trial excavation of a Geometric tomb at Knossos. The purpose of the dig was to check the stratigraphy of the site, and therefore the British did not deem it worthy to request a formal excavation permit from the Greek authorities nor to notify the Ephor of Crete. In all fairness to Evans, permits had not been required in the past, although such were formally required by Greek law.[2] The breach of protocol raised an important issue in the mind of Marinatos: if his position as Ephor of Crete were undermined, this might encourage arbitrary excavations by other foreign archaeologists. On the other hand, if he were to cross swords with Evans, the consequences might be severe for him personally.[3] In the end, he decided to take the risk of displeasing Evans and asked the guard of Knossos, David Kanakis, to stop the dig. The suspension order was accompanied by a letter addressed to Evans personally. It is cited here in full.

June 2, 1929

My most respected friend Sir Arthur,

I think there has been a misunderstanding between us; nobody ever has doubted that the British School has the right to excavate Knosos [sic] and its environs. Here is the issue. The archaeological law since Nov. 30, 1927 requires that permits be renewed every year, and you will agree with us, that it is not possible for a nation to function properly if foreign excavators conduct their digs without previously informing the archaeological service of the ministry. It is precisely because similar misunderstandings have taken place in the past that the law in question has been passed. I am enclosing for your inspection a document (please return it) which I have just received from the French excavators at Malia and which shows the renewal of their yearly excavation permit. You can see there that the Archaeological Council and it alone has the authority to grant permits. As you can see, this is a mere formality but it is necessary that both you and I observe this formality. You, alone among all foreign guests [xenoi] digging in Greece constitute an exception and this has been silently accepted by the ministry because it takes into account that you began your work at Knosos [sic] before the establishment of these Greek laws and because of your exceptional position as a pioneer in the field. But we cannot extend this privilege to other excavations of the British School because this would set a precedent of privilege and it would correctly lead to protests from the other archaeological schools.

I am truly sorry that the lot fell on me to apply a law which my predecessors had neglected but please believe me that I am just executing orders and that, in my capacity as a civil servant of the state, I must oversee the observance of the laws of my country. I repeat that the matter is a formality but the law must be observed. If Mr Payne wants a systematic excavation anywhere, he must ask permission either directly, or through me, from the ministry of education. Regarding the present case, because he has already begun the excavation of a tomb, as the guard Kanakis informs me, I think that I can allow the dig to continue taking responsibility on my own shoulders but under the condition that no other exploration be conducted without the permission of the ministry.

I take the opportunity to repeat to you that I think you ought to excavate a few tombs in the land of Paterakis where I think there is a temple. In the next season the vineyard will have grown more and the owner will ask for compensation whereas for this year I have asked for 'compulsory excavation' [*anagkastiki anaskafi*] which does not necessitate expropriation of the land. I would thus advise the British School to take advantage of this, since from the point of view of topography we know little about Knossos environs.

With all due respect,

Yours Spyr. N. Marinatos[4]

The letter is highly respectful and cleverly crafted since it allows a way out of the conflict. Marinatos states that the dig *may continue* with the provision that no similar one be undertaken in the future. Also, the author ends in a conciliatory tone, proposing a common project between British and Greek archaeologists, the excavation of the land of Paterakis.

Evans, however, did not bite the bait of the common project and got very angry instead, exactly as Marinatos had feared. He considered the young man impertinent and, in his vexation, called him discourteous. Since the dig was only a small trial excavation, he said, he did not think that a permit was necessary – it had never been required in the past. In defiance, Evans ordered that a second trial dig be started.

When Marinatos was informed about the second dig, he was greatly insulted, and his anger was made even deeper when he received a letter by Evans where he was called 'discourteous'. He responded in an angrier tone. This letter too has survived in the archives of the British School at Athens, and it is an invaluable document because it contains Evans's comments written in the margins. The letter is reproduced below, translated from Greek with Evans's comments inserted in brackets.

3 June 1929

Most respected and honoured Sir Arthur,

Thank you for your letter which I received today. Unfortunately the matter has not been satisfactorily resolved yet because the law, which I enclose, stipulates that the excavators of the trial digs must be named. Mr Payne is mentioned only for Eleutherna, not Knosos [sic]. Today you write to me that he was excavating on your behalf. But I could not have known this since I had not been informed; and because I knew that you were not especially interested in Geometric graves, I had to act the way I did. I think that the heavy-handed phrase of your first letter is unwarranted. My action has been neither 'abrupt' nor 'discourteous'. On the contrary, I ordered the guard to come in the evening and in all politeness announce that the excavation is suspended, so as to avoid being offensive to you. I wonder why you think my position is 'quite indefensible'. If it is not my job to interfere in archaeological matters of my district, then I do not know whose job it is. In any case, I must declare to you that the law has not been observed; the British School has requested a permit to excavate in many places but not this one – I attach the relevant document [*comment by Evans: impertinent to School*]. I do not know of any document which might justify the present excavation, an excavation which ignored my own authority. If you have such a document in your possession, I should be grateful if you made it known to me. In any case, because I have been informed that today you are continuing and excavating another grave, and because I consider this an act of hubris [*comment by Evans: impertinent to me*] but still do not wish to push the matter to extremes, for example to send the police to suspend excavations which I consider illegal, I am sending a report to my ministry, asking for instructions about what is to be done.

Believe me, I feel miserable when I must face a dilemma, a choice between my duty to the law and my personal relations towards the international family of our profession, especially when I am dealing with guests [*xenoi*] on the soil of my country. Unfortunately, having come so far, I must insist until the end. I ask you, on your part, to believe that should I be proven wrong in the present case, I should not only offer my apologies instantly – of which you remind me in both your letters – but I should also ask for my immediate transfer away from Crete [*comment by Evans: much better!*] so that another man may replace me, with whom you may have a better collaboration. I repeat today once more that this bitter cup[5] is what I have inherited from my predecessors. Because if they had imposed order from the beginning, the present incident would not have arisen; indeed such events have not taken place in any other archaeological district. In any case, I am not willing to commit the very mistakes for which I once blamed them.

Yours ever S. Marinatos[6]

The distress of the writer is evident. He foresees that the ministry in Athens will reprimand him (which it did) and perhaps transfer him elsewhere. To forestall such a possibility, Marinatos offers to resign of his own accord. A letter sent to Evans by the Director of the British School at Athens, Allan Woodward, confirms that Marinatos's fears were fully justified. Woodward writes:

Not that Marinatos has any shadow of real support for his attitude; Kourounioutis[7] admitted that much, and surely it is no fault of yours or mine if an ephor, fresh from Germany or elsewhere is not properly informed of the arrangements carried forward from the previous permit.[8]

Woodward's comment that Marinatos was fresh from Germany reveals another fact. There must have been talk at the British School that the Greek ephor was pro-German because the same assumption was made by John Pendlebury when he writes to his father Herbert: 'This is not the first time that Marinatos has gone out of his way to be insulting to us. He has been in Germany and is utterly Γερμανόφρων [German-minded]'.[9]

The accusation was hardly the point. Marinatos was indeed an admirer of German culture but did not act on behalf of German interests but Greek ones; nor was he, politically speaking, anti-British. On the contrary, in matters of foreign policy he was on the side of Great Britain, being a follower of the pro-British Greek politician Eleutherios Venizelos (and hence on the side of the Entente).

There is no evidence that Evans shared the view of his compatriots regarding the alleged Germanophilia of the Greek ephor. He more rightly diagnosed a case of personal pride fortified by a sense of national dishonour. And he was right because Marinatos described his own feelings of hurt pride in a letter to Humfry Payne some years later:

But I too have my weaknesses, if so they may be called, and they are my propensity at taking offence and a tendency to observe rules that my predecessors neglected. This led to one fatal misunderstanding with the British School, the School of a man such as Evans, whom I admire and love above all others.[10]

Pride was a sentiment that Evans could understand, but he was less tolerant of what he perceived as ingratitude on the part of the Greek ephor. In the past he had become angry at his ward, James Candy, for sulking unjustifiably during a game of tennis. He had turned to the boy, eyes blazing, and had shouted: 'You bad-tempered, ungrateful child! go home, go home, at once'.[11] However, when the boy apologized, Evans behaved as though nothing had happened and promptly kissed him.[12] A not too dissimilar sequence of events occurred in 1929: Marinatos eventually regretted his behaviour and apologized whereupon Evans forgave him. However, the affair took some time to come to this happy conclusion.

To return to the Knossos of 1929, Evans decided to stop the dig but also to report the behaviour of Marinatos to the latter's superiors in Athens. He subsequently sent a telegram to the Director of the Archaeological Service, Konstantine Kourouniotis. This is what he wrote:

Regret to trouble you with rather vexatious matter. Payne Director elect of the British School is working here on Geometric pottery from tombs Knossos including material supplied from excavations of my own. Finding debris from Tombs near Knossos, including pair of vases found by me on the spot in 1896, asked Payne to dig it for my own satisfaction and this with workmen detached from the Palace work at my expense, informing Kanakis who was deputed by you to act as *epistates*[13] in such case. This was clearly *dokimastike*[14] and within my rights but Marinatos actually ordered Kanakis to stop the excavation and wrote alleging that I had no *adeia*[15] for this year. I then wrote him protesting strongly against his action and saying that I relied on the right conferred by *adeia* to continue. Today Monday further exploration showed that the contexts were unimportant but another tomb having appeared beside it, I ordered men to explore it. It proved to be Late Minoan and I decided that it should be filled in and exploration postponed for another season. Now I have another letter from Marinatos saying that exploration of second tomb was

insulting to him and referring matter to ministry. Woodward
is arriving here on Thursday and I am asking him to call on
his return from Crete on you. He could report to you on
Marinatos's whole attitude which is very different from what
has hitherto been customary. Hitherto, I have been able to
act cordially with Ephor but he is making it impossible with
his generally obstructive attitude on which Woodward can
report to you. There has been no question of anything but a
small dokimastic dig and I surely have a right to employ
Payne. [...] This telegram is merely to explain facts and
needs no reply as excavation is now over.[16]

In Evans's version of the affair, the actions of the Greek ephor
are presented as unpredictable, and yet one detects a tone of mild
apology in the voice of the roaring lion: 'there has been no question
of anything but a small dokimastic dig'. Most important is an
additional handwritten comment at the bottom of the draft of
the telegram, added as if by afterthought: 'I cannot understand
why Marinatos should object to my employing Payne under my
direction.'
    This last sentence shows genuine puzzlement on the part of Evans:
why had Marinatos overreacted to a mere trial dig and why had he
broken with precedent? And yet, despite his anger, he recognized
steady principle behind the act of the Greek ephor's defiance. During
his own youth, Evans had opposed Austrian authorities in Ragusa
(Dubrovnik) by taking the side of oppressed Slavs. He paid dearly for
this defiance and ended up in prison in Ragusa.[17] Evans actually
secretly enjoyed a certain opposition, as Piet de Jong remembered.
The latter once had a personal row with Evans but it resulted in the
strengthening of their relationship.

But the impatience of Sir Arthur and my expressed annoyance
with him never impaired our friendship. I think, on the
contrary, it cemented it. He liked a certain opposition
particularly when results showed. [...] He was a very
remarkable man.[18]

Having stopped the dig, Evans took no further action, but Marinatos felt guilty because he recognized the grace shown by the older scholar. He thus offered (as he had promised) an official apology.

The clash marked the beginning of a true rapport between the older and younger scholar. Before that time, their relationship had been polite – even cordial – but impersonal. Now each man was suddenly revealed plainly and lucidly to the other. Commonality of principles, even when argument and conflict were involved, was the mode of communication that Evans understood best. Casual chatting and small talk were not his way.

The Excavation of the Temple Tomb

A year went by. In the meantime, the Ring of Minos made its appearance, and Evans was motivated to locate its source, searching the environs of the Palace for the alleged find-spot of this spectacular gem. The result was unexpected since he found not one but *two* important buildings. The first was surnamed House of the High Priest (because of its evident similarities to a Christian chapel) whereas the second was baptized the Royal Temple Tomb because it included a tomb as well as a shrine. On this latter building the subsequent discussion will focus because of the direct involvement of Marinatos (see Figure 31).

First, there can be no doubt about the fact that the building was close to the alleged find-spot of the Minos ring and this is why Evans considered its discovery proof that the ring was genuine. The gem, he said, had accidentally escaped the Minoan robbers of the Temple Tomb and had rested in the soil for more than 1,000 years! Marinatos did not believe this and had a different interpretation of why the building was found.[19] He knew that Evans had a trusted man whom he had personally trained to survey the soil for ruins. This man was named Manolis or Manolakis Akoumianakis and was also his foreman at Knossos (Figure 32). It was this Manolis who noticed unusual slabs on the surface of the soil near the Palace and told Evans about them. The latter understood that a building was concealed there and began excavations immediately. Marinatos did not find it so remarkable or unexpected that a large building was situated close to the Palace, and its existence did not prove in his eyes the authenticity of the Ring of Minos. Evans thought otherwise, however, and regarded this new discovery as miraculous.[20]

A more important issue on which Evans and Marinatos agreed was the function of the new spectacular two-storey building. Was it indeed a tomb? Contemporary scholars have disputed this fact on the grounds that no skeleton was found in the so-called burial chamber, and they intimate that Evans found only what he wished.[21] And yet there is incontrovertible evidence that the building was indeed a combination of grave and sanctuary since John Pendlebury reports a disarticulated skeleton of a man of middle age from the entrance of the burial chamber.[22] It was dedicated simultaneously to the royal cult and the chief divinity of the Minoans.

Built in ashlar masonry, the Temple Tomb was fronted by a solid gate reminiscent of Egyptian tombs. Passing the gate, the visitor would enter an interior court that passed to a vestibule; a stairway led to the upper storey. The vestibule led to a pillar crypt of the type well known from the Palace and the Royal Villa (Figure 33a–b). It contained two pillars and ashlar blocks marked with double axes, recalling not just similar Pillar Crypts but the Tomb of the Double Axes as well.[23] An added feature was that the door of the crypt could only be locked from the inside, and this could only mean one thing: there was a trap door in the crypt that led to the sanctuary chamber above. The guardian of the holy place could thus reach the upper chamber in privacy.[24] Evans felt that the Temple Tomb and the House of the High Priest, the two last buildings he excavated in Crete, added important information about the organization of Knossian society and considered the possibility that the guardian of the crypt was the same man who lived in the House of the High Priest. His job might have been to conduct rites connected with the royal cult (for such a practice he found Egyptian parallels). Some of the rites were performed next to the central pillar of the crypt of the Temple Tomb. This is why the latter was furnished with rectangular offering pits, recalling similar arrangements in the Pillar Crypt of the Royal Villa.[25] The pillar in the centre verified the hypothesis of a

Figure 31   Spyridon Marinatos in front of the Temple Tomb, 1934.

sepulchral *baetyl* cult. The spirit of the deceased resided in the pillar and received the offerings placed in the pits.

If Evans was right in his interpretation, the association between royal cult and funerary cult is firm. Marinatos's testimony lends support. He comments on how the tomb was robbed already in Minoan times: so eager were the thieves to get hold of its treasures, that they drilled a large hole in the wall from the outside and cleaned out the chamber thoroughly.[26] He had never witnessed such an efficient and violent method of plunder before, he writes, and it gave him the chills. The body and the valuables must have been contained in wooden caskets so that everything was taken away together, body and burial gifts. Indeed, the existence of wooden caskets has been verified by later excavations and is supported by Pendlebury's report.[27] Only a stone seal with

Figure 32 Manolis Akoumianakis and his wife (1934/5). He was Evans's favourite foreman, but Marinatos did not entirely trust him.

an engraved lion and some other minor objects escaped the mania of the robbers.

The entire building came to a violent end in Late Minoan I at about 1500 BCE, the same time as Amnisos was destroyed (see Appendix 2). It was abandoned for a time, but its crypt was reused again as a burial place in Late Minoan III.[28]

It was a disappointment to Evans that he did not find the hoped-for valuables that would prove that Knossian tombs had been

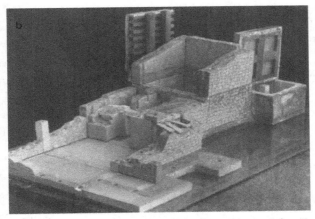

Figure 33a–b   Model of the Temple Tomb constructed by Zacharias
Kanakis, friend of Marinatos and restorer of the Herakleion Museum.

as rich as the graves of Mycenae, but the excavation of the building
was rewarding in many other respects. Not only did it prove the
association between pillar crypts and grave cult, but it furnished
new evidence about the direct communication between pillar crypt
and upper storey by means of a trap door. This communication
between the storeys confirmed Evans's hypothesis that Minoan cult
practice entailed chthonic and celestial cults within one and the
same building.

The practice of rites in the upper sanctuary was also inferred on the basis of evidence. The strongest indication was a pair of so-called sacred horns; another was vases that would have held floral offerings. For support of this latter thesis, concerning floral offerings to the deity, Evans turned to Marinatos's work:

> Thanks to the fruitful researches of Dr. Marinatos in some fine mansions belonging to Amnisos, the Eastern haven of Minoan Knossos [...] the fact is now established that by the MM III period, broad flower stands on a much larger scale were employed for similar garden decoration.[29]

Later in time, the excavations of Marinatos at Akrotiri, Thera yielded rich evidence of flowerpots standing on the windows of the West House, for example.[30]

The overall interpretation of the Temple Tomb was delivered in a lecture to the Society of Antiquaries by Evans in the autumn of 1931. The Temple Tomb, he said, recalled the description of an ancient monument by Diodorus Siculus (60–30 BCE) curiously named the 'Tomb of Minos'. The monument was a combination of tomb and sanctuary, the former being hidden beneath the earth and the latter (a temple to Aphrodite) being above it. Did the Sicilian tomb preserve the memory of Minoan royal cults? Evans wondered. This was a bold inference since Diodorus was a Hellenistic writer who had lived more than 1,000 years after the end of Knossos. Evans, however, used the method of analogy which he and Frazer inherited from Tylor.

Marinatos drew the same conclusion based on the same analogy in his own report sent to the Ministry of Education in April 1931.[31] At that time he could not have known what Evans said to the Society of Antiquaries, so he must have discussed this analogy directly with Evans. In any case Marinatos wrote the following to his ministry:

> The excavations of Mr Evans this season have brought to light a complex of buildings with an interesting design and obvious

religious function.[32] [. . .] Much more important is the structure
a few metres to the south which has revealed, as every
indication shows, a magnificent royal tomb which surpasses
every other monument on Greek soil.[33]

In a second report, sent to the ministry on 7 July 1931, he writes:

The sanctuary [i.e. pillar crypt] in front of the burial chamber
had an upper storey which is securely testified by evidence of a
stairway in the southern part of the building. The entire
complex curiously reminds the description of the tomb of
Minos by Diodorus (4.79); the tomb had a dual aspect, one
hidden part that contained the burial chamber and one
manifest, being dedicated to Aphrodite. In the case of the
Minoan Temple Tomb, there is a manifest sanctuary belonging
to the goddess and a hidden one, the burial chamber.[34]

It is said that John Pendlebury, who supervised the dig, was more
sceptical of this interpretation.[35] Indeed, the latter wrote to his father
that the restoration of the monument proceeded too rapidly: Evans
placed a pair of 'horns of consecration' on the roof although there was
no certainty about them.[36] However, a few years later Pendlebury
himself describes the Temple Tomb in accordance with Evans's
interpretation and restoration.[37] Pendlebury liked to defy Evans but
always came around and agreed with the old giant, as he called him.

After World War II, Marinatos asked his favoured restorer and
personal friend at the Herakleion Museum, Zacharias Kanakis,
to execute a model of the Temple Tomb and some views of this
model are shown here. The tomb itself is hewn into the rock.
The sacral horns have been multiplied in Kanakis's model (Figure
33a–b).

Spyridon Marinatos's Excavations in Crete 1932–6

Evans did not visit Crete between 1932 and 1935 because he worked
intensely on the last volume of *The Palace of Minos*. Marinatos,

however, wrote to him regularly to report about his new finds; Evans, in his turn, wrote back with comments or requests for information about objects in the Herakleion Museum, especially those objects that he incorporated in the last volume of *Palace of Minos*.[38]

In 1932, Marinatos had some good news. He had recently excavated a seaside villa of Amnisos, not far from Knossos, and had found there a set of masterful paintings of lilies executed in the highest Minoan quality, rivalling the murals of Knossos. This gave Evans the satisfaction to know that the burgher class of Minoan society was as sophisticated as he had always thought. What interested him particularly was the technique of impressing a motif on the still-wet gypsum of the mural and subsequently filling it in with colour paste. Marinatos writes that among the Amnisos frescoes depicting lilies he had detected this unusual technique:[39]

> The background is red whereas the flowers are blue and white. However, they are not painted; rather, the blue and white paste has been applied on a design previously impressed on the plaster. Thus, we have a true inlaid technique which is the prototype of the known dagger.[40]

This new evidence was very welcome to Evans because it verified something he had foreseen already. He had always believed that the inlay technique as evidenced on the decorated daggers of the Shaft Graves at Mycenae had been Minoan, but he had not managed to find the necessary evidence to prove this assumption. On the other hand, he had inferred that the technique of applying a material on an imprinted design had been utilised on frescoes. On the relief painting of the priest-king at Knossos, the lilies of the necklace had been first imprinted on the wet plaster and, after that, the flowers had been added as a paste. The paste had then been coloured in such a way as to represent metalwork. The plastic flowers had gradually become detached and left the imprints as a ruddy hue against the faded surface of the torso.[41] It is worth noting that few scholars then and now believed Evans on the grounds that there is no precedent for 'detachable' jewellery on frescoes.[42] Now we know that such evidence exists. Evans always tended to see more than others; and although some of his theories seem to go against common sense, he was more often right than wrong.

But the real satisfaction came from the fact that the villa verified his vision of Minoan civilization. The quality of its aesthetics indeed rivalled those of post-mediaeval European civilization itself. In the last volume of *Palace of Minos* he writes:

> The researches of Dr. Sp. Marinatos [...] have made highly interesting contributions to our knowledge. [...] In the seaport itself Dr. Marinatos has now excavated a townhouse with remains of frescoes [...] with elegant groups of flowers in garden stands and hints of artificial basins, singularly illustrative of the refined artificial development of Minoan life. It is a foretaste of Versailles.[43]

The reconstruction shown here (Figure 34) is made by an unknown artist whom Marinatos commissioned to render an impression of the hall of the lilies (possibly Gilliéron fils?). It is more accurate than the more recent version by Mark Cameron, who has included a woman in his colour reconstruction. For such a lady there is no evidence.[44]

Equally important for Evans's theories was Marinatos's excavation of the cave of Eileithyia situated close to the aforementioned villa. The most impressive feature of the cave was its stalactites and stalagmites, two of which resembled a mother and child and aroused a feeling of awe and wonder in the hearts of even the modern visitors, as Marinatos witnessed (Figure 35). Their cultic function could not be doubted since they were enclosed within a wall built in Minoan technique:[45] Evans was proven right once again that the goddess could assume an aniconic form as a *baetyl*. Marinatos sent him photographs and Evans suggestively reports in the last volume of *Palace of Minos* that the deity was 'visible through the gloom'.[46]

In 1934, Marinatos undertook a dig of another cave, next to the village of Arkalochori, east of Herakleion. This too yielded unexpected treasures and finds of religious significance. The cave had previously been explored by the Greek archaeologist Joseph

Figure 34   Reconstruction sketch of hall in the Villa of Lilies, Amnisos. It is unsigned. It is possible that it was executed by E. Gilliéron fils.

Hatzidakis, but the dig had remained incomplete. The new project began entirely by chance, as an eyewitness, Mr Mathianakis, reported to the present author. He was then a child of about seven or eight but remembers the incident well.[47]

A farmer detected an object glittering within the fissure of a rock close to the village of Arkalochori. Since the fissure was narrow, he could not enter it himself and therefore asked a small child to creep inside. The boy exclaimed that he saw many treasures and the news soon spread to the entire village. As people flocked in, the child was sent to retrieve as many valuables as possible, the looting lasting hours, perhaps days. However, at some point, the mayor realized what was happening and notified the gendarmerie (country police) and, of course, the Director of the Herakleion Museum. The informant remembers that Marinatos arrived in the middle of the night, riding a large motorcycle and wearing a black leather suit and hunting boots. He seemed quite formidable to the small boy and equally impressive was his passionate speech to the gathered villagers. He

Figure 35 Stalagmites in an enclosure, Cave of Eileithyia.

urged that the stolen goods be returned because they belonged to their island of which they were the sacred guardians. He spoke of the splendid civilization of Minoan Crete and of Evans's efforts to save it, mentioning that the English scholar had spent his entire fortune to help preserve it. He was also careful to remind that looting was severely punishable by law.

The crowd seemed numb at first but in the end many of the people returned the stolen treasures: precious double axes in silver and gold and dozens of swords. Marinatos stacked them in ordinary crates which he obtained from the local grocer, fastened them to the back of his motorcycle, and disappeared into the darkness of the night. This is the account of the informant.

Soon afterwards, a systematic excavation of the cave began with the assistance of Nikolaos Platon, and the English archaeologist Edith Eccles.[48] It turned out that the narrow fissure gave into a foyer which in turn led to the central cavity. There, the excavators found hundreds of bronze axes and swords piled up in total disarray, as though they had been thrown casually or hidden in an emergency. At first Marinatos thought that the bronzes were votive offerings placed on an altar, but their untidy disposition made him reconsider the case. Upon mature reflection, he decided that a smithy had been installed in the cave (this would explain why all the treasures were metal). Alternatively, he considered the possibility that some untoward event induced the inhabitants of the area to hide their treasures in the depths of the cavern. This emergency had to do with some great catastrophe; could it have been the same one that caused the collapse of the villa of Amnisos and the Temple Tomb at Knossos? The theory that the volcanic eruption of Thera was responsible for much of the destruction of Cretan villas and palaces in the period that Evans had designated as Late Minoan I A (c.1500 BCE) began to take shape in his mind. This theory was finally published in 1939 with the title 'The Volcanic Destruction of Minoan Crete' and was substantiated 30 years later with the excavations of Akrotiri, Thera (1967–74). In Marinatos's view Late Minoan I A and B were one and the same period.[49]

When Evans would finally come back to Crete in 1935 (see Chapter 9), he would visit the excavations of Marinatos at Arkalochori and would contribute a small sum towards its completion. This was a symbolic gesture of support but very much appreciated by the excavator since the Archaeological Service was very poor at the time and excavation funds had been severely curtailed.[50] The problem is evident from a letter Marinatos wrote to Mme Suzanne Goekoop in Holland:

We have made startling discoveries in the cave of Arkalochori. [...] In a fissure of this cave we have found dozens of double axes some of which are longer than 75 cm. [...] Unfortunately, this discovery has almost caused me to offer my resignation to the Archaeological Service. Can you imagine my psychological state? After having found these treasures and having been given an allowance of drs. 5,000,[51] I find that I do not have the means to either clean them or conserve them. This year the minister has completely abandoned the museum.[52]

Later that year, after Evans had already returned to England, Marinatos made the best find of all: a double axe inscribed with a dedicatory formula in hieroglyphic script. This script remains undeciphered, but the inscription on the axe constitutes a valuable addition to the corpus of Minoan hieroglyphs because it is an unusual combination of pictograms. Marinatos knew that Evans would be interested because the new signs took 'a medium place between the signs of the Phaistos Disc and that of the hieroglyphic class of the Cretan script'.[53] Evans too felt that the inscribed axe was important and included it in *The Palace of Minos IV*. A report was also made in *The Times* although not by Evans himself.

> Dr. Marinatos says the most important find is a copper double-axe bearing three lines of a hieroglyphic inscription composed of characters which now make their first appearance in the relics of Minoan civilization. The characters are similar to but not identical to those on the tray from Phaestos. The finds belong to the golden age of Minoan art, about the sixteenth century B.C. They have been taken to the Candia museum for cleaning.[54]

A month later Evans reports personally in *The Times*: 'Visiting the cave in the company of Dr. Marinatos, it was my good fortune to enjoy the spectacle of ordered piles of magnificent double axes'.[55]

Exciting as all this was to Evans (who could thus enrich his last volume of *The Palace of Minos* with fresh data) none was as rewarding as the discovery of a female statue of the 'Hellenic age' in 1935 because it confirmed his idea of the mother-goddess. It, along with two others, originated from the last significant excavation of Marinatos in Crete. Two years later, in 1937, he left his post. And in just a few years World War II broke out. Evans was not destined to outlive it.

The statues were made in bronze and were situated within the earliest Hellenic temple on Cretan soil. They represented a triad: two goddesses (one slightly larger than the other) as well as a god. It is the common opinion to the present day that they represent Apollo, Artemis and Leto. And since Leto was, as far as Evans was concerned, a survival of the Minoan mother, this find was of great importance for him. It will be remembered that the existence of a mother deity in Minoan Crete had been contested by Nilsson!

The statues originated near the ancient town of Dreros, close to the modern town of Neapoli, east of Herakleion. The account of their discovery has elements of a detective story and is worth recounting in full. One day in the autumn of 1935, an old farmer by the name of Georgios Koubanakis was in the process of digging his field along with hired labourers. Suddenly, his pickaxe struck against bronze, and it turned out that he had found the aforementioned three statues in fairly good condition. His immediate concern was profit and his predominant sentiment greed (he thought that the bronzes might earn him good money if sold as raw material). For this reason, he and his labourers agreed without scruples to mutilate and dismember the statues for easier storage and bury them within a container until the next day; at that time they could decide at their leisure where the statues could be sold for maximum profit. However, during the evening each of the parties decided to steal the treasures in secret.[56] In the middle of the night the labourers returned to the field, unearthed the mutilated statues, placed them in a sack, and fled as quickly as they could. Second to arrive was the owner himself, the old man Koubanakis, who found the containers empty. Rage gave speed to his old legs, which carried him swiftly to the neighbouring village of Vryses: there he found the culprits in the midst of negotiations with a buyer. The old man disclosed the whole affair to the police. They notified Marinatos, and so the statues ended in the Herakleion Museum, unfortunately in a severely mutilated condition. The head of the male statue was entirely missing.

The story had a happy ending, however. Being threatened with severe punishments by the Ephor of Crete, the robbers were finally persuaded to reveal the hiding places of the remaining pieces. This took a few days. The next stage was to excavate the find-spot of the statues, and Marinatos was fortunate to find the temple that originally housed them. The plan was unusual for a Greek temple since it consisted of a rectangular room with benches and annexes for storage; Marinatos suspected continuity with Minoan shrines. The main room contained a hearth in the centre and benches along the wall, one of which was filled in with horns of sacrificed goats (it appeared that the remnants of the goats were kept in the temple because they belonged to the god). It was on the aforementioned bench that the triad of the statues stood.[57] Marinatos wrote to Evans about it immediately, and received from him a congratulatory telegram on 9 November 1935: 'Hearty Congratulations important finds Dreros may I send short notice of your discoveries to *Times*? Evans.'[58] The title was 'Earliest Temple of Hellenic Age' and contained some thoughts of his own about the significance of the excavation:

> Thanks to the courtesy of the Ephor of Antiquities, Dr. Marinatos, I am able to call attention to the discovery by him of a temple which has good claims to be regarded as the earliest of the Greek Age in Crete, and at the same time shows remarkable connexions with pre-existing Minoan cult. [...] But the most remarkable find remains to be described. Above this Cretan horn altar were set up three bronze images ranging in height from 40 to 60 centimetres. Although these had been damaged by the village grubbers, it has been possible, reports Dr. Marinatos, to put together two of them in the Candia Museum in an almost perfect condition. One of these is a goddess, the other a boy god (kouros), the nude body of the latter well preserved, though the head is unfortunately wanting.

He adds with satisfaction, 'Dr. Marinatos's view that the sanctuary essentially represents a Minoan tradition is fully warranted.'[59]

Within a few days, Marinatos could report more good news: the missing head had been found and the male statue was now complete. He also discussed with him the civic and religious function of the temple within the Doric town of Dreros, and Evans answered that he thought the plan represented an intermediary stage between Minoan and Greek cult buildings. Marinatos fully agreed (Figure 36 a–b).[60]

As mentioned already, the Dreros goddess was an unexpected bonus for Evans's theories about the Great Mother Goddess and a

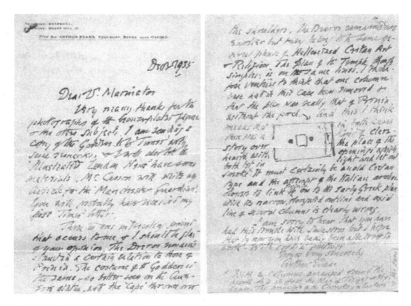

Figure 36a–b   Letter of Evans to Marinatos, December 1935.

lucky find for Marinatos since it made big publicity for him. In fact, Evans's piece from *The Times* was translated into Greek and was published also in the Greek newspaper *Eleutheron Bema* on 24 November 1935. An interesting detail is that the statues were restored by Emile Gilliéron fils. Is it possible that the fee came from Evans's pocket? Given the penury of the Greek Archaeological Service such a possibility is not out of the question.

As an epilogue to the discussion of the statues of Dreros, it is worth considering Evans's views from an aesthetic angle and from the point of view of his artistic sensibilities. He was very pleased about the survival of the Mother Goddess into Greek religion, but equally he was pleased by the ever-increasing realization of the superiority of Minoan aesthetics compared to the art of early Greece. It confirmed his general conviction – which has here been linked to the Darwinian conceptualization of progress – that time does not always bring improvement. His words when describing the goddess of Dreros

Figure 37   (a) Dreros Statue. (b) Maria from Fritz Lang's film *Metropolis*.

express his distance from the aesthetics of early Greek art, which he considers as being permeated by a military spirit.

> The austere image that we see before us, flat chested with squarely 'bobbed' hair and pointed nose and chin – in the attitude of attention, is the very impersonation of drill and discipline.[61]

The style of the Dreros statues was not entirely unfamiliar to Evans since starkness, angularity and minimalism mirrored the modernistic art of his times. It is hard to avoid the conclusion that when he expresses himself so strongly about the drill and discipline of the Dreros statues, he is also saying something about the style of his own age. The bob haircut of the Leto figure was fashionable in the late 1920s and 1930s, whereas the militaristic stance of the statues is curiously reminiscent of the robot-girl in Fritz Lang's cinematic masterpiece *Metropolis*, produced in 1927 (Figure 37a–b). Austere and stiff, the robot-woman was literally 'imprisoned in imperfect handicraft'.[62]

If Evans's taste was for soft looks, curly hairstyles and the pretty full-fleshed women of Renaissance and Baroque art, dressed in elaborate clothes and jewels (see Figure 29c), it is not hard to surmise that modernist art was not to his liking. One may even conjecture that he regarded this art as a symptom of a new and bleaker age that had altered Europe by 1935. And there may be an added message, unconscious even to himself, in the nostalgic statement he makes in the article, that no contrast could be greater between the Dreros statues and 'the great days of Minoan art'.[63]

CHAPTER 9

THE LAST VISIT OF EVANS TO CRETE

Honorary Citizen

We shall now revert to the spring of 1935 and discuss Evans's last visit to Crete. He was by then 84 and naturally wary of travelling long distances. The work at Knossos was completed and there was no compelling reason for him to return to Crete. Surprisingly enough, however, he did return for one last visit in April of 1935 to witness the unveiling of his bust at the entrance of the Palace of Knossos and be crowned with a laurel wreath as an honorary citizen of Herakleion. His sister Joan writes that he was so moved that upon return he refused to part with his wreath and carried it back to England.[1]

Another reason for his journey was that he wanted to see the latest excavations conducted by the British as well as the ones undertaken by Marinatos. He thus visited the Cave of Arkalochori together with the Greek ephor and saw hoards of double axes emerging from the depths of the cavern. Evans the excavator became the visitor and observer of others: time had brought about the natural reversal of roles between old and young.

Marinatos was actually the one who took the initiative to have Evans's bust erected at Knossos. He had conceived of the project already in 1930 but it took five years for it to materialize because of scarce funds and the severe economic depression in Greece. He persisted though and appealed to Cretan men of wealth to express their gratitude to Evans. He wrote to the Municipality Council that they should give some money as well. Evans was the first to have discovered their island's special role in ancient history, he argued, and the first to have called it the birthplace of one of the most brilliant civilizations of mankind. Due to Evans Crete had reaped substantial material profit stemming from the flow of tourists every year. He had spent his entire life and a huge part of his private fortune for Minoan civilization, but now that his life was nearing its end, honour and gratitude were long overdue. 'By honouring Sir Arthur Evans we will be honouring ourselves', Marinatos wrote.[2]

The funds were thus eventually found, and it was decided to hold the ceremony in April of 1935. The municipality of Herakleion made elaborate preparations for the event, and appeals were made to all members of the Herakleion communities to attend.[3] Municipal authorities invited judicial and military authorities, the press, farmers, commercial guilds, lawyers, doctors, the association of pharmacists, dentists, port authorities, public servants, school teachers, school children, Boy Scouts, athletic organizations, bank managers, presidents of unions (for agriculture, craftsmen, etc.), ambassadors and foreign representatives.[4] The invitation was published in the newspapers. The extensive list of the associations to which an appeal was made is worth noting because it reveals the social cohesion of the multi-class society of interwar period Herakleion. Marinatos prepared the people intellectually by lecturing on the importance of Minoan civilization and highlighting Evans's exceptional abilities to construct history out of disjointed material.[5] He spoke of him as a man of rare genius who had single-handedly created a new discipline, had sorted out its chronology, history, art and religion. He had understood its architecture, classified its pottery and all its artefacts. Such a man was Sir Arthur Evans, whose bust the Cretans were going to unveil in a few days!

Evans's long-standing collaborators came especially for this ceremony. One of the first to arrive was John Pendlebury, although he was no longer curator at Knossos. Also present was Evans's restorer and painter Emile Gilliéron fils, about whom much has been said in previous chapters. On this occasion he displayed his generous side because he made the clay template for the bust gratis. For Evans, the greatest surprise was the enormous size of the crowd that attended. It is estimated that some 10,000 people were present, the biggest crowd ever to have assembled in honour of a man of letters – and a foreigner at that.[6] He was taken aback by all this; he had no idea that he had been so popular.

The ceremonies began with a march performed by the small music band of the municipality. The Boy Scouts handed Sir Arthur a laurel wreath of which he was very glad, for he was particularly fond of the Boy Scout movement. Next, the Metropolite of the Greek Orthodox Church, Timotheos, gave a short introduction and was followed by Marinatos, who spoke once more about Evans's contributions to Crete and indeed to the whole of mankind. Finally, the mayor pronounced Evans an honorary citizen of Herakleion. Evans responded with a short reply delivered in Greek.

It was a humble speech. He was not a good speaker as his voice was thin and hardly audible, as I was told by an eyewitness of this event, Professor Stylianos Alexiou. He was a schoolboy at the time and remembered the ceremony as formidable. Of Evans he remembered only that he was a frail older man, but Knossos made a huge impression on his imagination. A series of pictures, taken after the ceremony, illustrate the atmosphere of that occasion. Evans stands in the centre, next to the Metropolite Timotheos. To the right of the priest (viewer's perspective), we see Marinatos (Figure 38). The mayor and other dignitaries are in the first row, to the left of Evans. In the second row, we see the representative of the gendarmerie and the mother of the curator of Knossos, Mrs Hutchinson, barely visible behind Evans. In the foreground stands one of the Boy Scouts, most likely the one who handed Evans his wreath. In the background stand the crowds, some men having climbed trees in order to get a better view. The whole scene is evocative of the Knossian frescoes, especially the Grand Stand mural which represents a crowd watching an unknown spectacle. In another picture (Figure 39), Marinatos and some other dignitaries stand in front of the bust of Evans.

Figure 38   Evans at the ceremony of his honorary citizenship at Knossos, 1935. Marinatos is first from the right, in the front row.

The event was followed by a reception hosted by Evans in his old home, the Villa Ariadne, which in the meantime had been handed over to the British School: a generous gift on the part of its owner. Evans was still in charge, however, and ordered the servants about, feeling somewhat anxious that he did not have enough sandwiches to feed the guests.[7] In the late afternoon, some more pictures were taken on the porch of the villa (Figure 40). On this occasion Marinatos took the picture of Evans dressed all in white and enthroned on his porch. He looks relaxed and exudes the contentment of a man who knows he is appreciated. To his left is the district governor (nomarch) Emmanuel Lydakis; behind him stands Gilliéron fils, half-hidden in the shadows and staring impersonally and uncomfortably. Mrs Hutchinson, the mother of the curator of Knossos, is the official hostess of the party. Hutchinson himself sits discreetly in the back.

Figure 39   Marinatos with some dignitaries in front of Evans's bust at Knossos, 1935.

In the next few days, Evans visited the site where the new museum was to be erected and was happy to learn that the old crumbling building was about to be demolished. Satisfied that a new home was

Figure 40   Evans seated in the porch of the Villa Ariadne, 1935. Next to Evans is the governor of Crete (seated); behind the latter stands Emile Gilliéron fils. To the left are the curator R. W. Hutchinson and his mother.

found for the treasures of Knossos, he left Crete for good on 22 April 1935. John Pendlebury wrote to his father the next day: 'Evans left yesterday. There has been a sad break in the continuity of splendour since our day. It was rather depressing'.[8] And he added, 'In the long run few of us found the old giant resistible'.[9]

As for Marinatos, he suspected that he would never see Evans again. He framed his picture and placed it on his desk where it stood, next to the picture of Georg Karo, for as long as I remember.

Evans's Last Speech and his Vision of Knossos

Evans's last speech in Crete differs from all others because it was more about a vision than about the scientific facts of his excavations. He chose a language that was deliberately poetic, rich in metaphors and allusions, and referred to the ghosts of the past: the vanished people who once inhabited Minoan Crete. He began humbly by expressing his gratitude to the present, the Cretan people who had been his hosts for so many decades. He was not sure that he deserved such an honour, he said, since his role had been but a small one as a mere mediator between the present and the past. The real glory belonged to the Minoans themselves. A fortunate conjunction of circumstances had led him 40 years ago to the discovery of a culture of such great brilliance.[10] Enticed by its 'heroic phantoms', he had visited their old habitation and excavated their Palace. He was quick to realize that its grandness was not least due to the geopolitical role of the island as a bridge between two worlds: 'Here Babylon and Egypt had met and had danced hand in hand.'

He also spoke of Minos and Daedalos: 'Now we know that old traditions spoke the truth. We have nothing here but ruins of ruins in front of us but they exude a spirit of order and rhythmical movement: the works of Minos and Daedalos'.[11]

Did he say all this because he was a naïve believer in the historical existence of Minos and Daedalos?[12] The answer is no! Minos and Daedalos are mere symbols of the exceptional political and aesthetic quality of Minoan civilization. Just as Freud utilized Oedipus and Electra to refer to conditions of neurosis, so Evans utilized the mythical king and his artist to express a cultural paradigm of excellence, a paradigm that was not dissimilar to the one articulated by Gibbon for the golden age of the *Pax Romana*.[13] He imagined the navy of the Minoan king defending the frontiers of its domain and carrying goods to the entire Aegean, spreading prosperity to the farthest corners of the region. Through the figure of Daedalos, he expresses the harmony and balance between well-crafted and disciplined art on the one hand, and free naturalism on the other. This paradigm of Minos–Daedalos was understood by his sister Joan Evans, who writes:

> Time and Chance had made him the discoverer of a new civilization, and he had to make it intelligible to other men. Fortunately it was exactly to his taste; set in a beautiful Mediterranean country, aristocratic and humane in feeling;

creating an art brilliant in colour and unusual in form, that drew inspiration from the flowers and birds and creatures that he loved. It provided him with enigmas to solve and oracles to interpret, and opened a new world for the eye and mind to dwell in: a world which served to isolate him from a present in which he had found no real place.[14]

Nostalgia

Evans's last speech in Crete is an example of the feeling of nostalgia that permeates his writings in the last decade of his life, when his productive years were behind and the prospect of another war lay ahead. It is true that some of his dreams had materialized. The ethnic groups of Slavs and Cretans, once under foreign rule, had been freed and had built their own nations. However, a different kind of oppression had arisen with Stalin in Russia, Mussolini in Italy and Hitler in Germany.

On the personal level, he must have felt lonely as members of his family and friends passed away one by one. When his wife Margaret died in 1892 he was still relatively young and bore her loss with fortitude; at that time years of exploration were yet to come. Still, he wrote to his father:

> You cannot know what Margaret's death means to me. [. . .] she was a helpmate as few have known. Her bright energetic spirit, undaunted by suffering to the last, and ever working for the welfare of those around her, made a short life long.[15]

As he grew older he must have felt her loss even more acutely than before because loneliness is more difficult to bear when one is not so active. Perhaps nostalgia for his wife is echoed in the interpretation of the Ring of Nestor in 1925 in which he saw the reunification of man and wife. He may well have imagined Margaret when he writes about the woman on the Nestor ring reciting some verses from Wordsworth's 'Laodamia':

No spectre greets me – no vain shadow this;
Come, blooming hero, place thee by my side!
Give, on this well-known couch, one nuptial kiss.
To me this day a second time thy bride![16]

The sentimentality of these verses reveals the emotional side of Evans, a feature of his personality that we can detect only in his writings because the secrets of his heart were seldom revealed to people. Margaret had died while he held her hand. He went to the field and plucked white daisies in order to make her a wreath of 'marguerites and mountain heath.' Allegedly he also wrote a poem.

Of Marguerites and mountain heath
And scented broom so white –
Such as herself she plucked, – a wreath
I wreathe for her tonight.
[...]
For she was open as the air
Pure as the blue of heaven
And truer love – or pearl so rare
To man was never given.[17]

Equally sentimental is the epitaph about his collaborator and field director, Duncan Mackenzie, in *Palace of Minos IV*. He died in Italy, just as Evans was correcting proofs of the last volume. The two had worked together since the beginning of the excavations at Knossos, and the latter had grown dependent on his field director because of the accuracy of information and sound judgement he supplied. So much did Evans trust Mackenzie's opinions that he adopted them in his own work.[18] The two men had different backgrounds and very different tempers and manners, a fact which often caused difficulties between them. Even so, they developed a strong intellectual intimacy, the *only intimacy that Evans ever knew* with anyone outside close family. As his sister writes, Evans 'was never cold-hearted – he could not be – but he kept himself remote and he grew up preferring impersonal relationships'.[19]

Mackenzie, for his part, held Evans in great esteem, although he found his electric personality difficult to bear. He confided to their mutual friend, Georg Karo, that despite their different characters not one high word had ever passed between him and Evans.[20]

In the preface to the last volume of *The Palace of Minos* he wrote the following:

> In the endeavour to carry out this comprehensive task it has been my grave misfortune to have been deprived through a now lengthening space of years – owing to a mental affection that had left no avenue for hope – of the invaluable services of my friend and colleague Duncan Mackenzie. [...] What, however, no training could have produced was his original and gifted nature, his whole-hearted devotion to the work, and his subtle artistic perception. In a material way, indeed, I have still gained frequent help from the rough notes in his 'day-books', chronicling progress made on various lines together with neat sketches of half-exposed plans. But nothing could replace the friendly personal contact and availability for consultation on difficult points with one of such great special knowledge.
>
> His Highland loyalty never failed, and the simple surroundings of his earlier years gave him an inner understanding of the native workmen and a fellow-feeling with them that was a real asset in the course of our spade-work. To them, though a master, he was ever a true comrade. The lively Cretan dances revived the 'reels' of his youth. No wedding ceremony, no baptism, no wake was complete among the villagers without the sanction of his presence, and as sponsor, godfather, or 'best man', his services were in continual request. There yet fall on my inner ear the tones of that 'still small voice' as he proposed a toast of a happy pair – with sly jocose allusions, fluently spoken in the Cretan dialect of modern Greek – but not without a trace of the soft Gaelic accent.
>
> Even as these words return from the printer's hands there reaches me from Italy the brief announcement that, a few days

earlier, on August the 25th that vexed Spirit had found release at last.[21]

What is most interesting is the existential thesis that an unhappy life is not worth living and it almost seems as though Evans's sorrow was less about the loss itself and more about the psychological torment that his friend had suffered. Mackenzie's last years had been plagued by mental illness 'that had left no avenue for hope'. Death had come as a relief when the spirit was finally released from its suffering.[22] Mental affliction was worse than death because it resulted in a serious distortion of personality and it was this that drove Mackenzie to reckless drinking and eventually madness. After a series of unfortunate accidents, Evans decided to suspend his duties and to give him a small pension out of his personal fortune as compensation.[23] Yet, he recognized that Mackenzie's removal from Knossos had 'broken his heart'. This is what he confided to Piet de Jong.[24]

Another friend and intellectual companion passed away in 1934 and was paid tribute to in the preface of the last volume of *Palace of Minos*: the Reverend A. H. Sayce, a scholar of Near Eastern literature. He had provided his constant and expert advice on the most challenging of all subjects, the decipherment of Minoan scripts. This advice would now be missed, Evans wrote, and he chose to express his personal loss by citing German poetry.

Zerstorben ist das freundliche Gedränge,
Verklungen, ach! Der erste Wiederklang.

Dead is that kindly crowd,
Hollow is the first echo that rings back.

The source is the first part of Goethe's *Faust*. The protagonist interacts with spirits that enable him to connect with happier days of a past era. However, then the spirits disappear and do not answer any longer: only a hollow echo reaches back to the caller.

This particular citation from Goethe was chosen to express sadness at the abrupt break between the past and the present, the inevitable consequence of death or change (Evans did not have the usual Christian faith in the afterlife according to his sister, but he did believe in the actuality of human memory). The nostalgia reflects his personal solitude as well as the transience of all historical moments. He employs similar vocabulary in *Palace of Minos* in order to describe the end of the best epoch of the Minoan age: '*vanished* is the power of individual characterization [. . .] *departed* is the strong sympathy with wild nature' (my emphasis).[25]

There is, however, another reason why Goethe is cited in German. Evans wants to pay tribute to the intellectual and artistic tradition of Germany, a tradition that he continued to cherish despite the alienation between the British and Germans caused by World War I. There is no doubt that his patriotism was awakened by the war, and his ward, James Candy, remembered well how it was announced to a group of Boy Scouts.

> August the 4th arrived and Sir Arthur came on foot and asked Frank to call all of us boys together, as he had an important announcement to make. When we had all gathered around in a circle he told us that Great Britain was at war with Germany. [. . .] Sir Arthur, on the outbreak of the Great War, erected four flag poles with the idea that should a victory be claimed by one of the allies, their national flag would be flown.[26]

He was so interested in the news that he called his friend at the *Manchester Guardian* to get information about the course of the war every morning at 11 a.m.[27] He also hosted meetings at his home: 'It was, I think, on July 1917, when Sir Arthur told me that a delegation from the War Office would arrive at Youlbury.'[28] However, the following incident shows how he separated his national identity from the brotherhood of science.

When German submarines sank the passenger ship *Lusitania* in 1915, the public in Britain and the US rose in outcry. A suggestion was made that all German scholars who were members of British Societies be immediately expelled. Evans, however, rose at a meeting of the Society of Antiquaries and objected to this motion. On the one hand, he condemned the sinking of the ship as an act of barbarism; on the other, he insisted that German scholars ought *not* to be expelled.

> I will not attempt to conceal from the society my own feelings on this grave matter. Public feeling is legitimately excited against a nation which has acclaimed the policy of murder without warning of civilian men, women and children on the high seas, and it is clear that professorial apologists for such action and doctors of medicine, who dishonour their humane profession, have put themselves beyond the pale. But strongly as I feel all this myself, I still dare express a hope that if any common action be agreed upon by this and other societies it may not be of a vindictive or indiscriminating character.
>
> In spite of the 'Gospel of Hate', let it be said to their credit, the learned societies and academies of Germany, with inconsiderable exceptions, have refrained from striking their English members from their rolls. In spite of official pressure, the Academy of Berlin has flatly refused to take this action. I myself am not ashamed of confessing that I have received, in the period of the war itself, cordial and even unsolicited assistance from a German archaeologist occupying a high official position. Even the temporary 'removal' of such names [...] will be a misfortune to our society.
>
> [...] we cannot shirk the fact that tomorrow we shall be once more labourers together in the same historic field. It is incumbent on us to do nothing which should shut the door to mutual intercourse in subjects like our own, which lie apart from the domain of human passions, in the silent avenues of the past.[29]

Evans practised these beliefs in earnest and this is why he maintained his friendship with Karo even during the War. This is what he writes in the preface of the last volume of *Palace of Minos*:

> But still less can I forget that, at a time when the Great War had already broken out, and national animosities were at their

height, as a friend and fellow worker in the same field of research, he [Karo] had found means to send me the first proofs of the text.[30]

Karo, on his side, said the most generous things about Evans both before and after the two world wars. A few years previously, in 1929, he had written to Humfry Payne, Director of the British School, *apropos* of Mackenzie's illness to defend Evans's decision to pension his collaborator off.

Evans revealed also on this occasion the enormous generosity of his nature which – quite apart from his greatness as a scholar – has secured the esteem and friendship of us all. In the thirty years I have known him he has not once disappointed me. And one cannot say this often about the same person.[31]

It has already been mentioned here that after Evans's death Karo rehabilitated his reputation, which had suffered from the negative evaluations of the Knossos restorations.[32] Their friendship was exemplary of the bond forged by the brotherhood of science despite the fact that both men had strong loyalties to their respective countries and were quite vocal about them. Evans considered German aggression in World War I to be an act of barbarism against civilization and was very suspicious of the terms of the Versailles Agreement.[33] Consider what he wrote to *The Times* to protest its mildness:

Sir the tremendous news of the acceptance of President Wilson's terms by the German and Austro-Hungarian Governments must not for a moment be allowed to disturb our saner judgment. May we, indeed exclaim, 'Nunc dimittis'? [...] Unless the 'will to resistance' in Germany is more thoroughly broken than authentic accounts have led us to believe, the acceptance of these terms seems almost unthinkable.[34]

Karo, by contrast, was highly resentful of the terms of Germany's surrender and considered them very unfair. Not only did he *not* accept his country's alleged guilt, but wrote a well-researched book on the subject of Germany's innocence while condemning British policy as hypocritical and imperialistic: 'England has ever possessed the art of adopting the semblance of the just man made perfect'.[35] He also writes that the persona of the grand, old, just gentleman is false; the Englishman is in reality a self-seeking imperialist.[36]

The two men differed also in their evaluation of Greek politics, in which they were both highly interested. In 1916, Evans rose in support of the party of Eleutherios Venizelos against the authoritarian (as he thought) monarch, King Constantine, whom he considered pro-German.[37] By contrast, Karo regarded Venizelos as the henchman of the European Entente and Constantine as the true hero of the land: the king tried to spare his people a civil war and was in no way to blame for what ensued. Karo regarded Venizelos as a detestable revolutionary.[38]

Given the deep disagreements in their ideology, it is a true miracle that Evans and Karo kept up their friendship with such consistency. They represented without a doubt the heroic generation of archaeology; they were like the two enemy officers of Renoir's cinematic creation, *The Grand Illusion*, gentlemen belonging to another world, another age. As Joan Evans said of her brother, he had found no real place in the present.[39]

A Troubled Island

When Evans came to Crete for the last time in 1935, he must have diagnosed that a political and economic crisis was at hand. On the one hand, the island had been transformed for the better since his first visit in 1894. After World War I, he had seen welcome renovations in Herakleion including a small *heroon* (hero shrine) designed in neo-Minoan architectural style and imitating the façade of the Palace of Knossos (Figure 41). The building symbolized Cretan identity of all ages and was due to the architect Kyriakos, who was aided by Spyridon Marinatos. It was a beautiful small building embellished with a park and situated in the central square of the town across from the archaeological museum.[40] Evans must have seen this *heroon* in

Figure 41   The Hero Shrine, 1931: a building designed in neo-Minoan architecture by the architect D. Kyriakos with the help of Sp. Marinatos (second from the left, second row, standing).

1930 since it was a tribute to his own restorations. By 1935, when he came to Crete again, a garden had been added, making it the jewel of the town. Herakleion was slowly turning into a European town, quite a different one from the Ottoman village that Evans found in 1901.

However, troubles of a different kind had arisen and, in some ways, the situation was worse in 1935 than in 1931, when Evans had last been in Crete. Greece had been severely affected by the worldwide economic depression and the government had constantly to borrow money from its European allies, cutting down salaries and funds for public works.[41] The island had been further weakened by the two strong earthquakes of 1926 and 1930 which turned entire neighbourhoods of Herakleion and other towns into dumps of debris (Figure 42). In the winter of 1935, immediately preceding Evans's visit, a third earthquake afflicted the inhabitants, and caused damages to the Archaeological Museum of Herakleion, about the fate of which something has already been written.

Poverty is a bad advisor and political instability makes things worse. As governments succeeded one another rapidly in Athens (often by *coups d'état*) Greek society became polarized. Tensions were especially strong in Crete where the royalist party (Laiko Koma) and the followers of Cretan Eleutherios Venizelos (Fileleutheroi) were at loggerheads. Since nobody knew who would be in charge next and what reprisals would follow if the wrong party took over, suspicion and fear spread. Another problem was that Venizelos, the most brilliant political star of modern Greece, had lost his credibility. In the past he had been regarded as the only man who could lead the country into a brighter future, but in 1935 he seemed a desperate figure even to some of his loyal followers.[42]

To backtrack to earlier years: Evans had known Venizelos personally and had hosted him in Britain as well as at Knossos. He had faith in his progressive views, but another reason he favoured him above all others was that Venizelos had been instrumental in uniting the Balkan countries and in getting Greece to sign a defensive treaty with Serbia, Montenegro, and even Greece's traditional enemy,

Figure 42 Afflicted house after the earthquake of 1930 near the town of Hagioi Deka.

Bulgaria.[43] Modern historians think that the agreement was precarious. Yet, as Evans diagnosed, the ensuing Balkan Wars brought to Greece unexpected and substantial gains. One of the effects was the elimination of Ottoman rule on European soil, for which Venizelos was given full credit by Evans. The latter wrote:

> Today in a little more than a month the whole political figuration of the Balkan peninsula has been changed. An Empire which has gone on for over five centuries has been

deprived of its European provinces and what all of Europe, and Great Powers like Russia, have in vain attempted to do, has been carried out [...] by the smaller powers joined in an alliance which a few weeks ago must have been undreamt of by those who thought they knew the Balkan country and Balkan people most thoroughly.[44]

This was the best example of what unity between nations could achieve against imperial oppression. The Balkan Wars were a moment of great triumph in European history. Little did Evans know what trouble lay ahead for Europe.

It has been mentioned already that Venizelos eventually lost his sway over the Greek people, one of the reasons being that he was held responsible for the national split between royalists and his followers. Back in 1916, when the split between Venizelos and the King had occurred, Evans and James Frazer had joined several other intellectuals in their unanimous support of Venizelos. A letter was sent to *The Times*:

We, whose love of Greece is founded in gratitude for all that Europe owes to Greek literature [...] have followed events since October, 1915 with profound sorrow and acute anxiety [...] the path of honour and safety for Greece was that marked out for her by M. Venizelos.[45]

On another occasion, Evans had sent a letter to *The Times* urging that the British follow their political principles rather than self-interest and that Venizelos ought to be supported.[46]

As time went by, however, it turned out that the national split was a very bad thing for Greece; by 1935 it was evident that Venizelos's policies had proved erratic and at times destructive. Evans would have read in *The Times* that the once great statesman had resorted to a *coup d'état* in March 1935 in order to regain the reins of government; and that while the coup was being manoeuvred by his collaborators, he himself had taken refuge in Crete. *The Times* then reported that he was responsible:

The attitude of M. Venizelos towards the rebellion is now clear, as it is known to-day that he has openly joined the insurgents in Crete. An official search of his house in Athens resulted in the discovery of five rifles, 2,000 cartridges, and some hand-grenades.[47]

By the time Evans arrived in Herakleion in April 1935, the *coup d'état* had failed completely, and its author had fled for Paris where he died a year later. However the repercussions of the attempted coup were felt by his followers, many of whom were incarcerated or driven out of their jobs.[48] One of the victims was Marinatos, who was accused of partisanship by some locals; fortunately nothing was found against him.[49] Evans was informed about all this and commented about the arrests in a letter to Humfry Payne.

The state of affairs [in Crete], consisting mainly of arrests and examination of prisoners, [is] very unsatisfactory, especially as the opportunity has been seized to shut up many of the quite moderate people who had nothing whatever to do with the insurrection.[50]

Georg Karo writes to Marinatos from Germany in sympathy and condemns the coup.

Now that the band of cowardly traitors has left Crete and the poor island has been made free, I can finally tell you how much I empathized with you about the earthquakes and the treasures trusted to you, not to mention how I care for those unfortunate ones who were affected by the misfortune.[51]

To add to the political tensions, class conflict became exacerbated that year. In August 1935, after Evans left Crete, dockworkers called a series of strikes and encouraged protesters. Six thousand armed men gathered at the harbour of Herakleion and were joined by a number of the populace. When violence broke out in the streets, the governor of Crete, Emmanuel Lydakis, feared a takeover of the town and declared a situation of emergency, asking at the same time for military help from Athens. In the meantime, the bells of the churches tolled and called the populace to assist the strikers. Civil strife broke out for a second time that year, but it was stopped in time.[52]

Evans chose the right moment to bid farewell to the island where a supreme civilization once flourished.[53] Conflict, violence and extreme ideologies would dominate Greece in the next dozen years: 'Every form of malice found its expression in ideas; and this was due to the civil wars that took place in Greece.'[54]

Figure 43 Spyridon Marinatos reads from the Bible during a religious ceremony in a village in Crete (1934). In the foreground (first from the left) is Evans's architect Piet de Jong. Next to him is Evans's foreman Manolis Akoumianakis. Effie de Jong is fifth from the left, her back turned to the viewer. The picture renders a vivid impression of society gatherings in Crete with people from all nationalities and social classes taking part in the ceremony.

CHAPTER 10

SUNT LACRIMAE RERUM: THE WAR AND THE DEATH OF EVANS

It is necessary to bear the daemons of fate with the
fortitude imposed upon us by necessity.

Thucydides 2.64.2

The Last Exhibition of Minoan Civilization 1936

The last years of Evans's life, although peacefully spent at his home at
Youlbury, were marked by further disappointment. One evening,
when his old friend Brice came to see him, they confessed to one
another a sense of failure. The world was moving on in ways that were
hard to grasp.[1] Not only was modernism incomprehensible to a man
who delighted in Renaissance, baroque and rococo paintings and the
music of Mozart,[2] but the new political constellations of absolute
power were troublesome to him. At the same time, British rule was
beginning to be contested everywhere, especially India: vanquishing
the British Empire was one of Hitler's stated goals. This must have
raised new questions in his mind about the justice of the British
Empire.[3] Also, traditional norms such as gender relations and social

hierarchies were questioned, a further disturbance to Evans, who was conservative in this respect. For his wife Margaret's sake he did not object to the Women's Colleges, but he did think that women in excavations were a disadvantage. This being said, he was very grateful for the assistance of young Edith Eccles at Knossos and at Oxford.[4]

As for his own written work, it had not been left uncontested. It must have been upsetting that Martin Nilsson's *Minoan-Mycenaean Religion* appeared more comprehensive – on the surface at least – than *Palace of Minos* on matters of religion. For this reason he insisted that the *Index* volume of *Palace of Minos* (1936) ought to be organized as an encyclopaedia of Minoan culture and religion, according to concepts and categories rather than keywords.

Still, at 85 he had the energy to bring attention to Minoan culture one more time by organizing an exhibition of Minoan artefacts in London in connection with the Fiftieth Anniversary (1886–1936) celebration of the British School at Athens.[5] It included the Ring of Nestor and, unfortunately, the forgeries of the so-called Thisbe treasure. On the other hand, it also showed many replicas of genuine objects, including the statues from Dreros. On 14 March 1936, he wrote to Marinatos to request that Gilliéron could make copies (in bronze) of the Dreros statues and some other Minoan objects from the Herakleion Museum and if they might be sent to London: 'one or two' he writes, 'would, I think, need Gilliéron's hand'.[6] Gilliéron was thus once more employed by Evans to craft replicas and Edith Eccles was asked to help out with the exhibition. She had become close with Marinatos in the last few years; they made excursions together and shared ideas (Figure 44). She writes him in the summer of 1936:

> I spend what time I can spare in Oxford helping Sir Arthur arrange his exhibition which is to be shown in London from October 14th to November 14th. Why not come? I am afraid you would be rather shocked. It is as much Gilliéronesque as Minoan – perhaps more.

In another letter she expresses the hope that Gilliéron will be eventually replaced by the Cretan restorer, Zacharias Kanakis.

Figure 44   Edith Eccles at Phaistos, 1934.

I am so pleased that you are allowing Zacharias to do these extra two replicas for Sir Arthur. I look forward to the time when Zacharias will have proved himself so good that there will be no need to cajole Gilliéron into coming to Candia![7]

In view of all that has been presented here about Gilliéron's possible role in deceiving Evans, it is interesting to know that Eccles had such a negative opinion of him.

Despite its 'Gilliéronesque' character, the exhibit was a great success and was visited even by the Duke of Kent on 14 October 1936.[8] Much was said on that occasion in praise of Greek and Minoan civilization, a very fortunate coincidence since Greece needed all the support and publicity it could get that particular year – we shall see why. Evans spoke with his usual passion, and yet we detect also the melancholy tone when he mentions that a culture 'most brilliant' had vanished from history. Indeed, nobody had suspected its existence until the fortunate accident of the excavations of Knossos. 'It is strange indeed,' he said, 'that a wholly new chapter [...] in the history of European civilization, should only have opened out to our knowledge within this generation'.[9] Who could have imagined that a culture of great sophistication had existed before the Greeks?[10] He dwelt on the ethical nature of its religion and emphasized once more that it foreshadowed the monotheistic creeds of later ages: 'Here indeed, we see a religious symbolism such as was never carried farther in Christian times'.[11]

Greece on the Eve of the War

Greece was again in turmoil in 1936. Anarchy, one of the results of factionalism, became intensified when the Communist Party gained 15 members in parliament and began to exert a crucial role in balancing the votes between liberals and royalists. This was 'a situation clearly pregnant with danger for what remained of the democracy', as one British historian assessed the situation.[12] The state of affairs gave rise to fears that a civil war was brewing similar to that of Spain. In March of 1936, a general strike supported by the Communist Party at Salonika turned out quite bloody.[13] Marinatos expresses intense anxiety in a letter to Mme Geokoop in Holland, 'every day we had fear that we would become a second Spain. [...] Communism has become dangerous'.[14] Indeed, the predicted civil strife did take place but only after the end of the German occupation.

These unrests in Greece induced the King and the premier of the government, General Ioannis Metaxas, to declare martial law on 4 August 1936. The parliament, which was dissolved for the summer vacation, was never reconvened. This event was bloodless but it marked the end of democratic life in Greece for several years to come since the dictatorship was followed by the German occupation.[15]

Evans surely viewed all these developments with disquietude and must have been suspicious of the dictatorship of Metaxas at first. On the other hand, he must have been relieved that there was some stability in the country. There had been so many *coups d'état* in Greece during the interwar period (almost three dozen) that the country was suffering from the ill-effects of political anarchy. For Evans the worry must have been not so much that Metaxas was an authoritarian as that he was perceived as pro-German. Edith Eccles evidently thought so and expressed this concern in a letter to Marinatos dated 9 September 1936:

> Both your letter and your parcel had been opened and sealed up again with paper saying ΕΛΕΓΧΟΣ ΣΥΝΑΛΛΑΓΜΑΤΟΣ [i.e. currency control]. Greece is becoming very German! On the other hand I had a letter from one of the Russian ladies today which has not been opened and is marked ΕΞΗΛΕΧΘΗ [i.e. censored].
>
> Why?[16]

Fears about the dictatorship of Metaxas and his alleged German sympathies were felt also by the American Ambassador in Athens, Ian MacVeagh, who writes accordingly to President Theodore Roosevelt:

> Mr. Metaxas is not only a German sympathizer personally, but a politically confirmed believer in the advisability of neutrality for his country vis-à-vis the Great Powers. Current rumours as well as the logic of the international situation as springtime approaches make this interpretation a possibility.[17]

MacVeagh adds that the British disapprove of Metaxas:

> Sir Sydney [Waterlow] did his best to circumvent Metaxas from putting his fascist policy into effect. Sir Sydney tried to persuade the king to get rid of Metaxas.[18]

The turn of events, however, eventually changed the attitude of the Great Powers when it was revealed that Metaxas was waiting out his time. Whereas he did not commit himself formally to any alliance between 1936 and 1940, he was actually carefully preparing his country for war with the axis. Apparently, he had secretly decided that the fortunes of Greece belonged with Britain: if Germany were to win, Greece would be a slave like other countries – he said. However, he hoped it would *not* win.[19] Thus, in January of 1940, MacVeagh writes to Roosevelt with great respect for Metaxas, giving him much credit for strategy:

> The Greek premier, general Metaxas, who is an excellent strategist trained in Berlin, where they called him the little Moltke, said to me the other day [...] that Russia is preparing an attack on the Straits.[20]

In any case, it is more than likely that Evans shared the opinion of *The Times* that Metaxas had managed to revive the deplorable economy and had 'achieved calm and order in the country'.[21] His broad historical judgement would have led him to regard the regime with cool sobriety as the symbol of a changing age where freedom of personal and political expression had been replaced by ideas of national self-sacrifice. It was too bad that the two (freedom and self-sacrifice) could not co-exist in Greece, for this had been Evans's dream and the ideal of civilization as he conceived of it. He must have agreed with the judgement of C. M. Woodhouse that 'the tragedy [...] for Greece was that two such brilliant men as Metaxas and Venizelos were seldom in agreement and never both right together. But neither was less a patriot for that'.[22]

In September of 1939 Hitler invaded Poland. Evans had already predicted this development and had said that 'the frontiers of Poland were not only morally but also strategically indefensible'.[23] He understood that the restlessness of German militarism had not been assuaged after the Treaty of Versailles and that Hitler was intending to upset the geopolitical balance of Europe. However, he saw other disturbing signs on the horizon: a most serious crack in the thin mantle of civilization was the persecution of the Jews in Germany. In 1938 he and many leading intellectuals in Britain, including Sir James Frazer, signed a protest in *The Times*:

> Sir, We wish to record our solemn protest, before the conscience of civilization, against the persecution of the Jews in Germany.[24]

Two Intellectuals under Hitler's Germany: Erich Bessel Hagen and Georg Karo

A digression will be made now to discuss the fortunes of two German intellectuals during the Nazi period, because their experiences typify the anxious times which Evans sensed in his final years. One of these men is Erich Bessel Hagen, a friend of Marinatos; the other is the archaeologist Georg Karo, the friend of Evans and mentor of Marinatos.

Erich Bessel Hagen was Professor of Mathematics at the University of Bonn. Stemming from a noble family, he inherited a tradition of philhellenism from his forefathers; one of his ancestors had actually served as an officer under the Republic of Venice in the seventeenth century and lost his life in Crete.[25] He met Marinatos in Berlin in 1925 when they both attended the lectures of the famous Hellenist Ulrich von Wilamowitz-Moellendorf at the University of Berlin. They became friends and stayed in contact until the war (shortly after its end Bessel Hagen passed away).

In 1928, when Marinatos went to Halle to study with Karo, Bessel Hagen also found himself in the same city. Eventually the latter was elected to the Professorship of Mathematics in Bonn and became a member of the country's intellectual and social elite. And yet he experienced the evil of the Nazi regime as acutely as those persecuted.[26] Terror spread slowly at first but eventually violence became manifest. In 1933 he writes to his friend in Greece:

> My beloved Germany is going through hard times. The National Socialist government that came to power on 30

January exercises an unbearable reign of violence intolerant of any freely expressed opinion. You will hardly know from your newspapers how terrible the situation is here; but I do not dare say more as the letters sent abroad undergo censorship.[27]

In 1936, the situation had become worse. Taking the occasion of a brief vacation in Switzerland, he expresses himself in greater detail and with greater freedom to his 'most dear Friend'. He begins the letter to Marinatos with a description of the beauty of the Swiss landscape, the splendid mountains surrounding the Lake of Thun, the beautiful Swiss autumn. He continues with a chilling account of life in Bonn under Hitler's regime.

In Germany, life has become *very* unpleasant since 1933 under the terror of Hitlerism. It is unbearable when I compare it with those earlier exhilarating times of freedom; the only consolation is that there have been worse times in world history, as for example the French Revolution of 1792–1794! At least now one is allowed to live and – if lucky – keep one's position.

The loud and mendacious propaganda, the shouting of National Socialists, the compulsion[28] to consent to things detestable just in order to save one's position is a horrible torture.[29] I and others, those of us who cling to ideas of liberalism, humanism and human dignity, are filled with unspeakable hatred which takes its toll upon health.

As long as I am in full possession of my bodily vigour, I am able to suppress the hatred through my scholarly work and positive thoughts about things beautiful. But when the body is weaker, during the slumber of early waking hours, or under circumstances of physical indisposition, the hatred overwhelms me with the force of a nightmare from which I cannot escape. The most objectionable aspect of the campaign is its anti-Semitism. My two best and most beloved colleagues (mathematicians, I mean) have lost their jobs because they are Jews. I experience the tragedy with them, I feel the worries that one of them has about his children, and still I can do nothing to help.

How horrible all this is I cannot adequately express in words. And that this heavy constant torture interferes with scholarly work is all too easy to understand.[30]

The letter ends with sentiments of gratitude towards Swiss hospitality: 'At least I am now in a friendly place', its author writes, 'unfortunately only for a few weeks. Here customs still exist, as I knew them'.[31]

The letter expresses the sentiments of an intellectual who suffered during the Nazi era although he was not Jewish. The German mathematician contrasts the gloom of Hitler's Germany with the ideals of previous days: beauty, order and freedom. He experiences brutality not just as corporeal punishment – to which he was not subjected – but as the mental compulsion to conform. His own complicity not openly to protest resulted in self-contempt, self-hatred and ultimately depression. The author was sensitive even to the unpleasant sounds of the shouting and propaganda of Hitlerism. He suffers because he cannot react or protect his Jewish friends. The only antidote, the only way to find balance, is to escape in the natural beauty of the Swiss Alps. The author does not adopt Freudian theory directly to explain his depression (although there is something Freudian there) but articulates his feelings in reference to a cultural ideal: a combination of aesthetics, freedom and moral principles that enable human beings to live good lives and experience happiness. Evans said very much the same when he spoke of the harmony between Minos and Daedalos.

Georg Karo also suffered under the Nazi regime. Like Bessel Hagen, he had family connections in Venice and was born there, but unlike him, he was Jewish. German and Italian were his native languages, but he also spoke English, French, and Modern Greek equally well: his ability for fluent conversation in many languages was not the least of his charms.[32]

It has already been mentioned that Karo lived in Athens for many years as Director of the German Archaeological Institute. He made friends there but also enemies. Some archaeologists, members of the American School of Classical Studies in Athens, mistrusted him on the grounds that he was a German nationalist; it was even said that he was a member of the German secret police during World War I. From this they inferred (perhaps unjustifiably) that he joined the Nazi Party and that the party made him an 'honorary Aryan' because of his great services to Germany before and after World War I. In 1936, we find him in Athens again. According to his own words, he sought to flee to the USA because he had been mistreated by the Nazi Party: they revoked his Aryan citizenship and made it difficult for him to use libraries. Fortunately, his friends at the American School of Classical Studies managed to get him a visa for America.[33]

We pick up the story of Karo's life again in 1939. By then he was settled in the United States and had a post as visiting professor at the University of Cincinnati. This is the year when the war broke out in Europe while Czechoslovakia was annexed to Germany, a fact to be noted.

It so happened that Marinatos also was in the United States that same year, giving a tour of archaeological lectures in the autumn. Karo naturally invited his former student to give a talk at the University of Cincinnati and Marinatos accepted; the visit, however, never took place because Marinatos contracted pneumonia and had to spend more than a week in hospital.[34] Since the two men did not manage to meet in person, Karo sent Marinatos a letter and asked him the favour of mailing some material contained in an envelope from Greece. In the envelope were 11 postcards, all identical and all bearing an etching of a building of the University Museum, Pennsylvania. The artwork was signed by the artist's name as 'Barbour 1939'. The messages on the back of all the cards were identical and contained a simple greeting. Most curiously, they were not signed by Karo's real name but the pseudonym 'George Barbour'. Most of the cards had German addresses, but three out of the eleven were destined for Prague, which had just been annexed to Germany. Why did Karo conceal his identity? Why did he want these cards to be sent from Greece and not be mailed from the US? Was he afraid that the American Federal Bureau of Investigation would note down the recipients? Or was it the case that he was protecting the recipients (assuming they understood that George Barbour was Georg Karo) from the government of the Nazis? Was he signalling to certain people that he was alive and well in America, or was he sending a message through a code that had been previously agreed upon?

These were hard times in which even friends could become suspects. Not being able to solve the dilemma and not wishing to engage in anything that might be doing service to the Nazis, Marinatos decided to leave the cards behind in America and asked his hostess, Mrs Elizabeth Humlin Hunt, to dispose of them as she thought fit. She thought the right thing for her to do was to hand them to the Federal Bureau of Investigation.

In the meantime, two American archaeologists by the names of Daniel Lewis (University of Pennsylvania) and Edward Capps (Professor of Classics at Princeton) brought forth accusations against Karo at the Federal Bureau of Investigation and declared him to be a dangerous spy of the Nazis. Now that the files have become declassified and we can study them, it is clear that these men were convinced that Karo had been a member of the German Police Force in Athens during World War I.[35] Subsequently, Karo was subpoenaed to testify in court, but nothing incriminating was found against him. Nevertheless, he was put under parole and was denied citizenship in the US. In the declassified records, he is categorized as 'Nazi'.[36]

All this was very humiliating to a man who had once held a dignified position in Germany. In a letter to an American friend, he writes movingly that due to nasty rumours he had to go before the Alien Enemy Board: 'At my age internment would have meant a death sentence'.[37]

After the war, Karo returned to Germany and lived a quiet life. The story about the mysterious postcards never found its explanation. Marinatos, in any case, decided to rehabilitate his teacher's memory after the latter passed away in 1963.

Karo's happy career was shadowed in his last years just when he had need of rest and peace to produce what he had still in mind. In 1936 the 'Partei' found that there was Jewish blood in his veins; he was expelled from Athens, and soon afterward from Germany. The United States received him as a refugee in 1939, and there he lived by writing and teaching at an advanced age at Claremont College.[38]

In his own *Memoirs*, the same ones where he talks about Evans, Karo has a very negative assessment of Hitler and describes World War II as a meaningless enterprise. Given with what fervour he had defended Germany after World War I, one wonders if these are words of wisdom or if they offer an apology. There is a distinct possibility, in my opinion, that despite his astuteness of judgement, Karo fell victim to the same mental compulsion as Bessel Hagen and could not face the truth. Perhaps he was blackmailed by the Nazis because of his Jewish blood. Or perhaps he realized in time that this regime was evil. About one matter I have little doubt: the experiences with the Nazi Party made Karo admire Evans even more than before because he appreciated his friend's boldness to always speak his mind about what he believed to be the truth. Evans, Karo wrote, stormed through life like a brave lion; in his courage he was comparable only to his great compatriot, Winston Churchill.[39] Joan Evans wrote similarly about her brother's strength: 'The secret fortress of his heart held firm'.[40]

The War and the Death of Evans, 1939–41

Evans was at his home at Youlbury in 1939 when he received two letters, one from Marinatos and the other from the American archaeologist Carl Blegen, informing him simultaneously that Blegen had unearthed a new palace at Pylos. The latter regarded the palace as the home of the Homeric king Nestor; namely it was a typical mainland palace reflecting the infallibility of Greek oral tradition. Evans was very happy with the news but insisted that it was a Minoan palace, defending his theory of the Minoan supremacy of the Peloponnese to the end. To that effect he sent a notice to *The Times*:

I venture to pass on to you the news that has reached me simultaneously with letters from the American excavator,

Dr. Blegen, and the Greek Director of Antiquities, Professor Marinatos, of the discovery near Navarino of a late Minoan palace, intimately connected with Knossos...[41]

He surely realized that he had lost the intellectual battle regarding the issue of the Minoan supremacy in the Peloponnese and that the younger generation was developing new ideas. By that time he was old and feeble, and even his beloved house at Youlbury began to show signs of neglect. The trees had grown and blocked the vistas, and the embroideries grew tattered and grim.[42] In a letter to Blegen, congratulating him on his discovery at Pylos on 23 April, Evans confides that he is under a cloud owing to a minor operation that he had to undergo about a year earlier. His days were shortened and his activities hampered.[43]

After the aforementioned operation, his sister Harriet came to keep him company. Then she herself was suddenly taken ill and did not survive. Her death was a severe psychological blow from which Evans never recovered because he was very close to his siblings. A sign of his resignation to the inevitability of death is the donation of his beloved Ring of Nestor to the Ashmolean Museum, Oxford in 1939.[44]

Two years later, he read in the newspapers that General Metaxas of Greece was dead, on 29 January 1941. His death was perceived by many British as a sign that Greece had lost its last small chance to resist Hitler or even to delay his advance in the Mediterranean. Metaxas was hailed a war hero in the leading article of *The Times*, and the British government declared national mourning. Evans would have read the following:

The body of General Metaxas was to-day laid to rest in Athens with the impressive ceremonies in which the Byzantine church is so rich, amid the lamentations of great crowds, including rich and poor, civilians and soldiers alike, who assembled along the route of the funeral cortège. [...] Flags on all Government buildings in London were yesterday flung at half-mast for General Metaxas. It was only the second time that anyone other than the Head of a State had been honoured in this way.[45]

Evans learned next in 1941 that Athens was taken and the German flag with the swastika was raised in the Acropolis. A few months later, in May, Crete was conquered and bombarded by the German air force. Unfortunately, the British navy was unable to offer protection against the enemy parachutists. His once curator at Knossos, John Pendlebury, was shot.[46] It was rumoured that when Evans heard the news he said: 'Here am I, still alive, and this young man with all his promise is gone'.[47] His foreman Manolakis Akoumianakis, to whom he owed the discovery of the surface slabs of the Temple Tomb (see Figure 31), was also shot.[48] The war had arrived at every place he had once loved and had taken its toll on his friends and collaborators.[49] When news of the bombardment of the island reached him, he was stirred to anger for the last time, thinking that the British had deserted it to the Germans, a betrayal not only of Crete but of the entire historic past of Greece.[50] Other rumours reached him that the King of Greece had taken shelter in the Villa Ariadne and that the curator Hutchinson had escaped. In fact, this was not true since Hutchinson and his brave mother remained in the villa until almost the moment the German parachutists dropped.[51] Nevertheless, it was a fact that the war was brought to the thresholds of the Palace of Minos.

One day, in the spring of 1941, he managed to drive to London and visit the British Museum. He found it ravaged by bombardments and its sight devastated him. Next, he took himself to the offices of the Hellenic Society to inquire about the fate of his British and Greek friends in Crete.[52] He did not find out much.

Some memories about his last days are recorded by his adopted son, James Candy, who visited him through the spring and summer of 1941. 'I asked him if he was not afraid that the Germans would steal or destroy the treasures of Knossos', writes Candy. 'No', Evans answered, 'the Germans have a department in their army which is responsible for preserving, where possible, archaeological sites. This also applies to our army, this department being under Sir Mortimer Wheeler'.[53] Evans spoke as a man who still maintained his faith in the brotherhood of science and the nobility of European civilization, and oddly enough he was right in some respects. The Nazis dropped fliers that informed their soldiers about the value of Minoan ruins. And Karo writes that the general who used Evans's villa as his headquarters showed respect for the ruins of Knossos and made sure they were preserved.[54] Evans was right on another count as well. 'The Cretans', he said, 'would carry on the war in Crete from the mountains as they had always done against any invader'.[55] And so they did.

A few weeks later, he was told that the Herakleion Museum had been bombed. This was true. Fortunately, the treasures of Minoan civilization had been stored away in the new museum's basement, thanks to the initiative of its new director, Nikolaos Platon, and the personal labour (under very dangerous circumstances) of the conservator, Zacharias Kanakis. However, Evans did not know any of this. It is best not to dwell on what he must have felt, if indeed he believed that so much of his life's work had come to such an end. Karo writes that Evans's end came 'in the midst of the most senseless war of our times'.[56]

Fortunately, his death in July of 1941 spared him the aftermath of the German invasion. He never found out that the Cretan villagers paid a high price for their insubordination; that wounded men were buried alive at a village of Kystomadon; that priests were shot and church altars desecrated; that some of the prisoners were forced to dig their own graves.[57] '*Sunt lacrimae rerum*', there are tears for human sufferings, he once wrote, citing Virgil. What would he have said about the sufferings of the Cretans, had he been alive in the autumn of 1941?[58]

In May 1941, James George Frazer had also passed away. A leading article in *The Times* discussed the philosophical content of his work. Like Evans, Frazer had spoken of a rich vision of civilization that man could attain. It was the irony of the closing years of both men that they witnessed Europe's plunge into chaos and darkness.[59]

APPENDIX 1

LETTERS BETWEEN SIR ARTHUR EVANS AND SPYRIDON MARINATOS

The letters published below represent only a portion of the correspondence between Sir Arthur Evans and Spyridon Marinatos. These letters are the ones that accidentally survived World War II because they were transported to Athens by Marinatos when he left Herakleion in 1937 and were placed in the back of a closet until they were found by the present author. Much of the rest of the correspondence of Marinatos has mysteriously disappeared.

— 1 —

Evans to Marinatos

(Figure 45)

Sir Arthur Evans, Youlbury, Berks, near Oxford

April 3 1930

Dear Mr. Marinatos,

I have been so desperately busy endeavouring to finish my Third Volume of *The Palace of Minos* that all my correspondence has fallen into sad arrears. I was, all the same, very much obliged for your letters and your discovery of the late tholos tomb in Messara

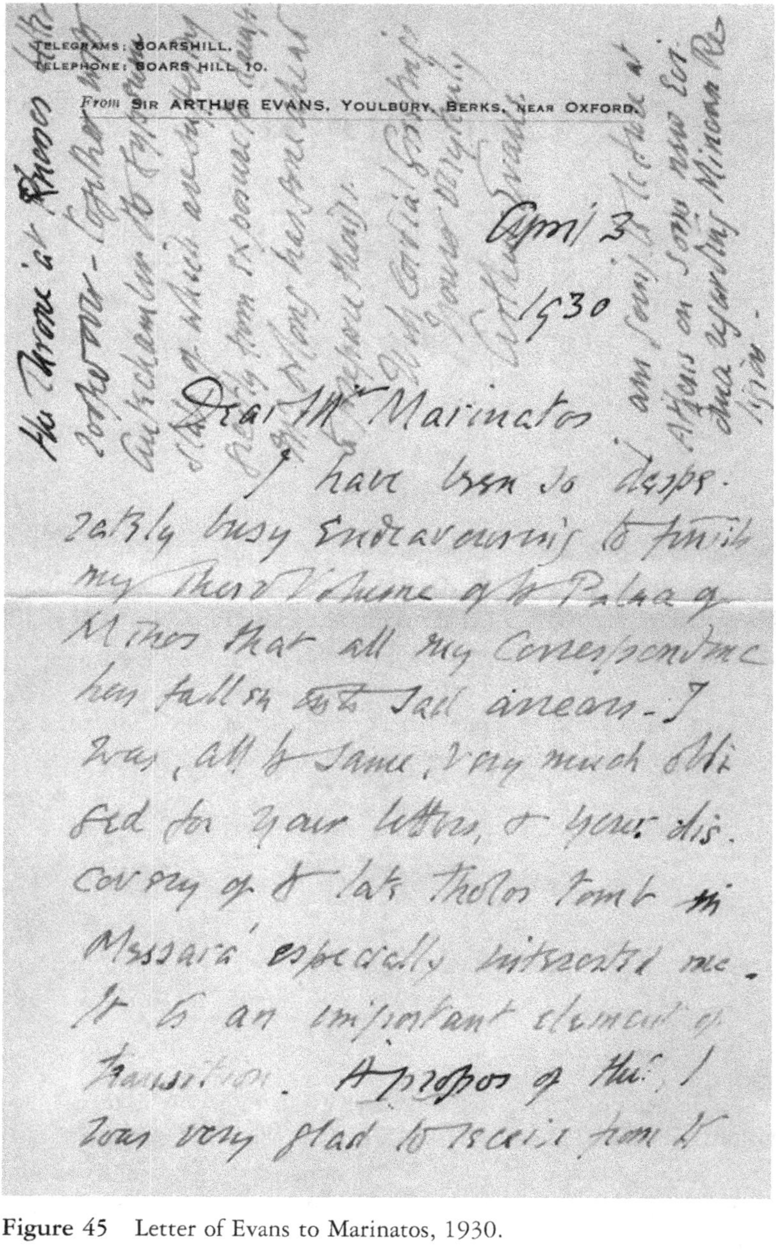

April 3
1930

Dear Mr Marinatos.

I have been so desperately busy endeavouring to finish my Third Volume of the Palace of Minos that all my correspondence has fallen sadly into arrear. I was, all the same, very much obliged for your letters, & your discovery of the late tholos tomb in Messará especially interested me. It is an important element of transition. A propos of this I was very glad to receive from the

Figure 45   Letter of Evans to Marinatos, 1930.

especially interested me.[1] It is an important element of transition. Apropos of this, I was very glad to receive from the late Professor von Duhn — whose death is very sad news — a letter in which he said that although it upset all his previous views after twice going through my work on the Shaft Graves he felt bound to accept its general conclusions and that many Rhinelauf archaeologists were coming to the same conclusion. Your evidence will signally help.[2]

I was glad to hear that you have not suffered more from the Earthquake, also that you are taking steps to secure an Earthquake-proof wing. That was promised by the Government after the 1926 earthquake but never executed.[3] Now I have got through my proofs of Vol. III I hope to hasten to Crete so I shall have an opportunity of talking over these things with you personally. I want to have the Room of the Throne at Knossos better roofed over — together with Antechamber, the Gypsum slabs of which are suffering greatly from exposure to dampness. M. de Jong has gone ahead to prepare this.

With cordial greetings,

Yours sincerely,

Arthur Evans

I am going to lecture at Athens on some new evidence regarding Minoan Religion.[4]

— 2 —

Marinatos to Evans

(In Greek, typed. Translated by N. Marinatos. Sent to the present author by N. Momigliano from Evans's Archives at Oxford.)

Directorship of the Herakleion Museum
Herakleion, 14 April 1932

My most respected friend, Sir Arthur,

With the present letter I deem it my duty to report to you a most interesting discovery at Amnisos. You know already that old traditions had placed the harbour of Minos there. Some exploratory excavations by the sea and near the foothill of the rock (which today is called Paleochora) brought to light very interesting finds that have surpassed every expectation. In the west foot of the hill, a large deposit of rubbish has been found consisting mainly of Middle Minoan ceramics. There were also remnants of buildings which have not as yet been dug. In the north side of the hill, within the sand, a small *megaron* has been found built in ashlar masonry.[5] One of the blocks has an incised double axe. The hall has not been fully excavated, but we found in it a small piece of gold and a fragment of a faience vase. These are promising signs!

Near the *megaron* a strange building was found with very thick walls (approximately 2 metres), also built in ashlar. I tend to believe that it was a fortification tower. But it must be fully excavated before any opinion is pronounced.

But the most important and rather unexpected find was a rich deposit of fresco fragments in the east side of Paleochora. We have so far found more than ten crates and more pieces still remain in the ground. The subject is floral decoration; I send you two samples.[6] The most valuable composition is the Fresco of the Lilies because it furnishes us with the prototype of the lily vases and reveals a thus far unknown mural technique which may be designated 'inlaid fresco'. The background is red whereas the flowers are blue and white. However, they are not painted; rather, the blue and white paste has been applied on a design previously impressed on the plaster. Thus, we have a true inlaid technique which is the prototype of the known dagger. Also reed-plants have been imprinted by the same method. After the cleaning of the frescoes, it may be possible to understand the whole of the composition because it seems that an entire programme is at hand. Various other finds from the top and the sides of the hill have given us a full picture of the history of habitation from Early Minoan times onwards. Amnisos seems as old as Knossos itself!

I have provisionally stopped the excavation. But if new finds are made, I shall keep you informed.

With respect and warmest greetings,

Yours, Spyr. Marinatos

— 3 —

Evans to Marinatos

Sir Arthur Evans, Youlbury, Berks, near Oxford
21 April, 1932

Dear Dr. Marinatos,

I should be much obliged if you would send me some plaster casts of two bead seals in the Candia Museum.[7] These are Xanthoudides Κρητικαί σφραγιδες no 59 (lion or cub) and 103 two ⚒ [double axes].

I was sorry not to have been able to visit Candia this year but I am so much engaged in trying to finish my last Volume (IV) of the Palace book. There is still a great deal of work to be done.

I hope that you are well and that you had a successful season.

With cordial greetings,

Yours sincerely,

Arthur Evans

— 4 —

Evans to Marinatos

(Figure 46)

Youlbury, Berks, near Oxford
Dec. 19 1932

Dear Dr. Marinatos,

Forgive me again for troubling you for information.

There is in the museum an early Minoan stone vessel in the form of an owl. I forget the exact shape. Could you let me have a photograph? Also I should like to know where it was found. Is there exact indication of dates?

Some years since I acquired an ivory seal of the same form from Southern Crete – probably Mesara [sic].

With best Christmas and New Year's wishes to you and Madame Marinatos.[8]

Yours sincerely,

Arthur Evans

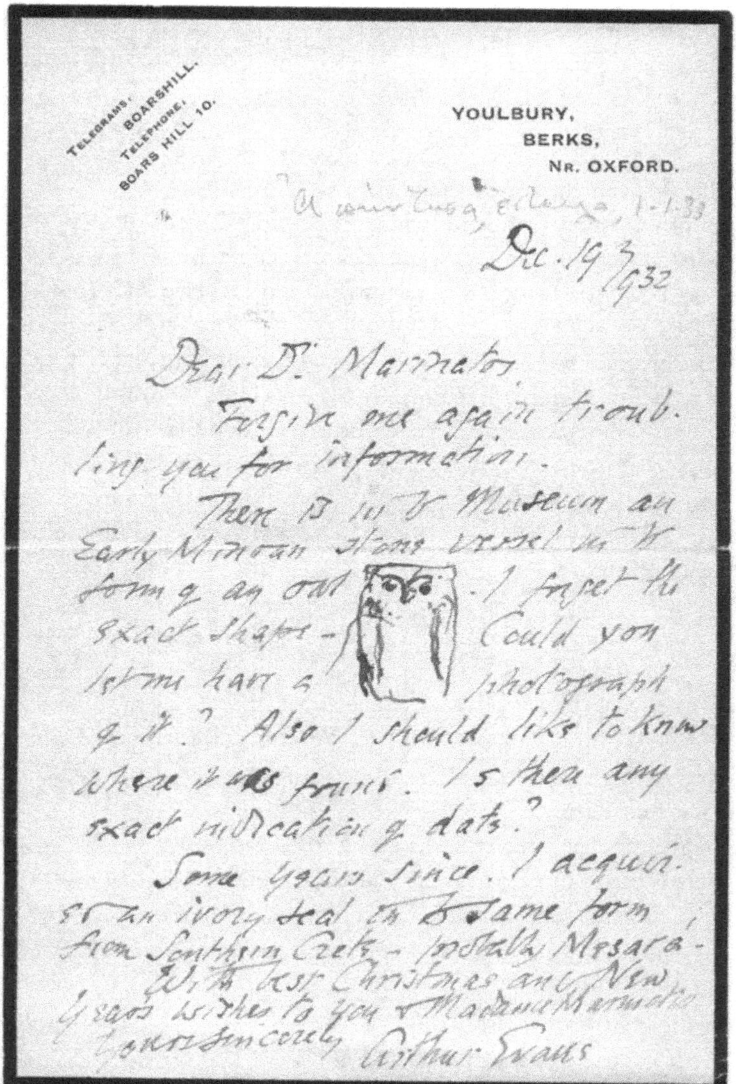

YOULBURY,
BERKS,
NR. OXFORD.

Ἀνω Πνωγ Ἐπαργο, 1-1-33

Dec. 19 3/1932

Dear Dr Marinatos,

Forgive once again troub-
ling you for information.

There is in the Museum an
Early Minoan stone vessel in the
form of an owl. I forget the
exact shape — Could you
let me have a photograph
of it? Also I should like to know
where it was found. Is there any
exact indication of date?

Some years since, I acquired an ivory seal of the same form
from Southern Crete — probably Mesará.

With best Christmas and New
Years wishes to you & Madame Marinatos
Yours sincerely Arthur Evans

Figure 46   Letter of Evans to Marinatos, 1932.

— 5 —
Marinatos to Evans
(Figure 47)

Herakleion, Mai [sic][9] 7th 1935

My dear Sir Arthur,

A further happy event from the excavations at Arkalochori has been just noticed:[10] A bronze double axe of medium size (length [...] cm)[11] shows 15 letters in three vertical lines. Two of these letters are not well preserved but the 3 letter of the second line seems to be an interpunction sign, like Nr. 5 of the first line.[12]

As it will be seen, these signs take a medium place between the signs of the Phaistos Disc and that of the hieroglyphic class of the

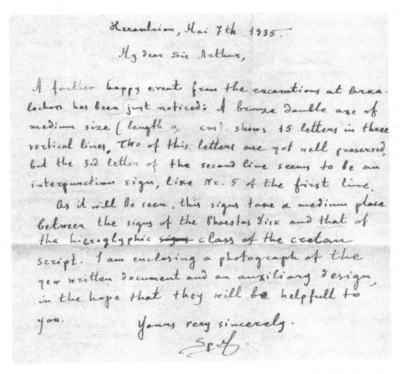

Figure 47   Draft of letter that Marinatos sent to Evans, 7 May 1935.

Cretan script.[13] I am enclosing a photograph of the new written document and an auxiliary design, in the hope that they will be helpfull [sic] to you.

Yours very sincerely,

Sp. Marinatos

— 6 —

Marinatos to Evans

Herakleion, November 20 1935

My dear Sir Arthur,

We have just finished the reconstruction of the first three statuettes, of which I enclose a photo. The other two statuettes will be not ready before two or three weeks. I send you too some other photos to make use if necessary in daily press. As to the building in Dreros, I am not sure about its identification. It may be the Delphinion (as we found two inscriptions inside it) but it could be too the prytanion of the town, because of the hearth.

The new Museum has not yet found its beginning, as Mr. Salustros, who is now not more in the service, has caused in the newspapers and in the coffee-houses a terrible reaction.[14] He is pretending that the old Museum must not be demolished. As it is impossible to found [sic] another place, he tells to built [sic] the new Museum out of town. He has excited much [sic] people but I have too, my partisans and a mortal duel is being fought now in the Ministry. I have mentioned, that I shall go out of Crete, better, than to undertake the danger of the transport of the museum far away from its actual place. I think that this week we shall begin to put down the great flight of the old building, that is already free from cases. It has not been possible to go to Kephallonia excavation this year.[15] The new museum absorbs all my time and I have put aside every other work.

It was splendid idea to publish a popular edition of *The Palace of Minos*. It was very necessary for the less specialized scholars![16]

With my best salutations and wishes.

Yours faithfully,

Sp. Marinatos

— 7 —

Evans to Marinatos

Sir Arthur Evans, Youlbury, Berks, near Oxford
Dec. 1935

Dear Dr. Marinatos,

Very many thanks for the photographs of the bronze plated figures and other subjects.[17] I am sending a copy of the Goddess to *The Times* with some remarks and shall also let the *Illustrated London News* have some materials. Mr. Casson will write an article for the *Manchester Guardian*. You will probably have received my first *Times* letter.[18]

There is one interesting point that occurs to me and I should be glad of your opinion. The Dreros remains stand in certain relation to those of Prinia. The costume of the Goddess is the same – as better seen on the Auxerre statue, with the 'cape' thrown over the shoulders. The Dreros remains are earlier but they belong to the same general phase of Hellenized Cretan art and religion. The plan of the Temple though simpler is on the same lines. I therefore venture to think that one column base had in this case been removed and that the plan was really that of Prinia without the porch. And this I think means that in both cases there was a kind of clerestory over the place of this hearth with openings which both let in light and let out smoke.* It must certainly be an old Cretan type and the attempt of the Italian archaeologists to link Prinia on to the Early Greek plan with its narrow elongated outline and axial line of several columns is clearly wrong.

I am sorry to hear that you have had this trouble with Salustros but I hope that by now you have really been able to set to work.

With cordial greetings

Yours very sincerely,

Arthur Evans

*With 4 columns arranged round the hearth this is in fact the plan of Tiryns only later [? writing illegible]. The principle of the clerestory or lantern is the same.

— 8 —
Marinatos to Evans
(Handwritten draft kept by Sp. Marinatos in his archives.
In possession of N. Marinatos.)

Herakleion Dec. 12, 1935

My dear Sir Arthur,

Very many thanks for your letter that I have become today [sic],
in the same time with the newspapers '*Proia*' and '*Eleutheron Bema*',
that they publish the article of Dr. Casson. Your own article of the
'*Times*' Nov. 20 has been already appeared [sic] in *Eleutheron Bema* of
Nov. 24.[19]

I reply with pleasure to your very suggestive questions. First of all I
have abandoned the idea, that the Dreros building could be a prytaneum
owing to its strange inner arrangement. It is unquestionably a temple,
the earliest temple of purely Minoan tradition.[20] Apart from the fixed
hearth, another stone table of offerings movable like the Minoan
examples, stood before the *keraton*. As we have found there two
inscriptions, it could be the Delphinion, that served as an archive of the
town (we know it from the inscription of the *orkos*[21] of the Drerians).

The question of the two columns near the hearth is highly
interesting, after your explanation of a possible 'lantern'. In every case
we have found only one column base, that of the entrance side, and,
curiously enough, in Prinias too only this column base has been
found *in situ* (cf. Pernier, Prinias, p. 61). But it is highly possible, that
in both cases we have to do with two columns. As to Pernier's
attempt to link the plans of the early Greek temples, I agree with you
that it is surely wrong. In fact, in the whole Greek period of Crete
predominates an un-Greek form of temple (Lato enceinte, Pythion of
Gortyn). We have to do clearly with a special tradition in the Cretan
temple form, a tradition that necessarily must be Minoan.

As to the statuettes, I have only splendid news for you. After my
different procedures[22] the unknown owner of the missing pieces has
been terrified and he has advertised[23] me, through an anonymous
letter, that he had deposited them in a hole of an old building near
Neapolis. I have been there with the police and we found indeed

6 new pieces, among them the head of the greatest statuette, that of the kouros. This magnificent piece will be now completed. Only the hands are missing, perhaps partly lost in old times. It is half size (75 cm) and the hair over the stern was formed in spiralform curls.

The two goddesses are almost identical and they belong to the series of the peplos figures known from East Greek terracotta plaquettes, and from the sculptures of Prinia, Eleutherna and Auxerre and seems to me advanced or belonging at least to a different school. But the style is different. I cannot yet tell my last word, but I think that Mr. Casson's chronology (8th century or beginning of 7th) is too high.[24] They may belong to the middle of the 7th century. The archaic smile, of which the earliest examples were the Ephesos ivories, is already present here, especially on the kouros, that may be the latest example of the series. There are good reasons to believe that on the heads of the statuettes stood poloi.

The question of the new museum has happily ended. The half of the old building has been already put down and we hope that till April we shall have the new flight. But the unexampled demagoguery of Mister Salustros and his similars has caused to me much trouble. I have been called a not indigenous (*anemozoxaris* in their own dialect) and I have been invited by a newspaper to go away from Crete. I am sorry that I am obliged to abuse still of their hospitality!

With my cordial wishes for Christmas,

Yours very sincerely,

Sp. Marinatos

— 9 —

Evans to Marinatos

Sir Arthur Evans
Youlbury, Near Oxford
17 March, 1936

Dear Dr. Marinatos,

I gather that this may find you in Athens. Gilliéron has informed me, privately, that you might be kind enough to arrange for him to supply the Ashmolean Museum, Oxford with copies (in bronze) of the Dreros images. W. E. T. Lead would be glad to purchase and Gilliéron might perhaps give him the rough estimate of the cost.

I am wanting some reproductions of Minoan objects from the Candia Museum for an exhibition to be held in London — at the Royal Academy in October of this year in connexion with the jubilee celebration of the British School in Athens. I have given Miss Eccles (who is about to start for Greece and Crete) a list of those and she could arrange with you about the matter. One or two would, I think, need Gilliéron's hand.

With cordial greetings!

Yours sincerely,

Arthur Evans

APPENDIX 2

LETTERS BETWEEN EDITH ECCLES AND SPYRIDON MARINATOS

Introduction

A biography of Edith Eccles (see Figure 44) has been compiled by Nicoletta Momigliano; references to her may be found also in Dilys Powell, *The Villa Ariadne* and I. Grundon, *The Rash Adventurer: A Life of John Pendlebury*.[1]

She was an energetic, witty British archaeologist who, after her studies in England, came to Knossos to help John Pendlebury in the stratigraphic museum. She studied there the history of gems of the Late Minoan period and Sub-Minoan pottery.

In 1934 she became friends with Marinatos, who took her as a collaborator in his excavations of the cave of Arkalochori (Chapter 8). Their friendship reinforced the friendly ties between Greek and British archaeologists, which were strained in the earlier years of Marinatos's directorship in Crete (see Chapter 8 and Appendix 3). In 1936, Eccles helped Sir Arthur Evans to organize the exhibition of Minoan artefacts in London and undertook to write to Marinatos on behalf of Evans.

After this task, she spent a year at Bryn Mawr College in 1936–7. In 1938 she returned to Greece and excavated on the island of Chios. Marinatos and Eccles remained friends even during the war and even afterwards when Marinatos got married to his second wife Aimilia.

Eccles's promising career came to a halt after she became ill with multiple sclerosis after the end of World War II. As stated in her obituary in *The Times*, for someone of her energy and intelligence the illness was a particularly cruel blow.[2] In 1946 she joined the Research Department of the Foreign Office (Greek and Turkish section), where she worked until her retirement in 1965.

Eccles's letters to Spyridon Marinatos testify to a romantic friendship. Eccles was ten years younger than Marinatos and evidently respected and idealized him. She asked his opinion on several matters but also offered her own views in matters of common interest. It is indicative of her sentiments that she asked him to write a reference letter for her when she applied for admission at Bryn Mawr College; the other referee was Sir Arthur Evans.

During the excavations at Arkalochori, Marinatos developed his theory about the destructive consequences of the Theran eruption on the palaces of Crete and confided them to Eccles. The excavations at Amnisos had given him the idea that a huge tsunami had struck the north coast of Crete. A few words must be said about this theory in connection with Eccles.

At Amnisos, Marinatos found substantial quantities of volcanic pumice in a building just north of the villa. He noticed another curious fact: the heavy exterior walls of the villa had been violently dislocated, as though they had been sucked by a wave retracting towards the sea. If a volcanic eruption had occurred, it might account for a tsunami as well as the pumice found in the buildings. Surely, this volcano was the well-known one in the nearby island of Thera. The accompanying earthquakes would have damaged the Temple Tomb, the excavation of which by Sir Arthur Evans and John Pendlebury Marinatos had observed in 1931. In fact, the earthquake that struck the Temple Tomb had been so sudden and violent that it had trapped human victims in its ruins.[3] The Palace of Knossos had also suffered during this destruction but, because it was so quickly repaired, Evans had not realized the magnitude of the catastrophe in Late Minoan I A (*c.*1500 BCE).

The cave of Arkalochori had also collapsed suddenly at about the same period, and Marinatos shared the idea with Eccles that the same earthquake had caused the destruction of the building as well as the cave. They both realized that *all the Minoan sites* on the north coast of Crete were affected at the same time: Nirou Chani, Amnisos and Arkalochori. They also disagreed with Evans that there was a discrepancy of 50 years between Late Minoan I A and I B.[4] On this (still very controversial) subject Marinatos was supported by Eccles, and this is why her role in the formation of the theory is important. She writes in 1939 reviewing Pendlebury's book *The Archaeology of Crete*:

> At Sclavokampos vases with the 'LM Ia', floral style of decoration and others with that of LM Ib, marine style were found together. The same was the case at Tylissos, Nirou Chani and Gournia. Neighbouring ateliers were decorating pots with marine and plant motives at one and the same moment. The differences between the two styles are clear, but purely stylistic, and are no indication of a difference in date. Yet Pendlebury can still speak of 'the later phase of LM I pottery as LM Ib.'

After Evans's departure from Crete in April 1935, Marinatos asked Eccles and the curator R. W. Hutchinson[5] if they would accompany him on an exploratory visit to Thera in order to survey the field for Minoan pottery of Late Minoan I A or B. The intention of Marinatos was to seek evidence of contemporaneity between the Theran eruption levels and the destroyed Cretan sites. It was known that small exploratory digs had been conducted by the French geologist F. Fouqué and the German archaeologist Robert Zahn in the middle of the nineteenth century and that both men had found pottery in their investigations; yet, the specific location of their digs and the exact dates of their finds were not known.[6] Evans was aware of these explorations as well.[7]

The Anglo-Greek party arrived in Thera in May 1935. Foreign visitors were so scarce those days that the visit was recorded in a local newspaper.[8] Walking through the black rocks of the volcanic island, they agreed that the pottery they saw was stylistically very close to the vases from Amnisos.[9] Oddly enough, the party never reached Akrotiri (which was then accessible only by donkey), the very spot where Marinatos would eventually uncover the ancient town buried under the ashes. After the party returned to Crete, Marinatos told Eccles that he was certain of a connection between the fates of Crete and Thera. He asked her to check the publication by the German and French excavators in the libraries in Athens, and Eccles writes back on June 14 1935 to suggest excavation (see letter no. 4).

In the same letter she predicts a war – which in fact happened. After the end of the war, Evans had passed away and Eccles became very ill. Marinatos barely escaped with his life when he was almost arrested by partisans during the civil war that followed the German occupation. In the post-war years he became preoccupied with his new excavations in the Peloponnese and the project to excavate Thera was indefinitely postponed.

In 1962, however, Marinatos returned to the island and began methodical investigations by collecting reports from villagers and conducting surveys. The reason he returned to Thera then was that his old collaborator and assistant at the Herakleion Museum, Nikolaos Platon, had found pumice at the Palace of Zakros in the south end of the east coast of Crete. Platon had always been convinced of the correctness of Marinatos's theory regarding the eruption of the Theran volcano as a cause of the destruction of the Cretan coastal sites.[10] Delighted with Platon's discoveries at Zakros, Marinatos was inspired anew to excavate Thera, fulfilling his intention of three decades before.

It is not known how Eccles reacted to the Theran excavations in 1967, but it is hard to imagine that she did not know about them despite her illness. She would have witnessed the success of these excavations and would have seen how close in conception the buildings at Thera were to the restorations of Evans at Knossos.

Ill as Eccles was, she actually survived Marinatos by three years and must have read about his fatal accident of 1 October 1974 at Akrotiri in an obituary in *The Times*.[11]

Letters

— 1 —

Αγγλική Αρχαιολογική Σχολή
[British School of Archaeology]
3 June 1935

My dear Marinatos,

My many thanks for the photograph and the enlargement. It will be a souvenir of the one occasion in my life when managed to keep still for the whole length of an exposure — and a souvenir of a very happy evening.

I've had my Santorin films developed and some are not too bad; but I've no time now to wait for pictures to be made (I leave for England tomorrow) so I'll send them to you after I reach home.

Athens is much too hot.

Yours sincerely,

Edith Eccles

— 2 —

4 Ιουνίου 1935

My dear Marinatos,

I found your letter almost as soon as I'd posted mine and it made me very happy. You know as well as I do what a link Arkalochori is between us. Even if I never see the site again, whenever I read or think about Arkalochori I shall think of you at the same moment and thank you each time for having let me go there so often with you. I'm glad too that we paid one last visit on such a lovely evening. It made me sadder than ever to be leaving such a beautiful country.

But I shall come back χωρίς άλλο.[12] I love Crete far too much to stay away from it for long.

I'll write again from England and send the photographs.

Yours very sincerely,

Edith Eccles

— 3 —

21 June 1935

My dear Marinatos,

Would you be very kind and, *me tin ypomoni sou*,[13] have another look at seal impression No. 136 in the Knossos case? It's the one with a human head on it and a pointed cap which I drew just before I left. I mentioned it to Sir Arthur the other day and he referred me to *Palace of Minos* Vol. IV.2, p. 626, Fig. 613. But when I look at Fig. 613 – as I hope you will do – I find that Gilliéron's drawing makes the top of the head round and not square. I hope this is another case of Gilliéron's inaccuracy but I fear it may be a case of mine. So would you look at it again and tell me sometime? I suppose Sir Arthur is right about the part of a leonine body and what must certainly be regarded as a grain of barley in the field. It was quite unintelligible to me. But I thought the top of the head was clear.

It looks too as though there must be another sealing with a facing head and two grains of corn somewhere in the Museum. Or has it disappeared?![14]

I've had to start and think all over again about plans for next year because I've remembered that the Prehistoric and Protohistoric Congress will be in Oslo in August and I can't afford that *and* Crete. At least I don't think I can. I must talk to my father again!

I enclose one of my Thera photographs which I didn't include last time. Remembering your love of Manolaki, I think you may like to have it.[15]

I hear that you now have Miss Benton to amuse you! Please give her my kind regards.

Yours very sincerely,

Eddith Eccles

These stamps have just fallen out of my writing case. Will you have them? They're no possible use to me here.

— 4 —

Leyfield Road
Liverpool 12
14 June 1935

My dear Marinatos,

I enclose photographs of the New York and Boston impressions – almost actual size. I've written the catalogue number and the materials on the back of each.

I enclose too a few photographs of Santorin, the ones of the finds from beneath the pumice are pretty bad but fortunately it doesn't matter because I find that they've been published already. Karo reported their discovery in the *Anzeiger* for 1930 (135) with a couple of photographs by Lehman-Hartleben. I needn't quote it to you because, although I know you haven't the *Jahrbuch* for these later years, Karo is sure to have given you an offprint. Pendlebury has not yet sent me the film he took of the two pots Zakhari[16] restored but as soon as he does I will let you have prints.

I hadn't realized how much had been found at the Minoan site at Akrotiri – the one we never reached! I had imagined that all Fouqué's attentions were confined to Therasia. But not so. Do you know his Akrotiri finds which are in the French School at Athens? I don't. I know only Renaudin's description of them in *B.C.H.* for 1922; they seem worth having a look at. And how much did the Germans find in their big excavations? Dörpfeld in describing his 1901 *Inselreise* in *Jahrbuch* XVI p. 105 mentions the finding of a Mycenaean sherd under the pumice at Zahn's dig of prehistoric houses at Akrotiri but I don't remember any report of that dig. But that is probably due to my bad memory, for in the second volume of the big German publication they mention Zahn's report as about to appear soon and it would be very unlike the Germans if they failed to produce it. In any case I grow more and more convinced of the importance of Thera and of the need for someone to do a good dig there. If you go this year you must write and tell me all about it; and if you go next year I shall probably come over for a few days to see what you find. For I plan now to come to Greece for the months of June, July and

August – though of course anything may happen in the meantime to upset the best of plans. We may be in the middle of a war with Italy by then!

I am leading a very peaceful and eventful life for the moment. I enjoyed the trip to Gla and Orchomenos though the Copais was like a furnace and after three days we fled to Delphi in the hope that it would be cooler up in the mountains. We went back to Levadia by way of Arachova and the Monastery of Osios Leukos [sic][17] which I'd never seen before. (Incidentally, apropos of your Neolithic pottery from the Eileithuia cave which resembles Vasiliki ware, I suppose you know the similar ware from Hagia Marina which is now in the Chaironeia Museum? It reminded me, too, of course of Mrs. Walker-Kosmopoulos' pottery which is in the Corinth Museum – I think from Gonia.)

My journey home was quite pleasant (except for the bit from Brindisi to the Italian-Swiss frontier, which I loathed as much as ever!). By chance I left the Piraeus on the 'Kephallonia' (how many things conspire to prevent my forgetting you!) and the next day actually stopped at Same, or Samos, or whatever you call it. But there wasn't time to land, so I still haven't set foot in the lovely island. And it *did* look lovely that day. Still – καμιά φορά ...[18]

Much to my delight I continued to talk Greek until, and even after, I landed in England on Saturday. For a passenger on the Kephallonia was coming right through to England to board a ship; and as he didn't know any English – or very little – I had the great joy of being able to help him a bit on the channel steamer and in getting through the customs. It's the first time I've ever had the chance to return to any Greek in England the hospitality which we meet everywhere in Greece. I wish we had the chance more often. But wait till you come to England in the autumn ...

Meanwhile let me know what happened in the last stages of Arkalochori. And all good wishes for Amnisos!

Yours very sincerely,

Edith Eccles

I'm sorry so many Arkalochori people had to be punished. But I suppose it was inevitable.[19]

— 5 —

18 June

Sorry to have been delayed but I found that the prints I'd made for you were very bad and ordered some more. These are a little better but where they are quite indecipherable I've attached a better print from my note book and enclose it. I don't recommend England. A storm of hail yesterday has killed all our roses. EC

— 6 —

Royal Holloway College
Surrey
10 December, 1935

My dear Marinatos,

I write to you in haste to remind you – though you probably need no reminder – of the passage in Pausanias iii. 17.6. It seems to me it may have some significance apropos of the new Dreros bronze figures. For were not Dipoenus and Scyllas natives of Crete and may they not have been members of the school which had produced the Dreros figure?

It is a mere suggestion.

Kind regards,

Yours,

Edith Eccles

Sir Arthur has kindly had copies made of the photographs you sent to him and has given me some.[20]

— 7 —

18 August 1936
Leyfield Road
Liverpool 12

Dear Marinatos,

I saw Evans today and he asked me to write to you to ask if Zacharia may make two more plaster casts (coloured) for him.

May he make copies of

1. Palace of Minos I, p. 92, Fig. 60
2. – – – – – – – – – – –, IV, p. 980, Fig. 939

and send them by post to the Ashmolean Museum, Oxford, marking the parcel IN BOND. They must be here before the end of September because Sir Arthur wants them for his exhibition; so could you have them sent from Crete before September 8? Let Zacharias colour them as well as he can. There is no time for Gilliéron to come.

Would you write to me immediately to Liverpool to tell me if this is possible or not?

Fearing you may be away to Kephallonia I am writing also to Zacharias but I suppose he has no keys to get the originals for the cases!

I go to America on September 11th. Would you do something for me? Would you be very kind to send me at Bryn Mawr College, Bryn Mawr, Pennsylvania copies of your photographs of the Gazi goddesses? I hesitate to put you to this trouble and expense but I should find them so valuable in my work on the Sub Minoan period and perhaps someday I may be able to pay you. Meanwhile you will have my deep thanks.

I send Sir Arthur's kindest regards together with my own.

Yours very sincerely,

Edith Eccles

— 8 —

Sept. 9, 1936
Bryn Mawr College
Bryn Mawr Pa, USA

Dear Marinatos,

You really are too kind. I am delighted to have Sheffer's book. It is a most handsome return for Weickert's little book.

I am very glad too to have the Gazi photographs and the news about your recent work there. It sounds a promising site and I hope you will find the time and money to dig it – but vines are expensive things!

I am sorry our king did not come to Crete but he seems to have very much enjoyed what he has seen in Greece. I hope it will not be a fashionable tourist ground as a result!

I sail for America on the 18th and am busy packing. I spend what time I can spare in Oxford helping Sir Arthur arrange his exhibition which is to be shown in London from October 14th to November 14th. Why not come? I am afraid you would be rather shocked. It is as much Gilliéronesque as Minoan – perhaps more.

Both your letter and your parcel had been opened and sealed up again with paper saying ΕΛΕΓΧΟΣ ΣΥΝΑΛΛΑΓΜΑΤΟΣ [i.e. currency control]. Greece is becoming very German! On the other hand I had a letter from one of the Russian ladies today which has not been opened and is marked ΕΞΗΛΕΧΘΗ [i.e. censored].

Why?

By the way – why do you regard both the Gazi goddesses as Minoan? Have you found some recognizable pottery with the three new ones? Do let me know, because I had thought the one with the very angular profile certainly post-Minoan.

I am so pleased that you are allowing Zacharias to do these extra two replicas for Sir Arthur. I look forward to the time when Zacharias will have proved himself so good that there will be no need to cajole Gilliéron into coming to Candia!

Your saying that you are now 'quite alone' disturbs me. I do hope that this does not mean that your wife is now permanently in Athens.[21]

I should be very sorry.

Yours very sincerely, Edith Eccles

— 9 —

Posted in Boston
(Aboard the *Samaria*)
26 September, 1936

Safely so far. I'm just going ashore to see the famous goddess.[22] I should reach New York tomorrow night. I am so glad Zacharias has finished the extra two reproductions.[23]

Ever yours,
Edith Eccles

— 10 —

Bryn Mawr College
Pensylvannia, USA
9 November 1936
[note on top in pencil: answered]

My dear Marinatos,

I am liking America. I've been here six weeks now interesting too. Müller knows the Oriental material amazingly well – which pleases me a great deal, because until came here knew nothing much about anything East of Troy and Tell el Amarna. Of course he tends to see too much Oriental influence everywhere and, I think, underestimates the Minoan element not only on the late Helladic mainland but even in Crete. But even so I am learning much from him.

Rhys Carpenter is tracing the tribal migrations during our period (1100–700) and so far we have been dealing with mainly Hittites and Phoenicians and the Luristan Bronzes and such things. Soon, I suppose, we must tackle the problem of the movements of the Danube peoples and the great question of the 'Dorian Invasion'.

But it is, of course, the work with Miss Swindler on the pottery of the period which I am enjoying most. In the bottom of my heart I am so much more interested in pottery than in anything else so I think all our problems of this sort Mycenaean, Protogeometric–Geometric period will be cleared up by the study of the pottery, if they are ever cleared up at all. We covered as a background all the LH III [Late Mycenaean] pottery, going carefully into any data from Egypt or Palestine which would help with this tremendous problem of Sub-Mycenaean. It fell to my lot to study the Kephallenia material and explain it to the others and[24] wished I had you by my side to help me. I wished too that I had handled the actual pots in Argostoli. Still you have published it so well that it was not such a handicap not to have seen it. (Incidentally, if you have a spare copy of your first report in Εφημερίς for 1932 I should be most grateful for it, but please do not trouble if it would be difficult to send it).

I wondered as I read your remarks on page 45 of AE 1932, whether you still believe what you say there about the absolute dating of your finds. Schweitzer's dating seems much too early.[25] It seems preposterous nowadays to put the beginning of Geometric back to 1200. It is surely much more likely that the Geometric period lasts from say, 900 onwards. If then you date the fall of Mycenae to c. 1130–1100 and if the 'granary style' pottery goes on after this, as we see in the Lion Gate deposit in BSA XXXV, we must put the end of Mycenaean period down into the eleventh century – to perhaps 1075 or 1050. The period 1050–900 will then be covered by the sub-Mycenaean or protogeometric periods.

I find hard to agree that your Kephallenia pottery belongs to the period 1250–1150. At that time – if you accept Hutchinson's dating of LH III as he gives it to the Liverpool Annals 1932 – the Mycenaean pottery is vague at Mycenae in the granary style of which (admittedly) you have a great deal in Kephallenia. But much of your material seems later. Your Kylikes, for instance, proceed a long way from the standard LH III type as one sees it at Mycenae and Zygouries. You have the development into the swollen stem and the further development into the ridged stem. Thus, while *some* of your *kylikes* (the straight-stemmed ones) may go back into the thirteenth century with the Zygouries *kylikes*, I think your other *kylikes* – the vast majority of the whole number – show so much development that they probably come down to 1100 or even later.

These are some suggestions as you probably have most forceful arguments to refute them all – which I should be very glad indeed to hear. Incidentally I am interested to see that the Heurtley BSA XXXVIII accepts your 1250–1150 dating without question. This makes one think that his still unpublished finds from Ithaka must have produced corroborative evidence for you that we must wait some time yet before we know what it is. I think Miss Benton has already written her article. Perhaps you have read the proofs.[26]

It would help me very much to know your opinion on the sub-Mycenaean period, not only in the Ionian islands but in Crete also. I wish I had had a chance to talk to you about it but as you know,

I had very little time in Crete, after I knew that I was coming to America to study this period, and spent most of that time trying to find evidence of sub-Minoan period in the sherds from the little palace – with no success. I wish I had done more work on Vrokastro-Mouliana finds. Incidentally, if you are near the Vrokastro case some day, would you look to see if the circles are compass-drawn on the amphora illustrated in Vrokastro publication, Fig. 84, p. 143 and on the *oinochoei*[27] illustrated in Pl. XXXVII, 4? I should be very glad to know if the impression of the point of the compasses exists.[28]

I do apologize for bombarding you with questions like this. If only you were in America you should come to stay here and take part in our discussions.[29] As it is I can only write and hope that you may find time to reply. Your reply whenever it comes, will be very welcome.

How is the Museum? Hope it progresses well.[30] I shall be in Greece next summer to see. I think I may not come until September for I shall not return to England until July and I shall not want to leave immediately.[31]

It seems that the B.S.A. exhibition[32] has gone well. I wish I had been there to see it, particularly as I spent much of the summer helping to prepare it. But Hutchinson will have told you all about it. Please give him my very kind regards when you see him.

Miss Swindler and Müller send their best wishes. Send mine too – coupled with best wishes for the speedy rebuilding of the museum. May I come and help to arrange it when it is finished?

Yours ever,

Edith Eccles

You may reply that it was no use trying to trace the development of the *kylix* shape from the Mycenae *kylix* because the *kylix* dies out early in the lion gate strata. I agree. It is certainly a lacuna in our argument. It may even be that the *kylix* died out at Mycenae c. 1250 and at the same time began to become popular in Kephallonia. This would make your finds contemporary with the finds from the later strata at Mycenae. But I still think that you must bring your dating down somewhat. Still – please let me know if your opinion is the same as it was in 1932.

— 11 —

94 Cheyne Walk
Chelsea, S.W. 10
Flaxman 1537
[date sometime in 1955]

Dear Spyro,[33]

I am delighted to hear from you from Sinclair Hood that they have had the good sense to put you in charge of the Service again.[34] And what a moment of opportunity! I shall look forward to hearing news of your successes.

Meanwhile please give my best love to your dear wife and to the little Ourania (I suppose she is no longer 'little').

Kindest regards,

Yours,

Edith Eccles

APPENDIX 3

THE RELATIONSHIP OF JOHN PENDLEBURY AND SPYRIDON MARINATOS

This appendix does not consist of letters only but additionally supplies the background necessary to appreciate the relationship between Spyridon Marinatos and John Pendlebury. The story follows the pattern familiar from the conflict and ensuing friendship between Marinatos and Evans. The primary sources that have been utilized to reconstruct the narrative are: 1. the memoirs of Dilys Powell; 2. letters by Pendlebury to his father Herbert now in the British School at Athens; 3. archives of the 23rd Ephoreia; 4. newspaper clippings of the 1930s derived from Sp. Marinatos's archives; 5. two letters by J. Pendlebury to Marinatos.

Marinatos clashed with both Pendlebury and with Humfry Payne in 1930 when a student of the British School, Miss Hartley, was sent by Payne to study some ancient pottery. It derived from old excavations and was stored for unknown reasons at a private house in Herakleion (apparently Payne and Pendlebury had been informed by someone about its existence there). The Greek authorities were not informed about this. Dilys Powell (Humfry Payne's wife) reports the incident from the British point of view in her memoirs, *The Villa Ariadne*.

While she [i.e. Miss Hartley] was thus innocently employed the police burst in. The vases were seized; the owners were arrested together with the chauffeur who had taken the British party from the Villa to the house; John [Pendlebury] received a furious letter from the Director of the Herakleion Museum, Professor Marinatos; and the local paper published an article accusing the British School not only of trying to buy the vases in question but of being involved in large scale antique-dealing.[1]

Marinatos's point of view is represented by a telegram he sent on 25 March 1930 to the Ministry of Education in Athens:

Today police confiscated antiquities concealed in a house in Herakleion. Student of British School, Hartley, caught in the act. Has been ascertained that director Payne, to whom the finds were secretly announced, involved in operation. More details in letter. Ephor Marinatos.[2]

The case was taken up by the newspaper *Eleuthera Skepsis* on 27 March 1930. As may be gathered from Dilys Powell's account, the newspaper's tone was nationalistic and the British School was accused of illegal handling of antiquities, perhaps with the intention of exporting them from Greece. This was a serious affair, and the British Consul in Herakleion, Mr Eliadi, interfered. The incident was about to become a diplomatic disaster, as Pendlebury himself narrates to his father in a letter dated 31 March 1930.

My time this week has largely been taken up with an unfortunate incident (this by the way is strictly confidential). Payne and I went to see some vases in a house in Candia. They were proto Geometric and as Miss Hartley is engaged on such work, we went down to photograph them. While doing so she was interrupted by the police bursting in and confiscating the vases. The owners were arrested and so was the chauffeur who had taken us to see them.

Payne has left for Athens. But I later received a very rude and insulting letter from the Director of the Museum, who next day caused to be published in the paper a long article accusing the British School of wishing and trying to buy the vases and of dealing on a vast scale.

Having already been to the police and told them there was no question of buying or selling, I was furious and on the advice of our consul I sent the whole correspondence to Payne, telling him that I demanded an apology and I expected he would too. He will, I expect, take them not only to the Ministry of Archaeology, but also to the British Legation. This is not the first time Marinatos has gone out of his way to be insulting to us. He has been in Germany and is utterly γερμανόφρων.[3] He had to apologize to Evans and Payne last year and I think with the evidence I and the consul have collected, he is about done for the high jump.

The matter is resting till we get the word from Payne except that the accused men have written to the papers saying that the vases were found years ago and were taken immediately to the *makarites*[4] Xanthoudides who pronounced them valueless and gave them back to the owners as he did not want them to have been sitting out in the light of day for anyone to see. It is amazing how the cases seem to be tried in the paper before they come up in court. Anyhow I am out for my pound of flesh and blood and intend to demand a full apology to be published by the little tick in all the papers.[5]

The letter clearly expresses Pendlebury's sentiments. Things became exacerbated when another Herakleion newspaper, *Anorthosis*, which was not well disposed towards Marinatos and which rivalled the other newspaper, *Eleuthera Skepsis*, took up the cause of the British. On 30 March 1930 it published the testimony of the Cretan chauffeur of the British School, a man by the name of Myron Samaritakis, who said that the entire incident was a misunderstanding by the police. He had been arrested as an accomplice, but he was innocent because he had openly informed the guard of the museum about the vases. How could he have been a thief, he writes? Blame lay with an overzealous policeman who had followed him and made assumptions without proof. The same policeman had misinformed Marinatos, creating the impression that he and the British had been thieves.[6] It was all about nothing, for the vases were not valuable.

The Director of the Archaeological Service, Konstantine Kourouniotis, realized the seriousness of the situation and instantly advised Marinatos to use cryptic language in the future.[7] Payne complained to the Minister of Education, Georgios Papandreou, the same man who later became Prime Minister of Greece.[8] Papandreou personally reprimanded Marinatos in a letter sent to his official address at the Herakleion Museum.

As regards the incident of the confiscation of ancient vases in the house of Myron Manioudakis and the involvement of the British Archaeological School in this affair, as you describe it in your report of 29 March, the director of the British Archaeological School Mr Payne has sent us a copy of your two letters to him and Mr Pendlebury.

Having examined this affair on the basis of your reports and letters about the foreigners [xenous], we are convinced that your behaviour in this matter was not correct and that you have saddened and offended without reason your foreign colleagues.

Whereas in your letter to Mr Payne you assure him that you did not think that the British School intended to buy the antiquities, in your report to us you accuse the British School of photographing the antiquities with the possible purpose of buying them. And whereas in your letter to Mr Payne you confess that the antiquities were voluminous and (with one exception) without decoration and much originality and without much value, in your report towards us we discern a tendency towards exaggerating the importance of the confiscated vases.

And in your letter to Mr Pendlebury you accuse him and
members of the British School that they had been engaged in
illegal excavations and that the police knew much more about
this than they imagined.

We are truly sorry about all the above and we do not wish to
take any official measures against your action because we
believe that the reason for your rash behaviour was only
excessive zeal. Still, we hope that this sad event will be the last
cause for complaint by foreign guests [*xenoi*] towards you.

The minister, George Papandreou[9]

The reprimand of George Papandreou offended Marinatos and so
he offered his resignation instantly. It was not accepted. In the end,
Marinatos compromised and apologized to Payne and Pendlebury
officially.

The relationship of Marinatos and Pendlebury underwent a
transformation after that incident. Next, we find that they became
very good colleagues. In 1933, when Pendlebury had a problem at
Knossos with locals, Marinatos rushed to his aid and did it an
exemplary fashion which Pendlebury appreciated.

The occasion was this. An unruly man from the district of Lasithi
by the name of Mathioudakis claimed proprietary rights on the land
of the House of the Frescoes. The Greek law was too complex for
Pendlebury – at that time curator of Knossos – to understand but
Marinatos dealt more adeptly with local affairs and threatened to
prosecute the Lasithiote perpetrator. Pendlebury writes to Payne in
Athens:

The mad Lasithiote who bought the rest of the field in which
the House of the Frescoes has been prosecuted by Marinatos for
damaging that house. Legal proceedings interminable.
Marinatos, who is very helpful says ʼετρόμαξα απέναντι
του νόμου. Ο Νόμος είναι λαβύρινθος' [i.e. I was
perplexed by the labyrinthine complexity of the law]. He [i.e.
Marinatos] is very affable and will take all possible measures.

He says we have 3 things to choose from and will act out according to our instructions.

1. He will have a sale of the ground and we can buy it.
2. He can prosecute the Lasithiote for illegal possession, dispossess him and we can buy it from the government.
3. We can give it up to him.[10]

The point is you see that it was the property of a Turkish bey. After the expulsion of the Turks the Lasithiote Mathioudakis, bid highest ground and paid a deposit.[11] Meanwhile Evans had dug the House of Frescoes and, no one knowing who the owner was, had paid 5,000dr. to the lawyers. Though the Lasithiote got a claim on it yet by the fact of Evans digging it, it became archaeological ground and our property although we haven't a *symbolaion* [i.e. contract] for it, only a receipt for the lawyers. Manolaki[12] reckons it will cost 25–30 pounds. To my mind it most certainly ought to be bought, not only to save trouble in the future but because it will be one of the first places to dig.[13]

By 1935–6 Marinatos and Pendlebury developed a close scholarly collaboration and mutual trust as Pendlebury began exploring the Lasithi area. Marinatos lent his British colleague his own experienced foreman Ioannis Meliaras for the dig of the Trapeza Cave and promised him an exclusive spot at the Herakleion Museum for the display of his finds.[14] Then he asked Pendlebury to train his assistant Christos Petrou in excavation methods.[15] This token of respect meant a lot to Pendlebury, who wrote to his father that he deeply appreciated the 'compliment, kindness and respect' of Marinatos.[16] He added that Petrou was a good lad but he wanted a kick on the behind to make him turn up in time for the dig.[17]

On 18 May 1936, Pendlebury writes to Marinatos from Tzermiado, Lasithi:

Tzermiado
18/5/36

Dear Dr. Marinatos,

I am writing to tell you that today I went with one of the χωροφύλακες [policemen][18] at the request of the Stathmarchis to see some antiquities which had been found while they were making the road above Mesa Lasithi, fragments of Larnakes, some bones, a bronze pin and a small clay cup had been found. As far as I could see they belonged to the Geometric Period – but I am very ignorant of that and I should not like to say so definitely. The objects are now in the house of the schoolmaster of Mesa Lasith and strict orders have been given that if anything else is found you are to be informed at once. I may add that there are also a few Late Minoan III sherds by the metokhi of Tzermiado (also on the road) and a pithos burial further up at Palaiomandra.

I expect and hope that we shall see you soon. There was such a crowd last time that we didn't get a chance to talk. Meanwhile there are two things I wanted to ask you.

1. As you know the School at Athens is having an exhibition in London this summer. I wondered if it would be possible to get casts of our figurines.[19] I know that Zakhari is very busy and I shall absolutely understand if it cannot be done.[20]

2. In view of the new type of pottery and figurines here we are hoping to continue our explorations next year. Can you tell me whether it is still possible to get a 'dokimastic' permit for several sites, as Professor Hurtley used to in Macedonia.[21] Our new type of pottery seems to be Early Minoan I and it seems important to try and find the settlement to which the burial belongs. This may be on the Kastellos nearby – but the only sherds I can find there are Minoan. Can you tell me whether I could apply through the British School for a 'dokimastic' permit at the Kastellos, at Psychro, at Agiou Georgiou Papoura and Karphi?

We shall finish the dig very soon. In two or three days (though we shall stay at least a week after). Since you came we found very fine Egyptian scarab (XIIth Dynasty), a unique head in ivory (I believe Sumerian) and a number of γαλόπετρες.[22] Also we have at last found an undisturbed stratum.

With best wishes from us all.

Yours sincerely

John Pendlebury

When Pendlebury excavated the shrine of Karphi and found a set of clay goddess statues, he immediately sent his Greek colleague pictures and offered him the opportunity to publish them first (Marinatos had excavated a shrine at Gazi in 1937 and had found similar goddesses). Marinatos did not accept out of courtesy but mentioned the offer with gratitude in his report of the finds of Gazi.[23]

By 1938 Marinatos had left Crete and had become General Director of Greek Antiquities. He strongly encouraged Pendlebury to continue his excavations at Lasithi and sent a request to the president of the Lasithi district asking him to facilitate Pendlebury in all possible ways. The document was signed by Christos Petrou in Marinatos's absence.[24] Dilys Powell, wife of Humfry Payne, wrote in her memoirs that Marinatos was at that time on the best of terms with the British explorers, and apparently ventured to extend their permit on his own authority to include not only Tzermiado but the whole of Lasithi.[25]

John Pendlebury was shot by the Germans during the invasion of Crete in 1941.[26] His death was regarded as an act of martyrdom by Marinatos.

APPENDIX 4

LETTER OF SPYRIDON MARINATOS TO HUMFRY PAYNE

This letter, sent by Marinatos to the Director of the British School at Athens (1929–36), Humfry Payne, is from the archives of the 23rd Ephoreia at Herakleion. It is a carbon copy of the typed original that may still exist in the archives of Humfry Payne (Dilys Powell cites it in 1973).[1] It is an important document because it testifies to the complex relationship between Greek and British archaeologists at Knossos in the interwar period.

Marinatos was accused by Payne of having dug in secret the Geometric Tombs of Fortetsa, a district which was under the jurisdiction of British excavators. Payne also blamed him for preparing a report about the finds for the German periodical *Archäologischer Anzeiger*. Payne finally reprimanded Marinatos for having known about the existence of the tombs without notifying him.

Marinatos offers an apology and recognizes that there has been a misunderstanding. At the same time, he asserts the rights of Greek ephors to rescue and publish material found in their district in a preliminary fashion. He lays blame on the Cretan foreman of Evans at Knossos, Manolis (or Manolaki) Akoumianakis and says that his habit was to plant seeds of dissension. This is an interesting point of view since Akoumianakis is traditionally viewed as a true hero of Crete, especially since he was shot by the Germans during the battle of Crete (but see the sarcastic comment made by Eccles, Appendix 2.3).[2] Some additional evidence about Marinatos's opinion of Akoumianakis has been found by Theodoros Eliopoulos, who examined the correspondence between Marinatos and the middle-school teacher of Lasithi, Mavroeidis.[3]

By 1935, the year when Evans visited Knossos for the last time, the relations between the British School and the Greek ephor were utterly cordial. Some resentment may have remained in Payne's heart, however. This may be inferred from the fact that his wife, Dilys Powell, quotes this very letter in her memoirs, *The Villa Ariadne*, 40 years after the event. She does not mention Marinatos by name, but she ascribes the following quotation to 'a Greek archaeologist': 'Because we are a poor and oppressed nation, you know you can trample on us'.[4] Payne, she writes, was a true philhellene, and the comment of the Greek archaeologist was unfair. The quotation, however, is not accurate when compared to what Marinatos actually said (see below), because the latter did not intend to accuse, but to plead for more collaboration and respect to the Greeks.

When Payne died suddenly in 1936, Marinatos wrote a warm letter of sympathy to Dilys Powell and she wrote back that she was touched.[5]

Given the tensions between the Greeks and British in the interwar period, it is interesting to note that British intellectuals, following the path first opened by Sir Arthur Evans, bestowed great honours upon Marinatos in the last decade of his life. Just a few years before his death, he was elected corresponding member of the British Academy. The President of the Academy, Sir Denys Page, happened to be at Akrotiri, Thera in October 1974, when Marinatos breathed his last and practically expired in Page's arms. Page delivered the funeral speech for his colleague at the small church of Akrotiri in October 1974 and named him the greatest archaeologist of the twentieth century.

Sp. Marinatos to Humfry Payne
Herakleion 19 June 1933

Dear Friend, Mr. Director,

Upon my return last Sunday from Rhethymnon, where I had been on duty, I found your letter dated 14th of June. Perhaps you cannot even imagine what sorrow it caused me. Even so, I thought it is necessary to address the present letter to you because I wish to dispel any future misunderstanding between us.

I consider it a grave offence to the integrity of my character that you accuse me of having known about the Fortetsa tombs already last spring and of having concealed this fact from you. I only learned about the tombs in February; they were found by Mr. Platon, and he announced the news to me in Kephallonia by official letter; a similar one was sent to the Ministry of Education of which I enclose the copy of the Museum archives. Please return it when you have read it so that I can put it back to its place.

I am compelled to furnish you with this proof because obviously the 'other source' which supplied you with all the false information is no other than the terrible Manoli whose character you are still very far from understanding.[6] Since 30 years he plants seeds of dissention in the service,[7] and having managed (as he never ought to have) to win the limitless good will of Mr. Evans, he has created innumerable incidents. Several times the blessed Joseph Hatzidakis and Xanthoudides had asked Mr. Evans to remove this man from Knossos and Evans would answer that he would gladly do this only he would do it later. For the time being [Evans would say] Manolis kept notes about all the find-spots at Knossos and he [Evans] found this very useful. I assume that if you remove this man from your entourage as soon as his years of service are over, it would be a great thing because everybody except you, his superiors, know well what kind of a person he is.

It is also my opinion that the present circumstances give you the opportunity to investigate and learn the truth because when you arrive the day after tomorrow you may ask the other people at Knossos as well as the owner of the field;[8] he will be invited by me to testify (under oath if necessary) whether he had found the tombs before and had concealed the fact from us. In any case, you may rest assured about one matter which I assert in the most categorical fashion: we were informed about the matter in February for the very first time. Of course, I realized the importance of the finds only after I returned to Crete[9] and could go on the spot; at that time I notified you immediately and repeatedly. I believe that my behaviour has been beyond reproach in every way and did not deserve such suspiciousness on your part which is due to 'that other source', malicious and false, whichever it is. Why would I ever conceal that find from you? Do you really think that I am in need of another excavation and especially at Knossos which has been granted to your School? I have so many theoretical studies in the making, that I undertake new excavations only with the greatest reluctance and only when I am absolutely compelled to do so. I also assure you that if I had not happened to return from Kephallonia a little indisposed, I would have undertaken myself the cleaning up of this tomb and then I would have unhesitatingly asked you to publish the finds. But because Mr. Platon happened to begin this dig, and I could sense his enthusiasm, and because this is his first dig, I suggested that you publish the finds together. Of course, Mr. Platon's contribution would have been confined to the find circumstances and his observations relating to this matter. Neither would Mr. Platon be in a position to reflect on the interpretation of the finds, nor could our journals supply the funds for proper illustrations. For this reason, the collaboration of Mr. Platon would not have deprived our science of the British School's publication; on the other hand, such collaboration would have been very encouraging to Mr. Platon in his first steps. I am so sorry that you do not seem to be sharing these views, as I can judge from your silence on this matter of my proposal.

This much regarding your suspicion that I concealed the finds from you on purpose. As regards the second, and most important part of your letter, I have to confess that you charge me with a type of duty that I am not able to understand. In other words, you are of the opinion that the privileges of the British School forbid the local ephor from treading in your district! I think differently.[10] For me the

privilege entails only that other foreign Schools are kept from
[excavating] in your district. No law prescribes that Greek
archaeologists ought to abstain from treading on these zones of
privilege. And although Greek archaeologists actually abstain from
doing this, they do this only out of voluntary courtesy. Only on very
special occasions has there been a transgression of this custom as in
Strato of Akarnania[11] where Mr. Orlandos worked and then
published the temple since it had been abandoned by the French for
thirty years. On account of this matter they insulted him, called him
unworthy of his profession and I do not know what else.

I let you to be the judge of who is to blame in the above case. And I
am of the opinion that it is indeed outrageous that foreign schools
believe that we [Greek ephors] do not have the right to interfere in
cases of rescue excavations because it is our duty to save antiquities
from destruction, and this is exactly the case of Knossos. I also think
that if the [Greek] excavators want to publish finds in [their own
district], they may do so. In the present occasion I believe I have done
my duty and beyond.

You therefore realize how shocked I am by your own conception of
the matter, namely that I ought to have asked your permission before
writing a few words in *Archäologischer Anzeiger*. Let me, however, offer
an explanation anyway.

This matter was not contrived on purpose but by chance. Because
Dr. Karo asked me to personally write the *Fundbericht*[12] on Crete I
could not refuse to do my professor this small favour. I am surprised
that you think that a few pages and photographs of five pots (among
the 500), as well as some incomplete sketches of metal blades – made
by Mr. Platon without claim to scientific accuracy – constitute a real
publication.

But the most important issue is our difference regarding the
conception of the whole affair. If you like, we could pose the question
officially to the Ministry of Education and this would solve the
problem of the rights of the Greek ephor as regards small finds in the
zones of the foreign archaeological schools once and for all. A similar
problem arose with Mr. Pernier, when two years ago some significant
pithoi with reliefs of the 7th century were found close to the palace of

Phaistos. Mr. Pernier had the impression that he had the right to publish them and I wrote that I granted them gladly [as a courtesy] but that he did not have 'a right' since they were found by a peasant and I had excavated them. He accepted this immediately and so we reached an agreement. However, on another occasion, the Italians went so far as to request that Xanthoudides be deposed because he dared excavate the tombs at Kalyvia (found in the midst of winter) which, if he had not done, would have led to the looting of the tombs.

What I am trying to say with all this is that, as I think, we Greeks do what we can to please our foreign guests. When I visited Europe (I have not yet been to England) I did not witness any particular accommodation made to my person by my foreign colleagues. At the Louvre, I did not manage to get free entrance, nor was I permitted to photograph two insignificant ancient objects. I had much the same experience in Copenhagen; in Germany things were better by a small measure.

Of course we are a poor and weak nation and for this reason we must swallow many bitter pills. But even though this happens regularly in politics, I do not think it has a place in scholarly affairs where we all are one big family working towards the same ideals.[13] I have taken great offence, first because you gave greater credibility to the report of one of your unworthy servants than to my word, and second because you believe I ought to have requested your permission to write a simple *Fundbericht* when asked by one of your colleagues. I hasten to add that at the request of Mr. Veminion [?] from Algiers I have sent him a smaller report as well. I have not sent him pictures from Knossos but only because the vases were not ready yet. Such matters,[14] which many of my other Greek colleagues avoid, are burdensome but I thought and still think now that I better serve our science this way. On the personal level I serve foreign colleagues to whom I am attached. I was very far from imagining that this would cause displeasure. I believe it is a mutual misunderstanding between us. Note as well, that I keep Mr. Evans informed by letters and pictures about every find in Crete. I think this is a sign of my absolute willingness to be accommodating. But I too have my weaknesses, if so they may be called, and they are my propensity at taking offence[15] and a tendency to observe rules that my predecessors neglected. This led to one fatal misunderstanding with the British School, the School of a man such as Evans, whom I admire and love above all others. I hope that our misunderstandings will be resolved for good and I am ready to do everything towards this goal. Perhaps it will be difficult for you to think similarly since you believed – even for a moment – that I was not sincere. And for this reason, I hope that you will try to find out the exact truth. While expecting your answer, I hope you will receive the expression of my most friendly sentiments,

SpM.

APPENDIX 5

LETTERS OF PRIEST NIKOLAOS POLLAKES TO SPYRIDON MARINATOS AND HIS WIFE MARIA EVANGELIDOU

Nikolaos Pollakes was the priest of the Fortetsa district and doubling also as a teacher. He was the man who brought the Ring of Minos to the Museum of Herakleion in 1930. Marinatos suspected that the man was an illegal dealer of antiquities and therefore reported him to the police. The priest here protests his innocence.

— 1 —

Letter of Priest Nikolaos Pollakes to Maria Evangelidou[1]

To the most honourable Mrs Maria Sp. Marinatos, Teacher
Fortetsa/Herakleion, 20 July 1931

Honourable Mrs Maria Sp. Marinatos,

I am good friends with your much respected husband; for this reason I mention both your names during the holy service: [I say] 'for God's mercy, your life, health, and salvation of Spyros and Maria, their parents and relatives'.

Two months ago [your husband] turned against me in a hard way seeking to destroy me and did not hesitate to send me to court on the charges of stealing antiquities; I was investigated there yesterday. My large family and I are grieving terribly. I am innocent in every respect. Yet, there is no doubt that if one in power has the will, he can cause a great deal of harm to the weak.

My [priestly] office is the highest one. Nevertheless I beseech you to not inflict misfortune on me. Do advise your husband to withdraw his accusation from the court where I have never been sent because he may damage my health and life. If he insists to damage me and insult God, who is most high, whom I serve, he will suffer even more than Oedipus because the latter committed evil deeds in ignorance, whereas the former commits evil in full knowledge. Let him fear Divine Justice. But youth does not consider such matters! Respect my office, my age, large family. If you save me from the present danger, be certain, noble lady, that I shall be always the most fervent intermediary between you and God.

I expect a positive answer as soon as possible because if you are late, I shall write to him himself.

With high respect,
Father Nikolaos G. Pollakes

— 2 —

Father Nikolaos G. Pollakes to Spyridon Marinatos

Fortetsa/Herakleion, 20 July 1931

Dear Sir,

Your position is high but my own vocation is the highest of all. In this capacity I command you and entreat you

a) to reinstate our mutual friendship or love when you piously addressed me as 'Monseigneur, Monseigneur', [I was in such terms] with your predecessors I. Hatziddakis, S. Xanthoudides and F. Stavropoulos.

Stop taking actions against me; instantly withdraw your accusation against me; do not take me to court, a place where I have never been before. Desist from causing sorrows to my numerous family members, relatives and my parish. Nowadays, our advanced civilization does not allow the strong to harm the weak. My parish has taken the initiative to appoint a lawyer for my defence, and I shall appoint some more {lawyers}. But stop this unholy war, and rest assured that I shall always be your most ardent mediator towards God.

With high respect,

Yours truly,

Priest Nikolaos Pollakes

NOTES

Foreword

1. Cf. Fotiadis 2006, 5–27.
2. Alexiou 2000, 561–3. Translated from the Greek by N. Marinatos.
3. In addition to her frequent use of personal correspondence we much welcome the use of another particularly valuable source, probably to an extent unique in the field. This is the citation of reports published in Greek newspapers (many today obscure); usually these reports were written by the excavators themselves, or by educated and knowledgeable journalists.
4. For the influence of the ideas of Lubbock in particular see Harlan 2011, 210–30. Harlan emphasizes the evolutionist perspective of Evans but shows clearly his willingness to modify his views as new evidence became available; she also demonstrates how Evans's model of the associations of ancestors with stones, based on funerary architecture and megaliths, directly influenced the thinking in 'The Mycenaean Tree and Pillar Cult' (1901).
5. Marinatos was kind enough to receive me, simply a doctoral research student at the British School at Athens, in his house in Athens on 24 June 1964, and to converse on current topics in Minoan archaeology.
6. In Zervos 1956, 509–12. We note how his scheme is in fact more Evansian than that of Evans himself, with its division into three periods, Proto-, Neo- and Post-palatial, each of these divided into three subperiods and each of these latter 100 years long.
7. A foreword is a welcoming introduction to a book, not a review of it. Nevertheless I cannot resist the temptation, in this single instance, of confirming my different view from that of Nanno. I continue to accept the reliability of the reported find circumstances and consider the depiction of a standing figure (probably divine) using a steering oar *unique until the Theran ship fresco was found many years later* by Marinatos himself, to be crucial.

The steersman (or helmsman) on every ship on the fresco can only be at the stern of his vessel, facing the direction of travel, like the figure on the ring. The latter cannot therefore be a structural mistake.

8. See Dimopoulou and Rethemiotakis 2004 for the special exhibition of the ring in the Herakleion Museum after its dramatic reappearance.
9. Dimopoulou and Rethemiotakis 2004, Figs 13 and 22.
10. Lebessi, Muhly and Papasavvas 2004, 1–31.
11. Momigliano 1999, 147 Fig. 39 shows Mackenzie taking very careful measurements on the site.

Preface

1. 'A nuisance to the young scholars he had vowed to assist': MacGillivray 2000, 305. By contrast Myres 1941, 960 says that, 'he welcomed the notions and projects of the younger men'.
2. MacGillivray 2000, see text in jacket and 6. Following this trend, Gere 2009, 1–13, also implies that Evans's method is intuitive rather than scientific. This does not take into account the enormous task of classification of pottery and artefacts that Evans achieved.
3. See for example Blakolmer forthcoming.

Introduction

1. Evans, J. 1943, 380.
2. Evans, J. 1943, 305, 390.
3. Evans, J. 1943, 392–4, discusses her brother's artistic tastes.
4. Candy 1984, 27; Powell 1973, 39. This condition of Evans's night-blindness explains why in 1924 he needed the aid of a boy to cross Hyde Park after dark, a fact that has been curiously interpreted as evidence of secret homosexual tendencies by MacGillivray 2000, 281 (*The Times*, 4 February 1924). However, even superficial research in the newspapers of the period reveals that police arrests were frequent and often made without any basis. The police were urged by the Bishop of London to make arrests in order to purify society morals. The latter declared with some pride in 1923 that ten nights of observation had disclosed 746 cases of impropriety, indecency or immorality ('Hyde Park Morals, Protest by Bishop of London', *The Times*, 30 August 1923). Clearly, the police were instructed to make arrests. For MacGillivray's biography see the critical review by Warren 2001.
5. Piet de Jong to John Myres. Evans Archive, Ashmolean Museum, Oxford, in Momigliano 1999, 208.
6. Powell 1973, 42.

7. Powell 1973, 88.
8. Bowra 1966, 247–8.
9. Momigliano 1999, 210.
10. Hood 1998; Papadopoulos 2007.
11. Powell 1973, 44.
12. Powell 1973, 44.
13. Powell 1973, 44; MacGillivray 2000, 290.
14. See also Myres 1941, 959.
15. Candy 1984, 29.
16. Candy 1984, 15.
17. Myres 1941, 960.
18. Evans, J. 1943, 390.
19. Marinatos, Sp. 1964, 600–6 and Myres 1941, 960.
20. The dating has now been revised. Although Evans's arguments have not been taken into account, Wace's method of dating has been subjected to criticism; see Cavanagh and Mee 1999.
21. Evans PM III, 192–202.
22. Wace 1949, 119–31.
23. Marinatos, Sp. 1963, 185. Translated by N. Marinatos.
24. Cited by Blakolmer forthcoming.
25. For a thorough discussion and comparisons see Palyvou 2003.
26. The latter are depicted on a procession fresco from the building Xeste 4.
27. See Chapters 3–4.
28. Sp. Marinatos, notes 1973 (in my possession). Translated by N. Marinatos.
29. Evans PM IV, 1018.
30. Myres 1941, 960.
31. Some scholars (most recently Gere 2009, 123–9) rightly stress the psychological impact of the loss of a mother on a child. But I doubt that Evans created his scholarly work (e.g. the mother-goddess) to compensate for this loss. For the mother-goddess see Chapter 4.
32. For the stabilizing effect of solid value systems on the personality see Horney 1945, 23–33.
33. Darwin, F. 2000. The excerpts are taken from pp. 55 and 40.

Chapter 1   Tree and Pillar Cult

1. August (Greek translation 2009), 655–788.
2. Herod. 2.50.2 (reflecting Hecateaus). See Hoeck 1823–8.
3. On the term 'Minoan', see MacGillivray 2000, 84, 134–5; Karadimas and Momigliano 2004.
4. See the masterful discussion by Hall 2007, 41–59, which questions the methodology of the mytho-historical method.

5. Schliemann 1878, 149, 207, 291–2.
6. Marinatos, N. 2010, 186–96.
7. Evans 1912, 290. The claim of MacGillivray that Evans reconstructs Minoan history on the basis of legend is unsustainable: MacGillivray 2000, 84–5, 135–6.
8. Evans 1912, 277.
9. For the history of ideas concerning savagery and progress in Greek myth see Graf 1993, 9–34.
10. MacGillivray 2000, 70 and 200–10.
11. Darwin 1989, 40.
12. Darwin Correspondence Database: http://www.darwinproject.ac.uk/entry-2503 (accessed 3 September 2012).
13. Murray 1925, 2: http://www.sacred-texts.com/cla/fsgr/fsgr05.htm.
14. Harrison 1912 (second edn, 1927), ix, xiii.
15. President of Hellenic Society. Cited by Evans 1912, 277.
16. Evans 1936, 1. For an argument about the existence of Minoan literature see Evans 1912, 290.
17. Evans 1912, 277.
18. Evans 1936, 7.
19. Evans, J. 1943, 106; Darwin Correspondence Database: http://www.darwinproject.ac.uk/entry-3510 (accessed 2 September 2012); Owen 2008, 206–30.
20. Tylor 1871.
21. Darwin to A. R. Wallace, 22 September 1885 (accessed: http://www.darwinproject.ac.uk/entry-4896. http://www.darwinproject.ac.uk/entry-4896#backmark-4896.f7.)
22. See, for example, Darwin 1989 (*Emotion in Man and Animals*), 256, 259; (*Descent of Man*), 96, 106, 130, 162, 164, 203.
23. Tylor 1871, Preface to the second edn, v. 1, vii.
24. Evans, J. 1943, 160.
25. 'Presentation of Dr. A. J. Evans's Portrait to Oxford,' *The Times*, 9 December 1907; Evans, J. 1943, 284.
26. E. B. Tylor, 'Savages', *The Times*, 17 September 1888. See also Harlan 2010, 210–30.
27. Darwin 1874, chs. IV–V, pp. 10–65, argues that the ape-like ancestors of man had sympathy for their fellows and that this was the basis for their cohesion and morality. The latter was also the basis of civilization.
28. Tylor 1871, v. 2, 360–1.
29. Darwin 1989 (*Descent of Man*), 73: 'The Fuegians rank among the lowest barbarians; but I was continually struck with surprise how closely the three natives aboard the H. M. S. *Beagle* who had lived some years in England, and could talk a little English, resemble us in disposition and in most of our mental faculties'.
30. Tylor 1871, v. 1, 406–502.
31. Darwin 1989 (*Descent of Man*), 106.

32. Tylor 1871, v. 2, 215–27. For tree cult in the Greek *Hymn to Aphrodite* see Tylor 1871, 219. For the discourse on animism and a new definition (but not rejection of it) see Harvey 2006, 1–29. He claims that the old animism theory is not as objective as the discourse of modern scholarship requires, but he recognizes the legitimacy of the theory and speaks of new animism.
33. Haas 1982, 115–17 with Fig. 29; Mettinger 1995, 129–30 with references.
34. Mettinger 1995, 130.
35. Pardee 2009, 51–71. I thank David Sloan from the Oriental Institute, University of Chicago for valuable discussion on the stele.
36. Evans 1901, 106–7.
37. Evans 1901, 105, n. 5.
38. Evans 1901, 123.
39. Tylor 1871, v. 1, 1–10.
40. Evans 1901, 170.
41. Robertson Smith 1894 (repr. 2005), 201–6. Tree worship is integrated in the discussion of sacred stones.
42. Robertson Smith 1894 (repr. 2005), 197. See Judges, 9.37; Gen., 25.8.
43. See Evans 1901, 153–6, with Figs 30–34. Compare with Robertson Smith 1894 (repr. 2005), 197.
44. Robertson Smith 1894 (repr. 2005), 204–8. The term *baetyl* is used also by A. B. Cook in his *Zeus* to designate the stone swallowed by Kronos. Note, however, that Cook's book appears much later than Evans's article and that the inspiration may be due to Evans: Cook 1914, xii; 464–549.
45. Tylor writes: 'the curious passage in Sanchoniathon which speaks of the heaven-god forming the *baetyls*, animated stones (theos Ouranos Baitylia, *empsychous lithous mexanesamenos*) perhaps refers to meteorites or supposed thunderbolts fallen from clouds': Tylor 1871, v. 2, 166.
46. Marinatos, N. 2009a, 73–80.
47. For example, Tylor notes how solar festivals are manifested in a variety of societies, from Ancient Egypt to Polynesia, Africa, Rome and Christian lands, even though these religions are historically unconnected: 1871, v. 1, 285–9.
48. Evans 1901, 171.
49. 2 Chron. 3:15 NSRV.
50. Evans 1901, 144–5.
51. See the perceptive analysis of Harlan 2011 which demonstrates the indebtedness of Evans to both Tylor and Lubbock. She discusses Evans's unpublished monument on the megalithic monuments of Britain where the latter showed an interest in understanding pillar cult.
52. See Mylonas 1966, 149, n. 56 and now Vasilikou (Βασιλικού) 2011, 208.
53. Evans 1901, 108.
54. Evans 1901, 170.
55. Evans 1901, 108.
56. Evans 1901, 108.
57. Chapter 4.

58. Marinatos, N. 2009b, 22–8.
59. Schliemann 1878, 402–7.
60. Tsountas (Τσούντας) 1893, 157. Translated by N. Marinatos.
61. Tsountas (Τσούντας) 1893, 160–1.
62. Mylonas 1966, 150.
63. Evans, J. 1943, 99; Gere 2009, 135.
64. Candy 1984, 26–7.
65. John van Wyhe (ed.) 2002, *The Complete Work of Charles Darwin Online* (http://darwin-online.org.uk/), Notebook N (1838–9), CUL-DAR 126.

Chapter 2   Mourning Kybele: Arthur Evans and James Frazer

1. See Harrison 1912 (second edn, 1927), Chapters 11–12. For an assessment of her work see Beard 2000.
2. I have found only a few such designations: Evans PM III, 458. It is a common view that Evans was a follower of Bachofen's theory of matriarchy (Lapatin 2002, 71–3, 104, 174; Gere 2009, 123, 135). It is true that Evans would have read Bachofen, but the theory did not interest him much.
3. Evans 1901, 167. Although Evans toys with the idea that the young god may be the goddess's son, he decides that he is her consort in 1901. It must be stressed, however, that he does not suggest *that the god is both lover and son at the same time*.
4. Evans, 'Fresh Discoveries in the Palace of Knossos,' *The Times*, 28 May 1901. See also PM III, 463, where he prefers to call her Rhea. Kybele in 'Tree and Pillar Cult' is also called a mother (167) in her capacity as protectress of the city.
5. Graf 2004, 3–16; Burkert 2000.
6. Evans 1901, 168.
7. Evans 1901, 108, 130.
8. Tylor 1871, v. 2, 265, 270–3.
9. For the iconography of Near Eastern gods of this type see now Cornelius 1994, 235–63.
10. Evans 1901, 119.
11. Evans 1901, 121.
12. Evans 1901, 120.
13. Hepding 1903, which explores the relation of Attis to the great mother.
14. Fraser, R. 1994, xlviii.
15. Eller 2012, 75–88, mistakenly assumes that Evans was influenced by Frazer.
16. Evans 1901, 177–8. Mylonas 1966, 153, notes that there is no evidence that this posture connotes mourning.
17. Evans PM I, 432 with n. 1.

18. Evans 1901, 178.
19. Evans PM III, 142.
20. Goodison 2009, 51–7; Marinatos, N. 2010, 86–102.
21. Popham 1974, 195–257, with Fig. 14D. For an interpretation of all the related scenes as prophecy rituals see Goodison 2009, 51–7; Marinatos, N. 2010, 86–102.
22. The legacy of vegetation cults was established by Axel Persson rather than Evans. This model dominates post-war scholarship; see Alexiou 1976, 90; Dimopoulou and Rethemiotakis 2004.
23. Tylor 1871, v. 2, 410.
24. Robertson Smith 1894, 356–61.
25. Frazer 1922, Chapters 24, 52.
26. The citations are from the abridged 1922 edition (which is, of course, much later than 'Tree and Pillar Cult'). Frazer 1922, 487.
27. Frazer 1922, 264–74. For a discussion of Frazer and Christianity, see Robert Fraser's Introduction in Frazer (ed. Fraser) 1994, xxiv. See also Fraser 1990, 209.
28. Frazer 1922, 479. For a criticism of allegorical interpretation of myth and ritual, see Burkert 1979.
29. Frazer 1922, 316–27 and 335–7. In the original version of 1894, see v. 1, 278–300.
30. Lucian, *Dea Syria* 6–8.
31. Frazer 1922, 339.
32. Frazer 1922, 345.
33. Harrison 1903, 451.
34. Harrison 1912 (second edn, 1927), 160.
35. Harrison 1912 (second edn, 1927), 118–211.
36. Most recently by Eller 2012, 75–98.
37. Evans 1901, 128.
38. Frazer 1922, 332.
39. Evans, J. 1943, 389. The lectures were published two years later, Evans 1932.
40. Evans 1932, 248–88.
41. Evans 1901, 128; Evans PM III, 473, n. 3.
42. Evans 1932, 283.
43. Marinatos, Sp. 1974, 36.
44. Marinatos, N. 1993, 203–10.
45. Van Gennep 1960.
46. Harrison 1912.
47. For example Vernant 1984; Vernant 1995; Vidal-Naquet, 1986.
48. For references see Vlachopoulos 2007, 107–17.
49. For the sufferings of Isis and her son (they even mutually injure one another) see the story of Horus and Seth in Simpson 2003, 91–103, esp. 98.

Chapter 3   The Whirligig of Time: The Narrative of the Palace of Minos

1. Evans PM I, i.
2. For the popularity of this model and its effect on the general public see for example, 'Mental Anthropology. Sir James Frazer on Study of Uncivilized Races', *The Times*, 5 November 1921; MacGillivray 2000, 200. Nektarios Karadimas writes: 'they [i.e. German archaeologists of the Göttingen School] made extensive use of notions of growth, maturity, and decadence – notions that formed an important part of Evans's own Minoan chronology' (forthcoming MS, kindly given to me by Dr Karadimas).
3. Evans, PM IV, 944.
4. Evans, 'Further Discoveries at Knossos', *The Times*, 5 June 1903.
5. Karadimas and Momigliano 2004, 243–58; Karadimas forthcoming.
6. MacGillivray 2000, 69, describes the framework of Evans's thought as follows: 'Human history was charted as a linear evolutionary process beginning with a primitive stage of hunting and gathering, which was called "savagery", followed by the early farming stage, called "barbarism", until "civilization" was indicated by the use of writing'. This is a serious oversimplification of Evans's scheme.
7. Evans PM I, 191–201, 286–300.
8. Evans PM II, viii.
9. Owen 2008, 216–17.
10. Darwin 1989 (*Voyage of the Beagle*), 211.
11. Evans PM II, vii.
12. Evans PM I, 30–55.
13. Evans PM II, 1–21.
14. Evans PM II, 22–92, see esp. 46, Figs. 21–24. Throughout, Evans acknowledges his indebtedness to the work of the Greek ephor Stephanos Xanthoudides. The Libyan connection is rejected today although it was revised by Spyridon Marinatos who thought that Akrotiri in Thera had connections with Libya (Marinatos 1974).
15. Evans PM II, 564.
16. Evans PM II, 54–5, 258, 260–1.
17. Evans PM I, 15. See now Aruz 2008, 91–100.
18. Evans PM II, 253–66, 493–4.
19. A more sophisticated version of this model is found in C. Renfrew, *Emergence of Civilization* (1972). Significant contributions have been made to the understanding of Minoan religion by Warren 1990 and 1998, especially as regards *baetyl* cult.
20. Evans PM II, 267.
21. Evans PM I, 271–85.
22. Evans PM II, viii.
23. Evans PM II, 571.

24. Evans PM II, 277.
25. Evans PM II, 569–71.
26. Evans PM II, 439, 467.
27. Evans PM II, ix; see also 563–4.
28. Evans PM II, 562.
29. Evans PM II, 569. See also 466–7.
30. For the Minoan king as a priest-king modelled on the divine kingship of Egypt, see Evans PM II, 276, 773; PM IV, 988. For Frazer's version of the priest-king as a savage, see Frazer (ed. Fraser) 1994, 22–5. For the misunderstanding that Evans was indebted to the Frazer model, see Lapatin 2002, 81, who rightly stresses that Evans's model is the pharaoh but overstresses the notion that the young god was the goddess's consort. See also Gere 2009, 124.
31. Gere 2009, 115.
32. Evans PM II, 570.
33. Gibbon 1952, 50.
34. Evans PM II, 564.
35. Evans PM II, 571.
36. Evans PM III, 92–4. Some scholars are now sceptical about identifying ethnicity in Aegean art: Blakolmer 2011.
37. Evans PM III, 92–8.
38. Evans PM III, 98.
39. Darwin 1989 (*Voyage of the Beagle*), 203.
40. Evans PM III, 103–5.
41. MacGillivray 2000, 4–9; Gere 2009, 117–23.
42. For a critical assessment of MacGillivray 2000 see Warren's review (Warren 2001, 912–15).
43. Warren 2000, 208.
44. Evans PM II, 353; PM IV, 872.
45. Evans asked John Pendlebury to examine the sherds of the Temple Tomb and was informed that not a single one dated to the Late Minoan I B phase: Evans PM IV, 989 n. 1, 878, 988–9. This means that the Royal Temple Tomb remained in ruins for years until it was reoccupied in LMIII IA 1.
46. Marinatos, Sp. 1939, 425–39. See also Appendix 2.
47. Evans PM IV, xxii, 669. See also PM II, xiv.
48. Evans PM IV, 853–71.
49. Karo 1930–3, 345.
50. Evans PM IV, 987.
51. Evans PM IV, 987.
52. Evans PM IV, 944.
53. Evans PM IV, 322.
54. Evans PM IV, xxiii.
55. MacGillivray 2000, 272–5.
56. Evans PM V, 884–8.
57. Karo 1930–3, 344–5.

58. Evans PM II, 321–2.
59. Evans PM II, 322.
60. Darwin 1989 (first published 1839), 230.
61. Darwin 1989 (*Voyage of the Beagle*), 358, 366, 372–7.
62. Evans, 'Serbia in Danger', *The Times*, 30 October 1915; 'After Serbia, Montenegro', *The Times*, 13 January 1916; 'Montenegro Unsubdued', *The Times*, 25 January 1916; 'Kossovo Day', *The Times*, 28 June 1916; 'The French Fleet at Ragusa', *The Times,* 13 October 1914.
63. Evans, 'King Constantine and Venizelos. A Last Chance', *The Times*, 4 November 1916. See also MacGillivray 2000, 260.
64. Evans, 'The End of a Dynasty', *The Times*, 20 January 1916.
65. Frazer 1922, 328.
66. Evans, 'The Sixth Campaign at Knossos,' *The Times*, 31 October 1905; PM IV, 1018.
67. Darwin 1989, 125–6, 132–150. For the social struggle for existence see 143.
68. Shakespeare, *Twelfth Night*, Act 5, Scene 1, 372–8.
69. Evans PM IV, 1018.

Chapter 4   Monotheism

1. Fr. 67: Kirk, Raven and Schofield 2006, 190. The fragment reads: 'god is day night, winter summer, war peace, satiety hunger …'
2. Evans PM I, 514–15.
3. Eller 2012, 76 correctly writes that: 'the story of the Great Mother and the Boy God did not reach its full flower until Evans wrote his magnum opus on the Minoan excavations, *The Palace of Minos* (1921)'.
4. It is interesting though that already in 1901, Evans considers the possibility that the relationship of goddess to god may be that of a mother to a son rather than a wife to consort (Evans 1901, 168).
5. For the sacred nature of lilies and their hybridization as lily-waz see Evans PM II, 473, 476–9.
6. Marinatos, N. 2010, 122–3, 133.
7. For the merging of double axe with sacred knot, see Evans PM I, 432. For the goddess as a mother and queen of the underworld simultaneously see Evans PM I, 514–15.
8. Evans PM III, 457.
9. Evans 1913–14, 52–3, Fig. 70.
10. Evans 1913–14, 40, Fig. 52.
11. Evans PM I, 440–1. See also Evans 1913–14, 54.
12. 'Mr. Arthur Evans On Cnossos', *The Times*, 25 November 1903.
13. Additional snake goddesses saw the light of day in excavations. One was found in the Little Palace by Evans himself; others were found in minor shrines of later periods. See Evans PM II, 540, Fig. 344.

14. Evans PM I, 510.
15. In Egypt the divine cow is related to the night-sky goddess Nut. For a discussion of the iconography and conceptual framework of the Egyptian afterlife see Hornung 1999, 112–35; Wilkinson 2003, 140–5.
16. Evans PM I, 516.
17. Evans PM I, 514–15.
18. Evans PM I, 513. For the cross as a symbol of Babylonian Shamash see Collon 1987, 58–9, Figs 238–9. See also Nilsson 1950 (first edn, 1927), 416–25.
19. Evans PM I, 517.
20. Evans PM II, 335–44, esp. 339.
21. Evans PM I, 508.
22. Evans PM I, 508.
23. Evans 1932, 286.
24. Evans 1901, 176.
25. Evans PM III, 464.
26. Evans 1932, 287.
27. Evans PM III, 476.
28. Evans 1932, 287.
29. Evans PM II, 277.
30. Evans PM III, 144–5.
31. Lapatin 2002, 66–87.
32. Gere 2009, 79–81.
33. See Evans 1928. For the ivories see Lapatin 2002, 66–175. For the gold rings, see Chapters 5–6.
34. Assmann 2004, 17–31.
35. Evans PM II, 277; see also the title page of PM III.
36. Evans PM III, 155–6.
37. Tylor 1871, v. 2, 355–61.
38. Tylor 1871, v. 2, 361.
39. Breasted 1912, 165–98; 312–43.
40. Breasted 1912, 43, 318. Even today Egyptologists find the term henotheism useful: see Hornung 1982, 24–6, 236–7.
41. James Henry Breasted, 'The New Crusade' (1927–8): http://www.historians.org/info/aha_history/jhbreasted.htm.
42. Nilsson 1927, 335–6; for the citation, see Nilsson 1950, 390.
43. Nilsson 1927, 339–40.
44. Nilsson 1927 contradicts himself. He asserts on the one hand that the connections between Crete and Egypt are striking, more so than he ever realized at first, and yet further along he says that, 'all this is far from proving that Egyptian influence was the foundation of Cretan art and religion' (p. 9).
45. Nilsson 1927, 10.
46. Nilsson 1950, Figs 166–7, 175–6.
47. Nilsson 1927, 185–93.
48. Evans 1932, 254.

49. Evans PM III, 457–8 with notes.
50. Nock 1927, 297–8.
51. Hogarth 1908, 141–8.
52. Marinatos, Sp. 1937b, 290; idem 1941, 129–36; idem 1976, 26–9.
53. Platon, N. 1971, 260–1.
54. Alexiou 1976, 87–8.
55. Alexiou 1958, 268. Translated by N. Marinatos.
56. Persson 1942, 25–87.
57. Persson 1942, 89–90, follows Frazer's conceptual scheme and suspects that savage mutilations were imposed on the worshippers of the goddess.
58. Frazer (ed. Fraser) 1994, 111 (abbreviated version 1920, 142–5). See also Persson 1942, 147.
59. Picard 1948, 76, 81, 108–9, 111.
60. Picard 1948, 161.
61. Guthrie 1950, 54, intimates that the relationship between the prehistoric Mistress and the Master of Animals was one of sacred marriage (*hieros gamos*). It is not clear why he comes to this conclusion. Evans repeatedly wrote that there was nothing in art that indicated a sexual relationship between the two.
62. Sakellarakis, J. and E. 1991, 137–56.
63. See Brown 1993, 81–90.
64. Renfrew 1985, 11–26.
65. Dickinson 1994, 259. For more recent critical assessments see Goodison and Morris 1998, 113–32.
66. D'Agata and van de Moortel 2009, 1–8.

Chapter 5   The Ring of Nestor

1. For a discussion of Evans's acceptance of forgeries, see Lapatin 2002; Gere 2009, 132–9. The Ring of Nestor is considered genuine by Sakellarakis 1973, 303–18; Pini 1981, 135–58; idem 1987, 441–55; idem 1988, 1–13; Boardman in CMS VI 2, 448–50 with bibl. One must admit that the battered condition of the hoop argues for its authenticity, as suggested by Pini. However, against its authenticity we have the convincing arguments of Sakellariou 1994, 93–106.
2. On the two Gilliérons, father and son, see Stürmer 1994.
3. Stürmer 1994; Lapatin 2002, 120–1.
4. Marinatos to S. Xanthoudides, 27 June 1928. Sp. Marinatos archives, Gennadius Library, Athens.
5. Karo 1959, 111.
6. Nilsson 1927, 549–57.
7. Marinatos to Xanthoudides, 14 July 1928. Sp. Marinatos archives, Gennadius Library, Athens. Nilsson's first edition of *Minoan-Mycenaean Religion* had just appeared in 1927.

8. Bossert 1937, 9. Translated by N. Marinatos.
9. Evans PM III, 145. See also Lapatin 2002, 157.
10. Evans, Knossos notebook 42, pp. 82–3 (Box 10), Ashmolean Museum, Oxford.
11. Evans PM I, 707, Fig. 531.
12. Evans, J. 1943, 377.
13. Evans 1925, 46. For full bibliography and the view that the ring is genuine, see Boardman in CMS VI 2, 448–9.
14. Evans 1925, 46.
15. Evans PM III, 145. See also Lapatin 2002, 157.
16. Evans 1925, 46. (Italics added.)
17. Evans PM III, 145; Lapatin 2002, 157.
18. Evans 1925, 48–50.
19. Evans 1901, 162.
20. For funerary scenes on papyri see Faulkner 1995, 51.
21. Sir Wallis Budge edited and translated this papyrus before World War I and provided interpretation and illustrations. See Budge 1966.
22. Karo 1930–3, 304.
23. It should be noted here that despite the many criticisms that Evans's reconstruction of the priest-king has received, iconographical evidence that fully supports it has emerged. A god or prince is shown in a landscape of plants together with a griffin or sphinx. See Poursat 1977, v. ii, pl. xxxi and esp. xxxvii. Alexiou 1969, 429–35, published a Cretan seal which shows a robust divine figure holding a galloping griffin on the leash.
24. 'Crete and the Nile Valley. Sir Arthur Evans on the Knossos Finds', *The Times*, 12 December 1923.
25. Evans 1925, 48–50. See also notes 13–14.
26. Evans 1925, 50.
27. Evans 1925, 51, n. 18. Evans refers to the tales recorded by Jacob Grimm, *Deutsche Mythologie* (1878).
28. Evans PM III, 154.
29. Evans, PM III, 157.
30. See the excellent discussion in Fraser (ed.) 1994, xxi.
31. Frazer 1922, 159–61, 661, 665, 701–11.
32. 'The Golden Bough, No Mistletoe at Kew', *The Times*, 31 December 1920.
33. The allusion here is to Casaubon's ambition to write a key to all mythologies in George Eliott's *Middlemarch*.
34. Edith Eccles to Sir Arthur Evans, 23 November 1935. I owe a copy of this letter to Nicoletta Momigliano who has kindly sent it to me.
35. Lapatin 2002, 120–39.
36. Betts 1981, 34.
37. Grafton 1990, 40–1, in his study of forgeries suggests that personal ambition rather than money is often the motive.
38. Karo 1930–3, 304.
39. Karo 1959, 111.

Chapter 6   The Ring of Minos

1. Karo 1959, 41.
2. Evans PM IV, 948.
3. Marinatos to Xanthoudides, 27 June 1928. Sp. Marinatos archives, Gennadius Library, Athens. Translated by N. Marinatos.
4. Nilsson's first edition of *Minoan-Mycenaean Religion* had just appeared in which forged objects were included.
5. Marinatos to Xanthoudides, 14 July 1928. Sp. Marinatos archives, Gennadius Library, Athens. Translated by N. Marinatos.
6. Lapatin 2002, 91–119.
7. Marinatos to Xanthoudides, 14 July 1928. Sp. Marinatos archives, Gennadius Library, Athens. Translated by N. Marinatos. See also Evans PM III, 219, Fig. 151; Boardman in CMS VI 2, 520–1 believes the Archanes ring to be genuine (with bibl.). Evans had two copies made of the Archanes ring and took them to Oxford: MacGillivray 2000, 190. See also the review of MacGillivray's book by Trail 2001.
8. The Archanes ring was eventually donated by Evans to the Ashmolean Museum, Oxford. See Boardman in CMS VI 2, 520–1.
9. This is suggested by a petition Pollakes made to the Greek Ephor of Antiquities in 1900. Archives of the twenty-third Ephoreia of Crete, 1 March 1900. I owe this information to G. Tzorakis.
10. Platon, N. 1984, 67–8. This fact is reproduced in the Cretan press: *Patris*, 24 December 1999 (http://www.patris.gr/archive/99/12/24/; http://www.greeka.com/news/news/307.htm; http://www.stigmes.gr/br/brpages/articles/minosring.htm; http://madamepickwickartblog.com/2011/01/gold-rings-in-a-cretan-dark-age/.) See also Warren 1987, 486.
11. Dimopoulou and Rethemiotakis 2004, 8–10.
12. I have obtained a copy of the entry through the kindness of Dr I. Galanakis of the Ashmolean Museum. Attention to the entry was drawn by my friend Peter Warren.
13. Dr I. Galanakis kindly sent me this information. He correctly observes to me that Evans refers here secretly to 'Νοτια of Παλατι' ('south of the Palace') rather than to the north of the Palace.
14. Warren 1987, 486.
15. Platon, N. 1984, 65–70.
16. Warren 1987, 486–7.
17. This may be inferred from the remarks of Marinatos, Sp. 1976, 101, n. 19.
18. Evans PM IV, 947–8. Evans could not have described details of the hoop if he had not seen the original.
19. Herakleion, archives of twenty-third Ephoreia. Document signed by Gilliéron on official letterhead of the Ephoreia, dated 26 June 1930. The story is thus more complicated than what is presented by Dimopoulou and Rethemiotakis 2004, 8–10, who do not mention that the ring was sent to Athens for evaluation.

20. Herakleion, archives of twenty-third Ephoreia, no. 1160/5-11-30.
21. Herakleion, archives of the twenty-third Ephoreia, no. 71082/3295. The decision of the council to reject the ring is dated 29 November 1930.
22. Evans PM IV, 947, n. 1.
23. For a recent account of the find circumstances see Dimopoulou and Rethemiotakis 2004.
24. Evans PM IV, 951.
25. Evans PM IV, 951.
26. Ring impression from Hagia Triada (CMS II, 6, 20). See also CMS VS.1A, 138. Warren 1987, 491, has noted the peculiarity of the boat on the Minos ring. See also Jung 1989. In general see the discussions of authenticity in Persson 1942, 101; Nilsson 1950, 42–3; Warren 1987, 485–500; Pini 1987, 449; Dimopoulou and Rethemiotakis 2004.
27. Evans PM II, 250.
28. Karo 1959, 41–42. Translated from the German by N. Marinatos. See also MacGillivray 2000, 284, whose translation differs slightly from mine.
29. N. Platon to Sp. Marinatos, 30 November 1938. Sp. Marinatos archives, Archaeological Society at Athens. Translated by N. Marinatos.
30. N. Platon to Sp. Marinatos, 30 November 1938. Sp. Marinatos archives, Archaeological Society at Athens. Translated by N. Marinatos.
31. Ch. Petrou to Sp. Marinatos, 29 November 1938. Sp. Marinatos archives, Archaeological Society at Athens. Translated by N. Marinatos.
32. An anonymous letter sent to Marinatos on 27 January 1939 contains the information that Kefalogiannis was involved in illegal operations. Sp. Marinatos archives, Archaeological Society at Athens.
33. Sp. Marinatos to N. Platon. Letter courtesy of Lefteris Platon. Translated by N. Marinatos.
34. Evans to Marinatos. Sp. Marinatos archives in possession of N. Marinatos. See Appendix 1.1.

Chapter 7   The Final Years: Evans's Restorations and his Vision of Knossos

1. Krischen and Tischer 1921. The book was in the library of Spyridon Marinatos and was probably bought by him in Germany in 1925. It is now a rare item.
2. Evans PM II, 790–2, Fig. 516.
3. Evans PM II, 790.
4. Evans did not believe that the breasts of Minoan women were always exposed and suggests they were covered by a thin gauze. The evidence is clear on certain of the miniature frescoes from the Palace: see PM III, 59.
5. Evans PM III, 56.
6. Evans PM III, 49; see also PM IV, 27.

7. Evans PM III, 58.
8. Evans PM III, 52.
9. Evans PM III, vii.
10. Waugh 1930, 137.
11. For pictures and description of the early stages of the restorations see Brown 1983 and Lapatin 2002, 120–39. For an eloquent defence of the restorations see Warren 2000, 203: 'much of what he found in the East Wing, above all the truly magnificent Minoan engineering achievement of the Grand Staircase, actually existed, but in a collapsed, crushed state. It would have been irresponsible indeed simply to have removed the remains from the site and not to have reconstituted the collapsed but actual floors and flights of stairs back into their original positions.'
12. Lapatin 2002, 126–34, offers an eminently readable account of the various stages of the experiments in the East and West wings and the involvement of the two Gilliérons, father and son.
13. For this I have the testimony of the civil engineer of the University of Thessaloniki, Eleutheria Tsakanika. She has made the study of Evans's restorations the subject of her doctoral thesis and found very few mistakes (except for the case of a few pillars). She has commented on the remarkable scientific accuracy of the works. See also the similar conclusions reached by Blakolmer 2008, 103–16.
14. Hilda Pendlebury to Herbert Pendlebury, 28 April 1929. British School at Athens archives, Hilda Pendlebury Letters, 351–441.
15. Sp. Marinatos to Ministry of Education, 16 May 1929. Herakleion, archives of twenty-third Ephoreia, no. 797/894. Translated by N. Marinatos. For a pictorial record of the restorations, see Brown 1983, 37–84. For comments see Lapatin 2002, 120–39; Gere 2009, 105–10. For dates, see Evans, J. 1943, 380.
16. He means in the Queen's Megaron.
17. Sp. Marinatos to Ministry of Education, 16 May 1929 (as above, n. 15). Translated by N. Marinatos.
18. Sp. Marinatos to Ministry of Education, 31 May 1929. Herakleion, archives of twenty-third Ephoreia, no. 811/908. See also the thorough collection of documents by Tsipopoulou 2010, 339–52.
19. Evans PM IV, 5.
20. Evans PM IV, 944.
21. Momigliano 1999, 129.
22. Evans PM II, 315–16.
23. Powell 1973, 45–6.
24. 'Halls of Priest-King's Palace, Restorations of Upper Storeys at Knossos', *The Times*, 10 December 1926; Evans PM II, 350–3.
25. Sp. Marinatos to Ministry, 8 March 1930. Herakleion, archives of twenty-third Ephoreia. Translated by N. Marinatos.
26. Evans to Marinatos, 3 April 1930. Sp. Marinatos archives in possession of N. Marinatos. See Appendix 1.1.

27. See the pictures of the early restorations at Knossos in Brown 1983, pl. 27.

28. Lapatin 2002, 127; Gere 2009, 109.

29. Evans PM IV, 925, 928. Criticisms of Evans concerning the restoration of the throne room have been voiced by all his recent biographers: MacGillivray 2000, 293–4; Lapatin 2002, 121–6; Gere 2009, 107–9.

30. Palyvou 1995; Palyvou 2003.

31. Kostas Ouranis, 'The ancient palace of Knossos' ('Τα αρχαία ανάκτορα της Κνωσού'), Proia, May 5, 1933. Translated by N. Marinatos.

32. Sp. Marinatos, Eleuthera Skepsis, June 1933 (exact date unknown).

33. Eleuthera Skepsis, June 1933.

34. Sp. Marinatos, 'The Italian Restorations at the Palace of Phaistos' ('Αι Ιταλικαί αναστηλώσεις εις το ανάκτορον της Φαιστού'), Eleutheron Bema, 25 July 1934.

35. Karo 1959, 18. See also letter of Karo to H. Payne, 13 December 1929. Archives of the British School at Athens. Knossos, year 1929. Translated from German by N. Marinatos.

36. See Tzorakis 2014, 121–55.

37. 'Earthquake in Crete. Four Lives Lost', The Times, 26 February 1935.

38. 'Earthquake in Crete. Four Lives Lost', The Times, 26 February 1935.

39. Sp. Marinatos to Mme S. Goekoop, 18 March 1935. Sp. Marinatos archives in possession of N. Marinatos.

40. Evans, 'Inexhaustible Crete', The Times, 29 July 1935.

41. Sp. Marinatos to Evans, Herakleion, 20 November 1935. Appendix 1.6. The letter was written in English and has some mistakes in English idiom.

42. Newspaper Anorthosis, 21 February 1930.

43. Sp. Marinatos to Evans, 12 December 1935. See Appendix 1 for full letter (in the possession of N. Marinatos).

44. See the testimony of Mackenzie about Kalokairinos trespassing on the property of Evans at Knossos in Momigliano 1999, 192, 196; Lapatin 2002, 42–3, 47.

45. Evans to Sp. Marinatos, December 1935 (undated). See Appendix 1.7 (in the possession of N. Marinatos).

46. For a full report on the struggles of Marinatos for the new museum, see Tzorakis 2014, 121–55.

47. Newspaper Drasis, 18 February 1939.

48. Evans's preface to Pendlebury 1933 (reprinted 1954), 8.

49. Sp. Marinatos to Mme S. Goekoop, 20 November 1945. Sp. Marinatos archives (in possession of N. Marinatos). For the policy of the Archaeological Service see Petrakos 1994, 87–116.

Chapter 8   Sir Arthur Evans and Spyridon Marinatos

1. Marinatos to Xanthoudides, 27 June 1928. Sp. Marinatos archives, Gennadius Library, Athens.

2. Evans, J. 1943, 384.
3. This episode is also referred to by Grundon 2007, 122–7.
4. Archives of the British School at Athens, Knossos correspondence of 1929. Translated from Greek by N. Marinatos.
5. A biblical reference to Christ's bitter cup, namely crucifixion.
6. Sp. Marinatos to Evans. British School at Athens Archives. Woodward files, Knossos correspondence, 1929. Translated by N. Marinatos.
7. Konstantine Kourouniotis was the Director of the Greek Archaeological Service.
8. Woodward to Evans, 25 June 1929. British School at Athens Archives. Knossos correspondence, 1929.
9. John Pendlebury to Herbert Pendlebury, 31 March 1930. British School at Athens Archives, Knossos correspondence 1930. Letter no. 1488.
10. See Appendix 4 for full letter.
11. Candy 1984, 30.
12. Candy 1984, 30.
13. Greek for 'foreman'.
14. Greek word for 'trial dig'.
15. Greek for 'permit'.
16. Telegram of Evans to Woodward, Archives of the British School at Athens. Woodward files, Knossos correspondence, 1929.
17. Evans, J. 1943, 255.
18. Momigliano 1999, 208–10.
19. Sp. Marinatos, 'Excavations at Knossos' ('αι ανασκαφαί της Κνωσού'), *Eleuthera Skepis*, 8 May 1931.
20. Evans, 'Temple-Tomb of Crete. The Gold Ring of Minos', *The Times*, 13 July 1931; 'The Temple Tomb at Knossos, Sir A. Evans on Recent Discoveries', *The Times*, 20 November 1931.
21. MacGillivray 2000, 298. He cleverly contrasts Evans's report with Pendlebury's insinuating that the former was not reliable whereas the latter was. But Marinatos's reports confirm Evans's suggestions to the full.
22. Pendlebury 1933 (reprinted 1954), 72.
23. Evans PM IV, 969–71. See also Chapter 4.
24. Evans PM IV, 994–5.
25. Evans PM IV, 974, 978, Fig. 937.
26. Sp. Marinatos, 'Excavations at Knossos' ('αι ανασκαφαί της Κνωσού'), *Eleuthera Skepis*, 8 May 1931.
27. Pendlebury 1933 (reprinted 1954), 72: 'it was probable that the original coffin was of wood...'
28. Evans PM IV, 1008–18.
29. Evans PM IV, 1002.
30. Sp. Marinatos 1974, pls 49, 77b.
31. Tsipopoulou 2010, 339–52.
32. He is referring here to the House of the High Priest.

33. Archives of the Ministry of Culture, 25946. 29 April 1931. Courtesy Metaxia Tsipopoulou. Translated from Greek by N. Marinatos.
34. Archives of the Ministry of Culture, 25946. 7 July 1931. Courtesy Metaxia Tsipopoulou. Translated by N. Marinatos.
35. MacGillivray 2000, 297–8.
36. Grundon 2007, 143. As Grundon shows (p. 126) Evans and Pendlebury sulked at each other occasionally but had mutual respect for each other as well.
37. Pendlebury 1939, 194–5. See also Grundon 2007, 142.
38. For the letters see Appendix 1.
39. Sp. Marinatos, 'Amnisos to Epineion tou Minoos', *Eleutheron Bema*, 20 April 1932.
40. Appendix 1.2.
41. Evans 1901, 16.
42. For an example of modern scepticism, see Gere 2009, 122.
43. Evans PM IV, xi.
44. Cameron, in Morgan 2005, col. pl. I.
45. Marinatos, Sp. 1940/41, 130–6.
46. Evans PM IV, xi. See also Marinatos, Sp. 1940/41.
47. It was reported to me personally in 2009.
48. For the friendship between Marinatos and Eccles see Appendix 2.
49. Marinatos, Sp. 1939, 425–39. For more information see Appendix 2.
50. Marinatos, Sp. 1935, 212.
51. Approximately USD 150.
52. Marinatos to Suzanne Goekoop, 21 November 1934. Sp. Marinatos archives in possession of N. Marinatos. Translated from French by N. Marinatos.
53. See Appendix 1.5.
54. 'Minoan Axes Found in Crete, New Hieroglyphic Lettering', *The Times*, 29 June 1935.
55. 'Inexhaustible Crete', *The Times*, 29 July 1935.
56. Marinatos, Sp. 1935, 196–220 esp. 196–211; Marinatos, Sp. 1937a, 222–43.
57. Marinatos, Sp. 1935, 203–12; Marinatos, Sp. 1936.
58. Herakleion, archives of twenty-third Ephoreia.
59. Evans, 'A New Find in Crete. Earliest Temple of Hellenic Age', *The Times*, 20 November 1935. See also Evans, 'Hellenic Age Temple; the Bronze-Plated Images', *The Times*, 7 December 1935.
60. Appendix 1.6.
61. Evans, 'A New Find in Crete. Earliest Temple of Hellenic Age', *The Times*, 20 November 1935.
62. Evans, 'A New Find in Crete. Earliest Temple of Hellenic Age', *The Times*, 20 November 1935.
63. Evans, 'A New Find in Crete. Earliest Temple of Hellenic Age', *The Times*, 20 November 1935.

Chapter 9   The Last Visit of Evans to Crete

1. Programme published by the newspaper *Ide*, 13 April 1935. See also Evans, J. 1943, 392. Evans's half-sister was not an eyewitness of the event but met him later in Athens. She reports about the laurel wreath being carried back home.
2. Archives of twenty-third Ephoreia no. 11/62/1212. 10 December 1930.
3. Newspaper *Ide*, 13 April 1935.
4. *Ide*, 13 April 1935.
5. *Ide*, 13 April 1935.
6. The number of people is estimated by Powell 1973, 56–7, based on what Dr Stylianos Giamalakis (a friend of Marinatos and a famous doctor in Crete) told her in an interview.
7. Reported by Powell 1973, 56.
8. Grundon 2007, 188.
9. Cited by Powell 1973, 96.
10. Evans uses this expression in the preface to PM IV, xiii.
11. The speech was published in summary form in the Herakleion newspaper *Ide*, 16 April 1935.
12. MacGillivray 2000, 191–9, speaks of Evans's mythical history; see also Hamilakis 2002, 2–28; Hamilakis and Momigliano 2006; Gere 2009, 75–95.
13. PM IV, 888. It is worth mentioning that Gibbon believed that the best form of government was monarchy if it was not absolute and if it was governed by virtue and wisdom. Gibbon 1952 (ed. Saunders, repr. 1985), 107.
14. Evans, J. 1943, 350. This remark has been discussed by Lesley Fitton (Fitton 1996, 115), who argues that Evans projected his own tastes on Minoan art. I find this argument unsustainable because the critic may be as much subjected to preconceived notions and tastes as the one whom he criticizes. Thus, the argument becomes circular.
15. Arthur Evans to Sir John Evans. Cited by Evans, J. 1943, 305.
16. Evans PM III, 153.
17. The wording of this poem is echoed by Evans's own words as his sister records them in Evans, J. 1943, 304, but, as she does not cite the above verses in full, they cannot be authenticated. They are derived from http://knowledgeweb.tk/Arthur_Evans.
18. Momigliano 1999, 132.
19. Evans, J. 1943, 94.
20. Mackenzie to Karo in Momigliano 1999, 204.
21. Evans PM IV, vii–viii.
22. Evans PM IV, viii.
23. Momigliano 1999, 139; Grundon 2009, 110–13.
24. Momigliano 1999, 136–42.

25. Evans PM IV, 880.
26. Candy 1984, 22–3.
27. Candy 1984, 23.
28. Candy 1984, 36.
29. Evans 1916, 134.
30. Evans PM IV, xii.
31. Archives of the British School at Athens. File of Duncan Mackenzie, 1929.
32. See Chapter 7.
33. Evans, 'The British Museum. Requisition Decided Upon', The Times, 2 January 1918. In this piece he urges that the British Museum not be requisitioned because it would give the Germans an excuse to bomb it.
34. Evans, 'German Terms Not Acceptable. General Repudiation. Foundations of Peace', The Times, 15 October 1918.
35. Karo 1922, 26.
36. Karo 1922, 29.
37. See the debate in The Times, 23 September 1916, 'The Neutrality of Greece. Indictment by M. Venizelos, "All The Agonies of a Disastrous War"'.
38. Karo 1922, 65.
39. Evans, J. 1943, 350. This remark has been discussed by Lesley Fitton (Fitton 1996, 115). He argues that Evans projected his own tastes on Minoan art. I find this argument unsustainable for reasons that have been explained in the Introduction and in n. 14 above.
40. Tzorakis 2010, 321–53.
41. Veremis and Koliopoulos 2010, 101–10.
42. For the position of Venizelos toward the King see Venizelos, 'M. Venizelos. A Reply to King Constantine. Special Statement to The Times', The Times, 11 December 1915.
43. Woodhouse 1968, 190–4; Veremis and Koliopoulos 2010, 101–10.
44. From notes taken by Sir John Myres at a lecture given by Arthur Evans on an unknown occasion. Evans, J. 1943, 366–7.
45. Cromer, R. M. Burrows, J. B. Bury, A. Evans, J. G. Frazer, F. G. Kenyon, W. Leap, G. A. Macmillan, W. M. Ramsay, W. Ridgeway, 'M. Venizelos and Great Britain', The Times, 16 December 1916.
46. Evans, 'King Constantine and Venizelos. A Last Chance', The Times, 4 November 1916.
47. 'Greek Revolt, Fighting in Athens, Insurgent Ships Bombed, Crete Held by Rebels, M. Venizelos and the Crisis', The Times, 4 March 1935.
48. Woodhouse 1968, 228–9. 'M. Venizelos Condemned to Death, Sentenced in Absence', The Times, 6 May 1935.
49. Marinatos to Mme Goekoop, 21 May 1935. Sp. Marinatos archives, Gennadius Library, Athens. Translated from French by N. Marinatos.
50. See Appendix 4.

51. Karo to Marinatos, 14 March 1935. Sp. Marinatos archives, Gennadius Library, Athens. Translated from German by N. Marinatos.
52. 'Strike Riots in Crete. A Revolutionary Threat, Order Quickly Restored', *The Times*, 6 August 1935.
53. Powell 1973, 96.
54. Thucydides 3.83.1. Translated from Ancient Greek by N. Marinatos.

Chapter 10 *Sunt Lacrimae rerum*: The War and the Death of Evans

1. Evans, J. 1943, 389.
2. Evans, J. 1943, 394, mentions that in the last years of his life he travelled to see paintings of the Old Masters in the Prado, Madrid.
3. Brendon 2007, 379–420.
4. Evans, J. 1943, 384–5.
5. Evans, J. 1943, 392.
6. Evans to Sp. Marinatos, 17 March 1936. Appendix 1.9.
7. Eccles to Sp. Marinatos, 9 September 1936. Appendix 2.8.
8. 'Discoveries in Greece. Burlington House Exhibition, Duke of Kent at Opening Ceremony', *The Times*, 14 October 1936.
9. Evans 1936, 1.
10. Evans 1936, 1–12.
11. Evans 1936, 7.
12. Woodhouse 1968, 230.
13. 'General Strike in Greece. Bloodshed at Salonika', *The Times*, 11 May 1936. See also 'Armed Revolt in Greece. Currant Growers' Violence, Martial Law Declared', *The Times*, 28 August 1936.
14. Sp. Marinatos to Mme Goekoop, 10 August 1936. Sp. Marinatos archives, in possession of N. Marinatos, Athens.
15. 'Communists and Strikes in Greece', *The Times*, 4 June 1936; 'Martial Law in Greece. Fear of Communist Revolt, Chamber Dissolved', *The Times*, 6 August 1936; 'Troubles in Greece', *The Times*, 6 August 1936. For a few modern assessments see Woodhouse 1968, 231–2; Close 1993. See in particular the introduction by Veremis in Higham and Veremis 1993, 1–22.
16. Eccles to Sp. Marinatos, 9 September 1936, Appendix 2.8.
17. Iatrides 1980, 149.
18. Iatrides 1980, 150. The letter is dated to 31 January 1939.
19. Iatrides 1980, 208.
20. Iatrides 1980, 183. Helmuth Karl Bernhard Graf von Moltke (26 October 1800 – 24 April 1891) was a general of the Prussian army who was often called Moltke the Great.

21. 'Dictatorship in Greece. Gen. Metaxas at the Helm', *The Times*, 21 May 1937.
22. Woodhouse 1968, 196.
23. Evans, J. 1943, 394. See also Evans, 'German Terms Not Acceptable. General Repudiation. Foundations of Peace', *The Times*, 15 October 1918.
24. Evans et al., 'Persecution of the Jews', *The Times*, 22 November 1938.
25. This information about Bessel Hagen's family is obtained from a letter Hagen sent to Sp. Marinatos 2 January 1933. Sp. Marinatos archives, Gennadius Library, Athens.
26. For Erich Bessel Hagen's life and his service to the Jewish community, see Segal 2003, 171, 199. The three letters that have survived in Sp. Marinatos's archives date to 22 January 1933, 1 March 1933 and 4 September 1936. It is clear that the correspondence between them was regular.
27. Bessel Hagen to Marinatos, 1 March 1933. Sp. Marinatos archives, Gennadius Library, Athens. Translated from German by N. Marinatos.
28. '*Zwang*'.
29. '*entsetzlich quälend*'.
30. Bessel Hagen to Sp. Marinatos, 10 September 1936. Sp. Marinatos archives, Gennadius Library, Athens. Translated from German by N. Marinatos.
31. Bessel Hagen to Sp. Marinatos, 24 September 1936. Sp. Marinatos archives, Gennadius Library, Athens. Translated from German by N. Marinatos.
32. Sp. Marinatos 1966, 73–4.
33. Davis 2009, 119–31.
34. This is shown by his letter to Mme Goekoop of 24 November 1939. See http://www.academia.edu/3433111/Letter_of_Spyridon_Marinatos_to_Mme_Goekoop_Holland_when_WWII_broke_out
35. Davis 2009, 32.
36. The FBI archives have now become declassified and I owe their discovery to my friend Jack Davis. Federal Bureau of Investigation: Declassified 9778084. In the files the informants are Mrs Elizabeth Hunt and John Franklin Daniel.
37. Davis 2009, 31.
38. Marinatos, Sp. 1966, 73.
39. Karo 1959, 22. The word I translate here as courage is '*Kampfbereit*', combat ready.
40. Evans, J. 1943, 305.
41. Evans, 'Nestor's Palace. Important Discoveries In Greece, Inscriptions of Thirteenth Century B.C.', *The Times*, 29 April 1939.
42. Evans, J. 1943, 393.
43. Archives of the Gennadius Library.
44. 'Minoan Jewels for the Ashmolean. Sir Arthur Evans's Gifts', *The Times*, 2 February 1939.
45. 'Last Homage to Metaxas. Funeral Ceremonies in Athens', *The Times*, 1 February 1941.
46. Grundon 2007, 304–18.
47. Bowra 1966, 247–8.

48. Grundon 2007, 319.
49. Evans, J. 1943, 389.
50. Evans, J. 1943, 395.
51. Powell 1973, 148.
52. Evans, J. 1943, 395.
53. Candy 1984, 81.
54. Karo 1959, 19.
55. Candy 1984, 81.
56. Karo 1959, 22.
57. 'Atrocities in Crete. Men Buried Alive by Germans', *The Times*, 15 October 1941.
58. For the effect of the occupation on Greece, see Mazower 1995.
59. 'Sir James Frazer. The Vision and the Tragedy', *The Times*, 16 May 1941.

Appendix 1 Letters between Sir Arthur Evans and Spyridon Marinatos

1. The excavation referred to here is most probably the tomb at Krasi. The issue here (for which Marinatos provides some evidence) is probably the stone method of constructing roofs.

2. Friedrich Karl von Duhn was Professor of Archaeology at the University of Heidelberg 1880–1920. Duhn's first volume *Italische Gräberkunde* appeared in 1924; the second volume appeared after his death. His broad knowledge of European archaeology made his judgement especially valuable to Evans. Among the scholars he influenced were Gerhard Rodenwaldt and Bernhard Schweitzer, both of whom were teachers of Marinatos in Berlin in the late 1920s. For more information on von Duhn, see http://www.dictionaryofarthistorians.org/duhnf.htm.

3. The earthquake referred to here is discussed in Chapter 7. It is interesting that Evans testifies to the unreliability of the Greek state, which due to the economic depression could not fulfil its promises.

4. This certainly refers to his thoughts on the Ring of Minos. Evans seems unaware that Marinatos believed it to be a forgery.

5. The preferred designation today is Minoan Hall.

6. i.e. photographs.

7. Evans was very dependent on the efficient collaboration of the Herakleion Museum to obtain casts of seals, which he could not inspect himself as he did not visit Crete again until 1935.

8. The first wife of Marinatos was Maria Evangelidou. They divorced in 1936 (see also reference to this by Eccles, Appendix 2.8). It seems that Evans had met the couple on a social occasion.

9. '*Mai*' is German for May. Marinatos's English was imperfect but his increasing intimacy with Evans emboldened him to write in English.

10. Evans had just been to Crete, had attended the excavations, had seen many of the finds and had helped financially.

11. The dimensions are not entered in this draft of the letter.

12. See Marinatos, Sp. 1962, 87–94.

13. Marinatos believed, like Evans, that several scripts were in existence in Crete at the same time.

14. Manolis Salustros (or Saloustros) was a conservator of the Herakleion Museum but was retired when the letter was written. Evans knew him well because he had employed him at Knossos. It is not known why he was so hostile to Marinatos nor why he was so opposed to the demolition of the old crumbling building. For details see Tzorakis 2014. In 1938, Salustros and Marinatos reconciled.

15. Marinatos excavated in Kephallonia during the summer every year from 1929 to 1934.

16. He refers to John Pendlebury's *A Handbook to the Palace of Minos at Knossos* (1933), which included a foreword by Evans.

17. We do not have this letter, which must have contained a full report about the finds from Dreros. See Marinatos, Sp. 1937a, 222–34.

18. The articles in *The Times* and *Manchester Guardian* were indeed published. See Chapter 8.

19. Marinatos is evidently thankful for the considerable publicity he received in the newspapers thanks to Evans. A Greek version of Evans's *Times* article had appeared in the newspaper *Eleutheron Bema*.

20. Evidently Marinatos agreed with Evans that the Cretan tradition was distinct from the mainland one. It has been argued that the Cretan tradition was influenced by Syrian architecture: Beyer 1976 and review by Coldstream 1981, 345–6.

21. i.e. oath.

22. He means methods of persuasion and threat mixed together.

23. i.e. spread rumours.

24. Coldstream 1981, 345–6, argues against Marinatos's dating and the designation of the Dreros statues as daedalic. He compares them with the closely related bronze figurines from Kato Syme. See also see Lebessi 1976.

Appendix 2   Letters between Edith Eccles and Spyridon Marinatos

1. Powell 1973 89; Momigliano: http://www.brown.edu/Research/Breaking_Ground/bios/Eccles_Edith.pdf; Grundon 2007, 174, 190.

2. *The Times*, 30 June 1977.

3. Evans PM IV, 963–4.

4. Marinatos, Sp. 1939, 433; Eccles 1939, 290–1.
5. Many references to Hutchinson in Grundon 2007, 178, 186–7, 191–2, 251–2, etc.
6. Marinatos, Sp. 1968, 12; Tzachili 2006, 155–87.
7. Evans refers to a Late Minoan I A vase: PM II, 473.
8. Newspaper Φωνή της Θήρας, 19 May 1935.
9. For a comparison of styles with special emphasis on Zakros see Platon, L. 2011a–b.
10. Platon, N. 1971, 265–330. For a recent assessment see his son Platon, L. 2011a–b.
11. *The Times*, 3 October 1974. The death was reported the day before: 'Archaeologist Killed on Site of Excavation', *The Times*, 2 October 1974.
12. Without a doubt.
13. With all your patience.
14. Eccles has here suspicions that some men stripped the museum of its valuables. See Chapter 8 for more details.
15. This is possibly the picture of Manolis Akoumianakis, found in Marinatos's archives in multiple copies, published here (Fig. 31).
16. This is Zacharias Kanakis, restorer of the Herakleion Museum and friend of Marinatos. See Fig. 33a.
17. i.e. Osios Loukas
18. Perhaps some day... The entire sentence speaks of the romantic feelings that Eccles had for Marinatos.
19. As is noted in Chapter 8, the people of Arkalochori stole objects from the cave. Most objects were returned voluntarily and those men were spared. But some others, who hid their treasures, were punished.
20. These are surely pictures of the Dreros statues (see Chapter 8).
21. Marinatos's first wife was Maria Evangelidou. The two had been having trouble for some years on account of Maria's mother who was living with them. The constant tensions resulted in divorce in 1936. Apparently Marinatos confided in Eccles that his wife had left him. The late Prof. Stylianos Alexiou told the present author that the mother-in-law had insulted Marinatos in public on one occasion in 1935.
22. She means the Boston Goddess (see Lapatin 1999), which she and Marinatos had evidently discussed as a forgery.
23. The restorer Zacharias Kanakis was executing the wishes of Evans for the exhibition and was gradually replacing Gilliéron because of his exceptional skill.
24. This sentence reflects the intellectual and emotional regard that Eccles felt for Marinatos. His excavations on his native island of Kephallonia had been ongoing from 1929 to 1934–5 until he got too involved in Cretan archaeology to have time to spare. The Kephallonia excavations were financed by Mme Suzanne Goekoop, a rich lady from Holland whose husband had been a patron of archaeology and had collaborated with Wilhelm Dörpfeld before his death. The correspondence between Mme Goekoop and Marinatos has been used as a

source of events for the present work because Marinatos wrote to his patroness regularly. As for Eccles, she was especially interested in the pottery recovered from Kephallonia because it belonged to Late Mycenaean phases which helped her better to understand transitions from Mycenaean to Geometric. The phrase 'it fell to my lot' is an allusion to her emotional attachment to Marinatos's beloved island.

25. Bernhard Schweitzer (1892–1966) was a famous German archaeologist particularly known for his work on the Greek Geometric pottery style. Schweitzer's father was Major Carl Georg Heinrich Schweitzer, a career soldier in the German infantry. He studied at the universities in Berlin, under Georg Loeschcke, and one of his fellow students was Georg Karo, who also studied with Loeschcke. He also studied under F. K. von Duhn. Both Karo and Schweitzer were Marinatos's teachers in Germany.

Schweitzer was a leading exponent of the *Strukturforschung* (structural research) school, a German theoretical art historical term attempting to replace the concept of style with a spatial structural analysis. It is noteworthy that there was an attempt to link this to cultural (and racial) identity. This school was followed later by Friedrich Matz. (See also http://www.dictionaryofarthistori ans.org/schweitzerb.htm)

26. Marinatos notes in red pencil on the margins 'NO'.
27. A type of ancient Greek wine-vessel.
28. On the margin with red pencil Marinatos notes 'Already LM II'.
29. Marinatos notes this passage with a red circle in the margins.
30. This refers to the building of the new Herakleion Museum (see Chapters 7–8).
31. In the next year Marinatos left his post in Herakleion to become Director of the Greek Archaeological Service. He may not have been in Crete in September 1937.
32. British School at Athens. For the exhibition see Chapter 10.
33. This is the one time that Eccles calls Marinatos by his first name. The post-war period must have brought some greater intimacy between them, whereas Marinatos's marriage to Aimilia Loverdos removed any romantic possibility and ensured a more relaxed relationship. The context suggests that she had seen his little baby Ourania (the present author).
34. Marinatos was made Head of the Greek Archaeological Service for the second time in 1955.

Appendix 3   The Relationship of John Pendlebury and Spyridon Marinatos

1. Powell 1973, 76.
2. Archives of twenty-third Ephoreia, no. 999/1132. Translated by N. Marinatos. See also Powell 1973, 76; Grundon 2007, 124, who reports the British side.
3. i.e. German-minded.

4. i.e. deceased.
5. Pendlebury to his father, 31 March 1930. British School at Athens archives.
6. Newspaper *Anorthosis*, 30 March 1930.
7. Archives of twenty-third Ephoreia, Herakleion, 20101/716, 28 March 1930.
8. Georgios Papandreou served three terms as Prime Minister of Greece (1944–5, 1963, 1964–5). He was also Deputy Prime Minister from 1950–2 in the governments of Nikolaos Plastiras and Sofoklis Venizelos and served numerous times as a Cabinet Minister. In 1930, when the aforementioned incident occurred, he was Minister of Education. His political career spanned more than five decades. His son Andreas Papandreou also became Prime Minister and so did his grandson, George Papandreou.
9. Archives of twenty-third Ephoreia, Herakleion, April 1930 (day unknown). Translated by N. Marinatos.
10. He means: we shall let the Greek Archaeological Service deal with the land in question.
11. Paid the highest price for the land.
12. Manolis Akoumianakis.
13. Pendlebury to Payne, 16 April 1933. Archives of the British School at Athens, correspondence of 1933.
14. Ioannis Meliaras had been trained by Marinatos in excavations and subsequently hired by him to be a guard in the Herakleion Museum.
15. Grundon 2007, 213.
16. Grundon 2007, 213.
17. Pendlebury to his father in Grundon 2007, 215.
18. Policemen.
19. He means the statuettes of clay goddesses found by Pendlebury at Karphi. See Grundon 2007, 216.
20. Zacharias Kanakis. The closeness between Zacharias Kanakis and Marinatos is shown also in the picture Fig. 43. Zacharias is the moustached man seated just to the right of Marinatos (viewer's perspective) holding a dish.
21. Pendlebury is careful to respect protocol, the breach of which induced Marinatos to clash with Evans in 1929 (see Chapter 8).
22. White 'milk stones'. This is how locals referred to Minoan seal-stones.
23. Marinatos, Sp. 1937b, 291; Grundon 2007, 216.
24. Archives of twenty-third Ephoreia, 324/369, 8 December 1938.
25. Powell 1973, 99.
26. Grundon 2007, 319–32.

Appendix 4   Letters of Spyridon Marinatos to Humfry Payne

1. Powell 1973, 75.
2. Powell 1973, 252.

3. Eliopoulos (Ηλιόπουλος) 2014, 157–203.
4. Powell 1973, 75.
5. Sp. Marinatos archives, Gennadius Library, Athens. A copy of the letter has been donated to BSA.
6. Manolis Akoumianakis or Manolaki.
7. i.e. the Archaeological Service, especially as concerned Anglo-Greek relations.
8. i.e. about the truth.
9. He was at Kephallonia excavating when the find was made by Nikolaos Platon.
10. The opposite ought to be the case, Marinatos thought. Thus when Pendlebury began his excavation at the cave of Trapeza in 1936, Marinatos asked a local teacher, Mr Mavroeidis, to keep an eye on the dig. 'Mr Pendlebury is conducting excavations there and I am not happy that there is no [Greek] supervision'. See Eliopoulos (Ηλιόπουλος) 2014, 157–203.
11. There was a temple of Zeus there, a fact which was eventually published by Anastasios Orlandos.
12. Excavation report.
13. This sentence is not accurately quoted in Powell 1973, 75.
14. Namely sending reports abroad and keeping archaeologists informed about finds.
15. This is my rendering of the Greek *euthixia*.

Appendix 5   Letters of Priest Nikolaos Pollakes to Spyridon Marinatos and his wife Maria Evangelidou

1. Maria Evangelidou is the first wife of Spyridon Marinatos. They divorced in 1936.

BIBLIOGRAPHY

Abbreviations

CMS: Corpus der Minoischen und Mykenischen Siegel (Berlin, 1964).
Evans PM: Evans, A. J. 1921–35. *The Palace of Minos at Knossos*. London:
G. MacMillan.
BSA: Annual of the British School at Athens.

References

Αλεξίου, Σ. 1958. Ἡ μινωική θεά μεθ᾽ ὑψωμένων Χειρών᾽. *Κρητικά Χρονικά*
(*Kretika Chronika*) 12: 179–299.
Αλεξίου, Σ. 1969. Παράλληλον δια τον βασιλέα-ιερέα της Κνωσού᾽. *Athens
Annals of Archaeology* 4: 427–35.
Alexiou, S. 1976. *Minoan Civilization* (third revised edn). Herakleion: Spyros Alexiou.
Alexiou, S. 2000. 'Sir Arthur Evans: το έργο και η αντίστασή του στην κριτική',
in G. Cadogan, E. Hatzaki and A. Vasilakis (eds), *Knossos: Palace, City, State.
Proceedings of the Conference in Herakleion Organised by the British School at Athens
and the 23rd Ephoreia of Prehistoric and Classical Antiquities of Herakleion, in
November 2000, for the Centenary of Sir Arthur Evans's Excavations at Knossos*.
British School at Athens Studies 12, 561–3.
Aruz, J. 2008. *Marks of Distinction: Seals and Cultural Exchange between the Aegean and
the Orient*. Mainz am Rhein: Philipp von Zabern.
Assmann, J. 2004. 'Monotheism and Polytheism' in S. Isles Johnston (ed.), *Religions
of the Ancient World*. Cambridge, MA: Harvard University Press, 17–31.
August, M. G. F. 2009. *Comte de Choisieul-Gouffrier*, Ελλαδος Περιήγησις.
Αθήνα: Εκδόσεις Μίλητος.
Βασιλικού, Ν. 2011. *Το χρονικό της Ανασκαφής των Μυκηνών* 1870–1878,
Αθήναι: Βιβλιοθήκη της εν Αθήναις Αρχαιολογικής Εταιρείας.
Beard M., 2000. *The Invention of Jane Harrison*. Cambridge, MA and London:
Harvard University Press.

264   SIR ARTHUR EVANS AND MINOAN CRETE

Betts, J. H. 1981. 'Some Early Forgeries the San Giorgi Group' in I. Pini (ed.), *Studien zur minoischen und helladischen Glyptik, Beiträge zum 2. Marburger Siegel-Symposium, 26. 30. September 1978, Beiheft 1*. Berlin: Gebr. Mann Verlag, 17–35.

Beyer, I. 1976. *Die Tempel von Dreros und Prinias und die Chronologie der kretischen Kunst des 8. und 7. jhs. v. chr.* 2 vols. Freiburg Berlin: Wasmuth.

Blakolmer, F. 2008. 'Die "Rekonstitution" des "Palace of Minos" in Knossos im *Spiegel des Art Déco*. Und warum Evans Recht hatte'. *Studia Hercynia* 12: 103–16, pls 28–32.

Blakolmer, F. 2011. 'Ethnizität und Identität in der minoisch-mykenischen Ikonographie' in *The Phenomena of Cultural Borders and Border Cultures across the Passage of Time (from the Bronze Age to the Late Antiquity), International Conference at Trnava, 22nd–24th October 2010*. Anodos Studies of the Ancient World 10, 29–40.

Blakolmer, F. Forthcoming. 'Artistic reception of Minoan Crete in the period of Art Deco, the reconstruction of the palace at Knossos and why Arthur Evans was right' in A. Farnoux and N. Momigliano (eds), *Cretomania: The Reception of Minoan Material Culture. International Round Table, École Française d'Athènes, 23– 4 November 2013*, Bulletin de Correspondence Hellénique Suppl. (forthcoming).

Bossert, H. 1937. *Altkreta: Kunst und Kunstgewerbe in agäischen Kulturkreise*. Berlin.

Bowra, C. M. 1966. *Memories 1898–1939*. Cambridge, MA: Harvard University Press.

Breasted, J. H. 1912. *Development of Religion and Thought in Ancient Egypt*. Lectures delivered on the Morse Foundation at Union Theological Seminary. New York: C. Scribner's Sons.

Brendon, P. 2007. *The Decline and Fall of the British Empire*. New York: Vintage.

Brown, A. C. 1983. *Arthur Evans and the Palace of Minos*. Oxford: Ashmolean Museum.

Brown, D. 1993. *Wondrous Realms of the Aegean*. Time-Life Books.

Budge, E. A. W. 1966. *The Book of the Dead: The Hieroglyphic Transcript of the Papyrus of Ani* (orig. publication 1898). New Hyde Park, NY: University Books.

Burkert, W. 1979. *Structure and History in Greek Mythology and Ritual*. Berkeley: University of California Press.

Burkert, W. 2000. 'Migrating Gods and Syncretisms: Forms of Cult Transfer in the Ancient Mediterranean' in A. Ovadiah (ed.), *Mediterranean Cultural Interaction*. Tel Aviv: Ramot, 1–21.

Candy, J. S. 1984. *A Tapestry of Life*. Braunton, Devon: Merlin Books.

Cavanagh, W. and Mee, C. 1999. 'Building the Treasury of Atreus' in P. P. Betancourt, V. Karageorgis, R. Laffineur and W. D. Niemeier (eds), *Meletemata: Studies in Aegean Archaeology Presented to Malcolm H. Wiener as He Enters his 65th Year*. Aegaeum 20. Liège: Université de Liège, 93–102.

Close, D. H. 1993. 'The Power Base of the Metaxas Dictatorship' in R. Higham and Th. Veremis (eds), *The Metaxas Dictatorship: Aspects of Greece, 1936–1940*. Athens: Hellenic Foundation for Defence and Foreign Policy and Speros Basil Vryonis Center for the Study of Hellenism, 15–39.

Coldstream, J. N. 1981. 'Review: *Die Tempel von Dreros und Prinias a und die Chronologie der kretischen Kunst des 8. und 7. jhs. v. chr.* by Immo Beyer'. *American Journal of Archaeology* 85: 345–6.

Collon, D. 1987. *First Impressions: Cylinder Seals in the Ancient Near East*. Chicago: University of Chicago Press.

Cornelius, I. 1994. *The Iconography of the Canaanite Gods Reshef and Ba'al: Late Bronze Age and Iron Age I periods (c. 1500–1000 BCE)*. Orbis Biblicus et Orientalis 140. Friburg: Academic Press Fribourg.

Cook, A. B. 1914–30. *Zeus: A Study in Ancient Religion*, vols 1–3. Cambridge: Cambridge University Press.

D'Agata, L. and van de Moortel, A. (eds), 2009. *The Archaeologies of Cult: Essays on Ritual and Cult in Crete in Honor of Geraldine C. Gesell*. Hesperia suppl. 24. Athens: American School of Classical Studies.

Darwin, C. 1874. *The Descent of Man, and Selection in Relation to Sex*. Reprinted from the second English edition. Revised and augmented. New York: A. L. Burt Company.

Darwin, C. 1989. *The Works of Charles Darwin: Descent of Man, and Selection in Relation to Sex*, ed. P. H. Barret and R. B. Freeman. New York: New York University Press, vol. 21, pt. 1.

Darwin, F. 2000. *The Autobiography of Charles Darwin*. Great Mind Series. Amherst, NY: Prometheus Books.

Davis, J. 2009. 'That Special Atmosphere Outside of National Boundaries: Three Jewish Directors and the American School of Classical Studies at Athens' in E. Greco (ed.), *Annuario della Scuola Archeologica Italiana di Atene* LXXXVII, series III, 9, Tomo I. Rome: Giorgio Bretschneider, 119–31.

Dickinson, O. T. P. K. 1994. *The Aegean Bronze Age*. New York, NY: Cambridge University Press.

Dimopoulou, N. and Rethemiotakis, Y. 2004. *The Ring of Minos and Gold Minoan Rings: The Epiphany Cycle*. Athens: Ministry of Culture.

Eccles, E. 1939. 'Review of *The Archaeology of Crete: An Introduction* by J.D.S. Pendlebury.' *The Journal of Hellenic Studies* 59, Part 2: 290–1.

Ηλιόπουλος 2014. 'Αρχαιολογικά Παραλειπόμενα από την ανατολική Κρήτη' in E. Matzourani and N. Marinatos (eds), *Spyridon Marinatos: His Life and Times*. Athens: Kardamitsas, pp. 157–204.

Eller, C. 2012. 'Two Knights and a Goddess: Sir Arthur Evans, Sir James George Frazer, and the Invention of Minoan Religion.' *Journal of Mediterranean Religions* 25: 75–98.

Evans, A. J. 1900/1. 'The Palace of Knossos.' *Annual of the British School at Athens* 7: 1–120.

Evans, A. J. 1901. 'The Mycenaean Tree and Pillar Cult and its Mediterranean Relations.' *The Journal of Hellenic Studies* 21: 99–204.

Evans, A. J. 1912. 'Mycenaean and Minoan Element in Hellenic Life.' *The Journal of Hellenic Studies* 32 (2): 277–97.

Evans, A. J. 1913/14. 'The Tomb of the Double Axes and Associated Group.' *Archaeologia* 65: 1–59.

Evans, A. J. 1916. 'The President's Address to the Society of Antiquaries.' *The Burlington Magazine for Connoisseurs* 29: 134.

Evans, A. J. 1925. 'The Ring of Nestor: A Glimpse into the Minoan After-World and a Sepulchral Treasure of Gold Signet-Rings and Bead-Seals from Thisbê, Boeotia.' *The Journal of Hellenic Studies* 45: 1–75.

Evans, A. J. 1928. 'The Fitzwilliam Goddess.' *Classical Review* 42: 61–2.

Evans, A. J. 1932. 'The Earlier Religion of Greece in the Light of Cretan Discoveries' in W. R. Dawson (ed.), *The Frazer Lectures 1922–1932 by Diverse Hands*. Oxford: Freeport (reprinted by N.Y. Books for Libraries Press 1967), 248–8.

Evans, A. J. 1936. 'The Minoan World.' Lecture delivered at the Royal Academy of Arts, 16 October 1936.

Evans, J. 1943. *Time and Chance. The Story of Arthur Evans and his Forebears*. London and New York: Longmans, Green and Co.

Faulkner, R. O. 1995. *The Egyptian Book of the Dead: The Book of Going Forth by Day, Being the Papyrus of Ani (Royal Scribe of the Divine Offerings)* (second edn). San Francisco: Chronicle Books.

Fitton, J. L. 1996. *The Discovery of the Greek Bronze Age*. Cambridge, MA: Harvard University Press.

Fotiadis, M. 2006. 'Factual Claims in late nineteenth century European Prehistory and the Descent of a Modern Discipline's Ideology.' *Journal of Social Anthropology* 6 (1): 5–27.

Fraser, R. 1990. *The Making of the Golden Bough: The Origins and Growth of an Argument*. New York: St. Martin's Press.

Frazer, J. G. 1922. *The Golden Bough: Abridged Edition* (reprinted 1949). London: MacMillan.

Frazer, J. G. 1994. *The Golden Bough: A New Abridgement*, ed. R. Fraser. Oxford and New York: Oxford University Press.

Gennep, A. van. 1960. *The Rites of Passage* (orig. publication 1909). London: Routledge.

Gere, C. 2009. *Knossos and the Prophets of Modernism*. Chicago: University of Chicago Press.

Gibbon, E. 1952. *Decline and Fall of the Roman Empire*, ed. D. Saunders (repr. 1985). London: Penguin.

Goodison, L. 1989. *Death, Women and the Sun: Symbolism of Regeneration in Early Aegean Religion*. Bulletin of Institute of Classical Studies Suppl. 53. London: Institute of Classical Studies.

Goodison, L. 2009. 'Why all this about Oak or Stone? Trees and Boulders on Minoan Gild Rings' in L. D'Agata and A. van de Moortel (eds), *The Archaeologies of Cult: Essays on Ritual and Cult in Crete in Honor of Geraldine C. Gesell*. Hesperia suppl. 24. Athens: American School of Classical Studies, 51–7.

Goodison, L. and Morris, C. 1998. *Ancient Goddesses: the Myths and the Evidence*. London: British Museum Press.

Graf, F. 1993. *Greek Mythology: An Introduction*, tr. T. Marier. Baltimore: Johns Hopkins University Press.

Graf, F. 2004. 'What is Ancient Mediterranean Religion?' in S. I. Johnston (ed.), *Ancient Religions*. Cambridge, MA and London: The Belknap Press of Harvard University Press, 3–16.

Grafton, A. 1990. *Forgers and Critics: Creativity and Duplicity in Western Scholarship*. Princeton: Princeton University Press.

Grimm, J. and Meyer, E. H. 1878. *Deutsche Mythologie*. Berlin: F. Dümmler.

Grundon, I. 2007. *The Rash Adventurer: A Life of John Pendlebury*. London: Libri.

Guthrie, W. K. C. 1950. *The Greeks and their Gods*. London: Methuen.

Haas, V. 1982. *Hettitische Berggötter und Hurritische Steindämonen: Ritte, Kulte und Mythen*. München: Philipp von Zabern.

Hamilakis, Y. 2002. 'Introduction: What future for the "Minoan" past? Rethinking Minoan Archaeology' in Y. Hamilakis (ed.), *Labyrinth Revisited: Rethinking 'Minoan' Archaeology*. Oxford: Oxbow, 2–28.

Hamilakis, Y. and Momigliano, N. (eds) 2006. *Archaeology and European Modernity: Producing and Consuming the Minoans*. Creta Antica (Rivista annuale di studi archeologici, storici ed epigrafici, Centro di Archaeologica Cretese, Universita di Catania) 7. Padua: Bottega d'Erasmo.

Hall, J. 2007. *A History of the Archaic Greek World*. Malden, MA: Blackwell.

Harrison, J. E. 1903. *Prolegomena to the Study of Greek Religion* (second edn, 1922). Cambridge: Cambridge University Press.

Harrison, J. E. 1912. *Themis* (second edn, 1927). Cambridge: Cambridge University Press.

Harlan, D. 2011. 'The cult of the Dead, Fetishism, and the Genesis of an Idea: Megalithic Monuments and the Tree and Pillar Cult of Arthur J. Evans.' *European Journal of Archaeology* 14: 210–30.

Harvey, G. 2006. *Animism: Respecting the Living World*. New York: Columbia University Press.

Hepding, H. 1903. *Der Attiskult*. Zur Erlagung der Doktorwürde der Philosophischen Fakultät der Gross. Hessischen Ludwigs Universität zu Giessen, Giessen: J. Ricker'sche Verlagsbuchhandlung Alfred Töpelmann.

Higham, R. and Veremis, Th. (eds) 1993. *The Metaxas Dictatorship: Aspects of Greece, 1936–1940*. Athens: Hellenic Foundation for Defence and Foreign Policy and Speros Basil Vryonis Center for the Study of Hellenism.

Hoeck, Karl. 1823–9. *Kreta. Ein Versuch zur Aufhellung der Mythologie und Geschichte, der Religion und Verfassung dieser Insel, von den ältesten Zeiten bis auf die Römer-Herrschaft*. Göttingen: C.E. Rosenbusch.

Hogarth, D. G. 1908. 'Aegean Religion' in J. Hastings (ed.), *Encyclopaedia of Religion and Ethics*, vol. 1. New York: Charles Scribner's Sons, 141–8.

Hood, R. 1998. *Faces of Archaeology in Greece: Caricatures by Piet de Jong*. Oxford: Lepoard's Head Press.

Horney, K. 1945. *Our Inner Conflicts: A Constructive Theory of Neurosis*. New York: W.W. Norton.

Hornung, E. 1982. *Conceptions of God in Ancient Egypt: the One and the Many*, tr. J. Baines. Ithaca: Cornell University Press.

Hornung, E. 1999. *The Ancient Egyptian Books of the Afterlife*, tr. D. Lorton. Ithaca: Cornell University Press.

Iatrides, J. O. 1980. *Ambassador MacVeagh Reports, Greece 1933–47*. Princeton: Princeton University Press.

Jung, H. 1989. 'Methodisches zur Hermeunetik der minoischen und mykenischen Bilder' in W. Müller (ed.), *Fragen und Probleme der Bronzezeitlichen Ägäischen Glyptik: Beiträge zum 3. Internationalen. Marburger Siegel-Symposium 5–7 September 1985*. CMS Beiheft 3. Berlin: Gebr. Mann, 91–109.

Karadimas, N. Forthcoming. 'The Unknown Past of Minoan Archaeology; from the Renaissance until the arrival of Sir Arthur Evans in Crete', Proceedings of an international PhD and PostDocConference, 23–7 March 2011, Heidelberg. AEGIS. Louvain-la-Neuve: Presses universitaires de Louvain (forthcoming).

Karadimas, N. and Momigliano, N. (eds) 2004. 'On the Term Minoan before Evans's Work in Crete (1894).' *Studi Micenei ed Egeo-Anatolici* 46: 243–58.

Karo, G. 1922. *The Responsibility of the Entente for the War in the Showing of Their Own Statesmen*. Halle: Niemeyer.

Karo, G. 1930–3. *Die Schachtgräber von Mykenai*. München: Bruckmann.

Karo, G. 1959. *Errinnerungen. Greifen am Thron*. Baden-Baden: Bruno Grimm.

Kirk, G. S., Raven, J. E. and Schofield, M., 2006. *The Presocractic Philosophers* (second edn). Cambridge: Cambridge University Press.

Krischen, F. and Tischer, G. 1921. *Ein Festtag am Hofe de Minos*. Berlin: Schoetz & Parrhysius-Verlagshaus.

Lapatin, K. 2002. *Mysteries of the Snake Goddess: Art, Desire, and the Forging of History*. Boston and New York: Houghton Mifflin Co.

Λεμπέσση, Α. 1976 *Οι Στήλες του Πρινιά. Δημοσιέυματα του Αρχαιολογικού Δελτίου 22.*

Lebessi, A, Muhly P. and Papasavvas G. 2004. 'The Runner's Ring: A Minoan Athlete's Dedication at the Syme Sanctuary', *Athenische Mitteilungen* 119: 1–31.

MacGillivray, J. A. 2000. *Minotaur: Sir Arthur Evans and the Archaeology of Minoan Myth*. New York: I.B.Tauris.

Mannhardt, W. von 1875–77. *Wald- und Feldkulte* (2 vols). Berlin: Gebrüder Borntraeger.

Marinatos, N. 1993. *Minoan Religion: Ritual, Image and Symbol*. Columbus: University of South Carolina Press.

Marinatos, N. 2009a. 'Meta-Mythology of Baetyl Cult: The Mediterranean Hypothesis of Sir Arthur Evans and Fritz Graf' in U. Dill and C. Walde (eds), *Antike Mythen. Medien, Transformationen und Kunstruktionen*. Berlin, New York: Walter de Greuyter, 73–80.

Marinatos, N. 2009b. 'The Indebtedness of Minoan Religion to Egyptian Solar Religion: Was Sir Arthur Evans Right?' *Journal of Ancient Egyptian Interconnections* 1 (1): 22–8.

Marinatos, N. 2010. *Minoan Kingship and the Solar Goddess*. Urbana, IL: University of Illinois Press.

Μαρινατος, Σπ. 1935. 'Ανασκαφαί εν Κρήτη', *Πρακτικά της Αρχαιολογικής Εταιρείας* 1934–1935: 196–220.

Marinatos, Sp. 1936. 'Le temple géométrique de Dréros.' *Bulletin de Correspondence Hellénique* 60: 214–85.

Marinatos, Sp. 1937a. 'Ausgrabungen und Funde auf Kreta 1936–1937'. *Archäologischer Anzeiger* 52: 222–34.

Μαρινάτος, Σπ. 1937b. 'Αι Μινωικαί θεαί του Γάζι.' *Archaiologike Ephemeris*: 278–91.

Marinatos, Sp. 1939. 'The Volcanic Destruction of Minoan Crete.' *Antiquity* 13: 425–39.

Marinatos, Sp. 1940/41. 'The Cult of the Cretan Caves.' *The Review of Religion*: 129–36.

Marinatos, Sp. 1962. 'Zur Frage der Grotte von Arkalochori.' *Kadmos* 1: 87–94.

Μαρινάτος, Σπ. 1963. 'Περί των πρώτων Αχαϊκών Εποικισμών της Κρήτης'. *Κρητικά Χρονικά* 16: 177–92

Μαρινάτος, Σπ. 1964. *Επετηρίς Φιλοσοφικής Σχολής Πανεπιστημίου Αθηνών*: 600–606.

Marinatos, Sp. 1966. 'Necrology [for Georg Karo].' *American Journal of Archaeology* 70: 73–4.

Marinatos, Sp. 1968. *Excavations at Thera I, First Preliminary Report*. Athens: Archaiologike Etaireia.

Marinatos, Sp. 1974. *Excavations at Thera VI*. Athens: The Archaeological Society at Athens.

Marinatos, Sp. and Hirmer, M. 1976. *Kreta, Thera und das Mykenische Hellas*. Munich: Hirmer.

Mazower, M. 1995. *Inside Hitler's Greece*. New Haven, London: Yale University Press.

Mettinger, T. N. D. 1995. *No Graven Image? Israelite Aniconism in its Ancient Near Eastern Context. Coniectanea Biblica*. Old Testament Series 42. Stockholm: Almqvist and Wiksell.

Momigliano, N. 1999. *Duncan Mackenzie: A Cautious Canny Highlander and the Palace of Minos at Knossos*. Institute of Classical Studies. School of Advanced Study. London: University of London.

Morgan, L. (ed.) 2005. *Aegean Wall Painting: A Tribute to Mark Cameron*. British School at Athens Studies 13. Sherborne: Remous Ltd.

Murray, G. 1925. *Five Stages of Greek Religion*. Oxford: Clarendon Press.

Mylonas, G. 1966. *Mycenae and the Mycenaean Age*. Princeton: Princeton University Press.

Myres. J. L. 1941. 'Arthur John Evans 1851–1941'. *Obituary Notices of Fellows of the Royal Society*, 3 (10) (Dec. 1941). Published by The Royal Society Stable: 941–68.

Nilsson, M. P. 1927. The *Minoan and Mycenaean Religion and Its Survival in Greek Religion*. Skrifter Utgivna av Kungl. Humanistiska Vetenskapssamfundet i Lund. Lund: Berlinsgka Boktryckeriet.

Nilsson, M. P. 1932. *The Mycenaean Origin of Greek Mythology*. Sather Lectures, volume 8 (reprinted 1972). Berkeley: University of California Press.

Nilsson, M. P. 1950. *The Minoan and Mycenaean Religion and Its Survival in Greek Religion* (second edn). Acta Regiae Societatis Humaniorum Litterarum Lundensis 9. Lund: C.W.K. Gleerup.

Nock, A. D. 1927. 'Review of Nilsson M.P., *The Minoan and Mycenaean Religion and its Survival in Greek Religion*'. *Journal of Hellenic Studies* 47: 297–8.

Owen, J. 2008. 'A Significant Friendship: Evans Lubbock and a Darwinian World Order' in A. McGregor (ed.), *Sir John Evans*. Oxford: Muswell Hill, 206–30.

Palyvou, C. 1995. *Akrotiri, Thera: An Architecture of Affluence 3,500 Years Old*. INSTAP Prehistory Monographs. Philadelphia, PA.

Palyvou C. 2003. 'Architecture and Archaeology: the Minoan Palaces in the Twenty-First Century' in J. K. Papadopoulos and R. Leventhal (eds), *Theory and Practice in Mediterranean Archeology: Old World and New World Perspectives*. Los Angeles: Cotsen Institute of Archaeology, University of California, 205–233.

Papadopoulos, J. K. 2007. *The Art of Antiquity: Piet de Jong and the Art of the Athenian Agora*. Princeton: American School of Classical Studies Athens.

Pardee, D. 2009. 'A New Aramaic Inscription from Zincirli.' *Bulletin of the American Schools of Oriental Research* 356: 51–71.

Pendlebury, J. D. S. 1933. *A Handbook to the Palace of Minos at Knossos* (reprinted 1954). London: Max Parrish and Co. Ltd.

Pendlebury, J. D. S. 1939. *The Archaeology of Crete: An Introduction*. London: Methuen.

Persson, A. W. 1942. *The Religion of Greece in Prehistoric Times*. Berkeley and Los Angeles: University of California Press.

Πετράκος, B.X. 1994. *Τα Αρχαία της Ελλάδος κατά τον πόλεμο 1940–1944*. Αθήνα. Βιβλιοθήκη της Αρχαιολογικής Εταιρείας αρ. 144.

Picard, C. 1948. *Les Religions Préhelléniques*. Paris: Presses Universitaires de France.

Pini, I. 1981. 'Echt oder Falsch? – Einige Fälle' in I. Pini (ed.), *Studien zur minoischen und helladischen Glyptik. Beiträge zum 2. Marburger Siegel-Symposium, 26–30 September 1978*. CMS Beiheft 1. Berlin, 135–57.

Pini, I. 1987. 'Zum Ring des Minos' in *Eilapine, Festschrift Nikolaos Platon*. Herakleion: Vikelaia Bibliothiki, 441–55.

Pini, I. 1988. 'The Ring of Nestor.' *Oxford Journal of Archaeology* 17: 1–13.

Platon, N. 1971. *Zakros: The Discovery of a Lost Palace of Ancient Crete*. New York: Scribner.

Platon, N. 1984. 'Minoan Thalassocracy and the Golden Ring of Minos' in R. Hägg and N. Marinatos (eds), *The Minoan Thalassocracy: Myth and Reality. Proceedings of the Third International Symposium at the Swedish Institute in Athens (31 May–5 June 1982)*. Stockholm: Skrifter Utgivna av Svenska Institutet in Athen 32, 65–70.

Platon, L. 2011a. 'Zakros: One or Two Destructions around the End of the LMIB Period?' in T. M. Brogan and E. Hallager (eds), *LMIB Pottery: Relative Chronology and Regional Differences. Acts of a workshop held at the Danish Institute at Athens in collaboration with the INSTAP Study Center for East Crete, 27–29 June 2007*. Monographs of the Danish Institute at Athens 11, vol. 2. Denmark, 595–612.

Πλάτων, Λ. 2011b. 'Το ανάκτορο και ο μινωικός οικισμός της Ζάκρου, λίγες μόνο ώρες πριν από την μεγάλη καταστροφή.' *Proceedings of International Cretological Congress (Chania 1–8 October 2006)*, v. A2. Chania, 439–60.

Popham, M. 1974, 'Sellopoulo Tombs 3 and 4: Two Late Minoan Graves near Knossos'. *BSA* 69: 195–257.

Poursat, J.-C. 1977. *Catalogue des ivoires mycéniens du Musée national d'Athènes*. Bibliothèque des écoles françaises d'Athenes et de Rome fasc. 230, 2 vols. Athènes: École française d'Athènes. Paris: Dépositaire, Diffusion de Boccard.

Powell, D. 1973. *The Villa Ariadne* (reprinted 1985). London: Michael Haag.

Renfrew, C. 1972. *The Emergence of Civilisation: the Cyclades and the Aegean in the Third millennium B.C.* London: Methuen.

Renfrew, C. 1985. *Archaeology of Cult: The Sanctuary at Phylakopi*. British School of Archaeology at Athens suppl. vol. 18. London: Thames and Hudson.

Robertson Smith, W. 1894. *Lectures on the Religion of the Semites* (reprinted 2005). London: Adam and Charles Black.

Sakellarakis, J. A. 1973. 'Über die Echtheit des sogeganneten Nestorrings' in *Pepragmena tou Γ! Diethnous Synedriou (Proceedings of the Third Cretological Congress 1971)* vol. A. Athens, 303–18.

Sakellarakis, J. and E. 1991. *Crete. Archanes*. Athens: Ekdotike Athenon.

Σακελλαρίου, A. 1994. 'Το Δακτυλίδι του Νέστορα.' *Εταιρεία Κρητικών Σπουδών*. Ηράκλειον: 93–106.

Schliemann, H. 1878. *Mykenai. Ein Bericht*. Leipzig: F.A. Brockhaus.

Segal, S. L. 2003. *Mathematicians under the Nazis*. Princeton, NJ: Princeton University Press.

Simpson, W. K. (ed.) 2003. *The Literature of Ancient Egypt: An Anthology of Stories, Instructions, and Poetry*, tr. R. K. Ritner, W. K. Simpson, V. A. Tobin and E. F. Wente, Jr. New Haven: Yale University Press.

Stürmer, V. 1994. *Gilliéron's Minoisch-Mykenische Welt. Eine Ausstellung des Winckelmann-Intituts*. Exhibition Catalogue. Humboldt-Universität zu Berlin.

Trail, D. 2001. 'Review of Joseph A. MacGillivray, *Minotaur: Sir Arthur Evans and the Archaeology of the Minoan Myth.' Bryn Mawr Classical Review*, 19 February 2001. (http://bmcr.brynmawr.edu/2001/2001-02-19.html)

Τσούντας Χ. 1893. Μυκήναι και Μυκηναϊκός Πολιτισμός. Εθνικό καί Καποδιστριακό Πανεπιστήμιο Αθηνών. Διδάσκων Γ. Κορρές. Βιβλιοπωλείον της Εστίας (reprinted by Athens University).

Tsipopoulou, M. 2010. 'The Work of Sir Arthur Evans at Knossos as Documented in the Historical Archive of the Greek Archaeological Service (1922–31)' in O. Krzyszkowska (ed.), *Cretan Offerings: Studies in Honour of Peter Warren*. British School at Athens 19. Athens, 339–52.

Τζαχίλη, Ι. 2006. Οι αρχές της Αιγειακής Προιστορίας. Αθήνα. Καθημερινή.

Tzorakis, G. 2010. 'Το Ηρώον του Ηρακλείου. Το Πάνθεον των Κρητών Αγωνιστών'.' Παλίμψηστο, 24: 321–53.

Τζωράκης, Γ. 2014. 'Ο Σπυρίδων Μαρινάτος στην Κρήτη του Μεσοπολέμου: Από τον σεισμό του 1926 στο νεωτερικό Μουσείο του Π. Καραντινού' in N. Marinatos and E. Matzourani (eds), *Spyridon Marinatos 1901–1974: His Life and Times*. Athens: Kardamitsas, 121–50.

Tylor, E. B. 1871. *Primitive Culture: Researches into the Development of Mythology, Philosophy, Religion, Language Art, and Custom*, vols 1–2 (reproduction of imprint from orig. 1871 and 1873). London: John Murray.

Veremis, Th. M. and Koliopoulos, J. S. 2010. *Modern Greece: A History Since 1821*. London: Wiley-Blackwell.

Vernant J.-P. 1984. *The Origins of Greek Thought*. Ithaca: Cornell University Press.

Vernant, J.-P. (ed.) 1995. *The Greeks*, tr. C. Lambert and T. L. Fagan. Chicago: The University of Chicago Press.

Vidal-Naquet, P. 1986. *The Black Hunter: Forms of Thought and Forms of Society in the Greek World*. Baltimore: Johns Hopkins University Press.

Vlachopoulos, A. 2007. 'Mythos Logos and Eikon Motifs of Early Greek Poetry in the Wall Paintings of Xeste 3, Akrotiri, Thera' in S. Morris and R. Laffineur (eds), *Epos: Reconsidering Greek Epic I*. Austin and Lyon: University of Texas, 107–17.

Wace, A. 1949. *Mycenae: An Archaeological History and Guide*. Princeton: Princeton University Press.

Warren, P. 1987. 'The Ring of Minos' in *Eilapine, Festschrift for Prof. N. Platon*. Herakleion: Vikelaia Vivliothiki, 485–500.

Warren, P. 1988. *Minoan Religion as Ritual Action*. Gothenburgh: Gothenburgh University.

Warren, P. 1990. 'Of Baetyls.' *Opuscula Atheniensia* 18: 193–206.

Warren, P. 2000.'Sir Arthur Evans and his Achievement.' *Bulletin of the Institute of Classical Studies* 44: 199–211.

Warren, P. 2001. 'Review of Joseph A. MacGillivray, *Minotaur: Sir Arthur Evans and the Archaeology of the Minoan Myth.' The English Historical Review* 468 (September 2001): 912–15.

Waugh, E. 1930. *Labels*. London: Duckworth.

Wilkinson, R. H. 2003. *The Complete Gods and Goddesses of Ancient Egypt*. London: Thames and Hudson.

Woodhouse, C. M. 1968. *A Short History of Modern Greece*. New York: Praeger.

Zervos, C. 1956. *L'art de la Crète néolithique et minoenne*. Paris: Cahiers d'art.

INDEX

CPSIA information can be obtained
at www.ICGtesting.com
Printed in the USA
LVHW052020211220
674809LV00012B/158